Sihpromatum

I Grew My Boobs in China

Savannah Grace

A Memoir

Sihpromatum Publishing House

Sihpromatum Publishing House
Contact: sihpromatum@gmail.com

Printed and bound in the United States of America

Library and Archives Canada
Cataloguing-in-Publication data
Watkins, Savannah Grace, 1990-
Sihpromatum: I grew my boobs in China /
Savannah Grace Watkins
Also issued in electronic format.
ISBN 978-1-4792366-5-7
1. Watkins, Savannah Grace, 1990 Travel – China.
2. Watkins, Savannah Grace, 1990 Travel – Mongolia.
3. China – Description and travel.
4. Mongolia – Description and travel. 5. Watkins Family. I. Title.
DS712.W38-2012   915.104'611092   C2012-904888-7

ISBN 978-1-4792366-5-7

eBook ISBN
ePub 978-0-9881231-1-3
Mobi 978-0-9881231-2-0
Visit our website at
www.sihpromatum.com

Typeset in Garamond and Monotype Corsiva

Cover photo courtesy of © Ammon Watkins 2005
Author photo courtesy of © Breanna Watkins 2011

Edited by JoAnn Cleaver
Cover design by Heather UpChurch at www.expertsubjects.com

To Mom, for dragging me around the
globe and making me the person I am today,
and to Kees, for always supporting me
and helping my dreams come true.

Thank you.

Note from the Author

Sihpromatum (Sip-row-may-tum) – A blessing that initially appears to be a curse.

I put this book together with significant prompting from blogs, post-cards, family reminiscences, and extensive journal entries.

Some original blog entries and postcards are reproduced directly in the book and identified by double stars. **

Some names were changed to protect the innocent.

Join our journey and check out photos along the way at: www.sihpromatum.com

The Four Year Journey

Map Legend
05/05/05 – 23/07/05

1. Stop over Seoul.
2. Starting point Hong Kong with Sandra
3. Yangzhou
4. Kunming Stone Forrest
5. Lijiang with Granny
6. Lost in the Tiger Leaping Gorge
7. Emei Shan – Sacred Mountain
8. Panda sanctuary nearby Chengdu
9. Songpan three day horse trek
10. Three day Yangzi boat cruise
11. Xi'an Terra Cotta Warriors
12. Beijing and Great Wall of China
13. Ulaanbaatar
14. Two-week loop with Baagii
15. One-week excursion with Future
16. Stuck in the Gobi Desert
17. Train headed to Russia

Distance Covered in this Book

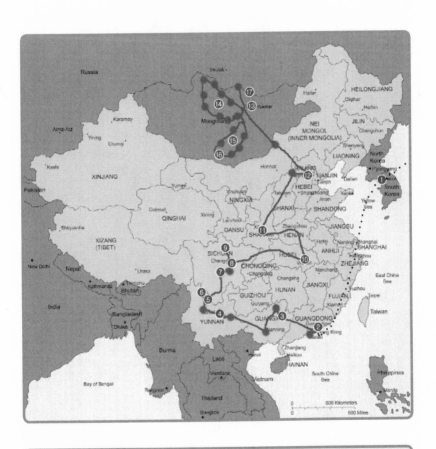

.... Flights
— Travel by bus or train
⬤ Places where we slept or spent time

Prologue

*H*is incredibly elongated shadow seemed to be one of the few anchors left in the desert.

"Do you think Future will come back?" I whispered to the solitary camel standing beside the van. My words expressed doubt, if only for a moment, wondering if our Mongolian guide had just abandoned us. But no. He was also our friend, and I knew we were all in this together.

"He'll come back." I guess Mom had been listening, and she affirmed my gut instinct about Future. "If he can, he will."

"If he can," I echoed with a profound sense of foreboding.

Her words reminded me of the seriousness of our situation. This wasn't just a game. It was real life, and I was all too aware of the perils we faced. Reaching toward the camel, I placed my open palm against the dusty window. Gazing into eyes that resembled golden flakes of sand framed with lavish dark lashes, a strange connection sparked between us. Maybe I was looking for reassurance of some kind or to somehow humbly share his intimate knowledge of the desert. My attention was diverted to my hand at that point and I thought it should have been sweaty or at least a bit moist against the glass, but I was already severely dehydrated. Every nail bed and wrinkle was caked with dirt. *What happened to you, Savannah?* I wondered, crinkling my forehead. This was not the "me" I remembered. *Where on earth did you go?* I asked myself.

"Like, Totally"
1

*I*t was May 5th, 2005 and I was reluctantly boarding a plane bound for Hong Kong. A whole new life was waiting for me, one I had absolutely no interest in living. As I took a cramped seat next to the window, I asked myself, *what the heck happened to get me to this point?* Listening to the pilot's confirmation of our destination, my young heart spun in my chest. As the engines roared and readied for take-off, my mind rewound five months to the last time I had enjoyed a final glimpse of normality before the turmoil of my deteriorating world hit me like a sledge hammer.

"Savannah, where are you?" I heard Kelly say, but she didn't mean it literally. A lot had been on my mind since my parent's separation, but the waving hand in my face brought me back with a start.

"Yah, you should totally get the pink one. That is so sexy," I said reflexively, noticing her well-developed figure.

She lunged through the hangers to reach for the last hot-pink T-shirt on the rack. Tidying herself and tucking loose red locks behind her ear, Kelly babbled on excitedly, "Hey, so did I tell you? I, like, totally found some receipts on my parents' dresser, and I am, like, almost one hundred percent sure my daddy's getting me an Infiniti G35 Coupe for my Sweet Sixteenth!!"

"Oh, wow," I simply said, trying to perfect the "Oh yah, that expensive thing, I know exactly what you're talking about" tone in two words, and I think it worked. She had no idea that I had *no* idea what, exactly, she was talking about.

Terri was in the change room, and I felt slightly abandoned being left alone with this Kelly person. Because I was shy and had attended so many different schools, I didn't have a whole lot of friends. My title was always the same – The New Kid. As soon as I'd start to fit in, we'd move again. Our little outing with Kelly was actually Terri's way of helping me to expand my circle of friends. Terri, with her tanned skin and dark, thick hair that came to her waist, was the Jiminy Cricket on my shoulder, the combined angel/devil, a sister from another lifetime – my best friend.

"You're so lucky. I'm totally jealous," I said, playing it cool and trying not to look too desperate or low class.

"Oh, shut up! I'm sure your parents will get you something amazing. You just have to wait two more years!" I couldn't tell if she was mocking me or not. *Could she really be that mean? Or is she simply clueless?* She didn't seem to grasp the effect her words had on me. *Is it my own insecurity?* I looked inquisitively at her with slightly narrowed eyes. *Does she feel superior because she's older and getting her driver's license? Or is she taking a jab at me 'cause she knows my parents could never afford to buy me a car, let alone a Infiniti?*

"Hey are you coming to my party? It's going to be epic," she went on. Clearly, she had not felt my awkward tension. *I'm in the clear!*

"What do you think!?" I replied, as if to say, "DUH! Of course! Where else would I be?"

As Terri came around the corner from the change rooms, she said, "I'm buying this, then let's just go. Our appointment's in ten minutes."

Kelly beat us to the cashier and was waiting to pay her grand total of three hundred and fifteen. Glancing at my almost empty hands, she asked, "Why didn't you get anything?"

"I did," I said, holding up a clear bag so she could see the lip gloss.

"Ok, but seriously! That doesn't count. I mean, those shoes were so hot on you," she insisted.

"Yah, you're right. I probably should've got them," I agreed, to avoid the embarrassing, "I don't have any money to spend" explanation. They each had their father's credit card, but I only had fifty dollars. If we were going to go for manicures, I should probably come home with my nails done, rather than shoes. Going out for a nail date and not getting your nails done would basically be a social disaster.

We quickly made our way past the mall's early winter shoppers, up the escalator, and through the glass entrance to the beauty salon.

"Yes, we have reservations for one o'clock,' Terri said to the little Asian woman standing behind the desk.

"Terri? For three?" she confirmed.

"Yup, that's us."

"We'll be with you in a moment. Please have a seat over here so you can soak your hands in these basins," she explained before she returned to reception.

"Thank you," we said in unison, then giggled.

"Where do you think she's from?" Kelly asked in a half whisper.

"Probably China," Terri guessed, dropping her bulging bags on the floor at her feet.

"Who cares?" I said, waving it off as I pulled out a comfy leather chair.

Kelly wriggled in her seat and fluffed her hair to draw attention before she announced, "So, did I tell you guys I have a new boyfriend!?"

"No way," Terri exclaimed, "Who!?"

"Tommy Jones. He's dreamy!"

With that, she began a long, drawn-out story of how he was so great, and how she was so great, and how they were so great together. She'd concluded her self-centred story by confidently professing that it was true love.

"But enough about me," she finally said. "Tell us about your love life, Terri."

"Who, me? Hah! Oh, no. No, no, no. I'm not interested," Terri assured us, and I knew it was true. Her heart lay in a career. Her adoration for her father, a well-respected medical doctor, had years ago inspired her dream of working right there next to him, saving lives.

"And Savannah?"

"She's not allo---"

"No, no! Nothing. No interest." I jumped in before Terri could finish her sentence. What she had been about to say was that I wasn't allowed to date until I was sixteen. Mom enforced strict, some might say ridiculous, rules about when her daughters should get involved with guys. Everyone but me had started to date and discover boys. I was willing to obey Mom's rules, but I sure didn't need other people to know how strict she was about that.

"Wasn't there a boy at Terri's house the other night that you thought was pretty cute? He was older, too," Kelly noted, twirling her hair and giving me the oooh-la-la look.

"Who? Grady?! Hah!" I objected. "He's my sister's best friend. Practically my brother!"

"Oh, don't lie. I saw the way you looked at him. You *so* like him!" Kelly said excitedly. Panicking a bit, I wondered if I'd really been that obvious. Thankfully, the manicurists showed up to end our conversation. I drifted into my own reveries as the rhythmic routine began with my left pinkie finger. *Could Grady ever see me as more than just "the little sister"? Could he? Maybe? Would he? Nah, I don't have a chance with him! He's so funny, everybody loves him, and what am I? Just plain geeky!* With that, I answered my own question before I scowled in the direction of Kelly's gorgeous four-inch heels. *Those things must have cost a fortune. No wonder she has a boyfriend. I am nothing like her. She's the kind of girl who'd catch any guy she wanted with those long legs that just didn't quit.*

Continuing my upward scrutiny, I envied the full breasts accentuating her elegant dress. *I mean, geez,* my mind wandered as I glanced cynically downwards at my flat chest, *I must be the only girl I know who has no boobs. Even her hair smells like it might actually be edible.* I flared my nostrils to inhale almost reflexively but instead, an overpowering whiff of manicure chemicals nearly choked me. *Grady would never be attracted to me! How much uglier could I get?! But maybe when I get my braces off, maybe then he'll see a beautiful girl* ... I pondered that thought, looking down as the woman held my fingers in her soft, delicate hands and watching as my nails were transformed beneath the file and polish. I naively thought a manicure might spark his interest.

Later that day we'd returned to Terri's house before deciding to spend the night at my place.

"Hey, Mom just called," Terri said, grabbing her coat and throwing me mine. "She's waiting at the top of the driveway."

"Why do you call *her* mom, Mom?" Kelly asked as she put an arm through her gorgeous red jacket accented with real rabbit fur.

"I really never see my real mom or talk about her. Plus, I'm always with Savannah – I'm practically part of the family. And that way, there's never any confusion about whose mom we're talking about," Terri explained. Over the years, we'd "adopted" many people into our family. Our home was always open and bursting with life. Friends, siblings, and foreign students we were hosting from abroad and all their friends were always welcome. Our family was often spontaneous and always very easy going, a situation that encouraged even unrelated people to think of Mom as a second mom.

Trudging up the driveway of my best friend's mansion of a house and stepping around to the back of the car, we threw our bags in the trunk. It was a cool night. Snow was forecast, and our breath was already forming ghosts in the air.

We hopped into the back of Mom's black, Mustang convertible. She interrupted her phone call to say hello as we climbed in before quickly returning to her conversation.

As I collapsed into the seat, my little dog, Harrison, leapt onto my lap to greet me.

"Why do you do that to him?" Kelly giggled and patted him on the head.

"Do what?" I asked, clueless.

"Paint him blue!" she exclaimed, as if it were obvious.

"Oh," I laughed at my blindness to it, "I didn't *paint* him!! It's just food colouring."

Because he was a white Maltese, it was hard to resist giving him a colourful coat.

I rubbed my nose on his black, button-shaped snout as I listened in on Mom's phone call. Trying to narrow down who could be on the other end was a bit of a game for me. She was always busy on the phone making preparations for work. This time, it wasn't work related. I knew that much, but I still couldn't figure it out. I overheard her saying, "pack up everything," "travel around the world," and "backpacks."

I'd heard enough. *Ugh! That sounds horrible. I just can't imagine why anybody would do that,* I thought sincerely, experiencing a rare moment of gratitude. *I'm so lucky I'm not that poor soul!*

Seconds later, Mom hung up the phone and presented her "great news." *We* were going to pack up everything, *we* were going to travel around the world, and *we* were going to live out of backpacks – for a whole *year*! Her mouth was still moving, but I heard nothing else. I was desperately trying to process what she had said. I couldn't fathom her words. They were dizzying. Suddenly bells rang, smashing about painfully in my skull. My jaw dropped in utter terror and my life transformed in a heartbeat. *We – as in us – as in ME!* I am going to travel the world, *I* am going to sell everything, and *I* am going to live out of a backpack for a *year*!

Aftershock
2

"**B**ut, what about my party? You can't leave before my party," Kelly muttered under her breath. *Leave it to Kelly to just not get it at all.* I acted as if I didn't hear her. *Who cares about your stupid party?!?!* I felt like shouting, *My life is gone! Did you not hear what she just said???* I wanted to scream. Instead, tears suddenly started flowing, and I bawled my eyes out. Harrison's long, soft fur was wet from my tears as I snuggled deeper into him. Kelly's eyes widened with surprise at the scene she witnessed in the car, and she didn't push further. Never before had anyone, other than Terri, seen me cry, and even then, only once. I'd become pretty much an expert at hiding my emotions, but Mom's announcement started a new trend for me that I could no longer control. I just couldn't figure out why it was happening. *Where the heck did all this come from?*

"Oh, Savannah! It'll be okay. You'll see. It's going to be lots of fun," Mom said, thoroughly convinced this was the right thing to do.

"No. It won't. Why do you want to do this? You can't," I panicked.

"I'm really so excited. We're going to go to China and see all those cool things. You girls should look at some of the pictures when we get home. It's gorgeous!"

"Mom, I don't care. I just want to stay here," a suffocating swell rose up in the back of my throat as I spoke. Without warning, without any hint or prior discussion or even THOUGHT, this calamity was laid right on me. It was as unexpected and bizarre as a blue whale falling out of the grey sky and landing on my head. The idea had never crossed my mind, and I still couldn't understand why it had crossed hers.

We'd rented houses for years, and every time the owners either sold them or moved back into them, it meant another new start – a new house, new school, new friends, and a heck of a lot of energy to move and get established again. But this! This was something else entirely. I felt many of the same feelings, except this time, there wouldn't be a new school, or new friends, or a new house. *It was--- It was just--- Just that---* Geez! I couldn't even form cohesive thoughts anymore.

We were home before I knew it, but the horror continued. Getting out of the car and walking up the driveway towards the house, I saw it with different eyes. I examined the towering forest above me and really breathed consciously, trying to taste the air before I stepped inside. I opened the door and noticed the colour of the doorknob for the first time. Everything went by in slow motion, colours and textures enhanced, as we walked up the carpeted stairway to my bedroom.

This is completely insane, I agonized as I sat, dazed, on my couch. My life seemed to be crashing around me like a pooling swirl of fragrant and delicate flower petals now drowning in the fury of a violent storm. Terri was gentle and attentive. She leaned in to tell me what she was sure of.

"It'll be okay, Savannah." It was simple, but it helped. She squeezed my hand in hers, attempting to comfort me. "There's no way Mom is actually going to drag you across the world. She's just going through a really hard time with this whole divorce thing." She must've believed what she said, and not just for my sake. I nodded absentmindedly.

"But I think it would be so cool to go to China and pray with the monks," Kelly threw in, now leaning over to hear our whispers. *She doesn't get that I would gladly give up my spot to her. What do I care about China? And what could Kelly possibly know about it?* I thought, standing and signalling for Harrison to follow with a quick tap on my thigh as I leaned over my couch and opened the window to let him out. At my request, Skylar, my brother nine years my senior, had piled firewood to create a ramp against the house that lead up to my second-story window. It had taken a while, but Harrison had learned how to climb in and out unassisted, and it worked like a charm. As I closed the window, I could hear Mom's footsteps in the hall before she came in with a big book filled mainly with photos of China. I watched him prance down the wood stack before I turned to face her.

"Look at this. Isn't it great?" she said, sitting next to Kelly and opening her book of treasures.

All I could think was, *Where the heck did she get this book? Is this what happens when I go away for the weekend? She completely changes our lives and announces it to the world without even asking me how I feel about it!?* Mom isn't the talkative type; she just makes things happen. I'd always known that about her. Unlike many other people, she doesn't make plans or come up with new ideas unless she intends to follow them through. That is what really scared me.

"I've always wanted to see the Terra Cotta Warriors, ever since they were discovered," Mom said dreamily. *Why would she want to do this? Isn't she over that childish dream of digging to China yet? Because that is what she is doing – digging and BURYING my life, starting with this very first scoop!* My eyes glassed over as I waited and stared out the window, letting her talk.

"All that history! Can you imagine? I'd love to have been with the farmers when they found them. Can you imagine what it took for the archeologists to put all the pieces together to rebuild those warriors?" she continued.

"Ok, Mom," I finally cut in, taking my eyes away from the window, "there is a big difference between buying a puzzle and doing it on your free time," the mention of puzzles put an even bigger smile on her face, "and giving up your entire life for one!"

"Oh, Savannah. It's not the end of the world. It's going to be fun. Trust me. And we're not giving up our whole lives. It's only a year. You have lots of years of your life to live. It will be an amazing experience for all of us."

"Oooh, wow. Look! This is really cool. Soooo pretty!" Beside me, Kelly was ogling the book that was open on Mom's lap.

"Seriously? What are you on? 'Cause that does not sound appealing to me – AT ALL!" It was easy for her to enjoy the photos and dream of going, but I knew she wouldn't be willing to sacrifice her life as she knew it – she'd never carried anything other than an expensive purse, let alone an ugly, heavy backpack. A faint clicking on the glass from Harrison's claws interrupted this train of thought, but it was quickly replaced by another as I began to generate an objection I hoped Mom would appreciate more than my angst.

"Bree isn't going to like this one little bit. You're seriously going to take her away from her boyfriend for that long?" I asked, slamming my palms down on the couch as I stood. Sliding the window open, I scooped Harrison up in my arms and dropped him on the couch.

My seventeen-year-old sister, Breanna, has always been my best friend and my worst enemy. As sisters tend to be, she is both a curse and a blessing. She has a very competitive, determined personality, which explains how it's possible for her to spend four hours, five days a week, training at gymnastics. She'd been dating Fernando for the last ten months, and I couldn't imagine her choosing China over him, or her gymnastics, either, for that matter.

"I already talked to her. She wasn't too upset. She figured that she might as well be out doing this as anything else, since Fernando is going away for his two-year missionary work anyway. Ammon is already busy planning a route for us." My eldest brother, Ammon, is a twenty-five year old "genius." When you get right down to it, he's not much more than a big brain carried around on a six-foot-two, surprisingly strong rack of bones. He's the kind of dude whose head is full of random facts and figures. Research and information flood his very being, but he is not so much a nerdy brainiac as he is a crazy scientist. Even so, his desire to wander the seven seas goes hand in hand with his lifelong search for knowledge. The yin and yang of his soul struggle for balance between the seeker and the wanderer.

The moment Mom told him about her desire to see the world, she and Ammon started buying travel books. Working together, they began exploring the world through maps and books, trying to decide where this year-long excursion would lead. Their whole scheme was beginning to fall into place. Her "pretty" little book was no accident. She had gone out of her way to purchase it. *Okay, this has gone far enough!*

"Why did I not know about this?! Everybody knew except me," I demanded.

"Well, you were away," Mom said meekly.

"That is not an excuse. You must've known before I went to Terri's. You just leave me in the dark and break it to me now? You don't even care how I feel about it!"

"I just figured there was no sense in worrying you until I knew for sure we were going," she admitted. *Like that makes me feel any better!* I took a deep breath.

"But why?! Why do you want to do this?" I questioned fearfully.

"I'm always jealous of Ammon when he goes away and does his three-month backpacking trips. I've always wanted to do that. Now is just the right time for me."

From what I'd heard of his travels, including the unbearably stingy budget and the food he ate, it was the very last thing I'd ever be envious of.

"I think the timing is right for him, too. He knows what he's doing. This is going to be our last chance to do something as a family; I mean, it won't be long before you'll all be moved out and we'll be living our own lives."

Isn't life always going to be gathering around the table and eating dinner with the family, laughing and telling jokes and stories? I sure don't want anything else. I was forced to face the current family situation I'd been too scared to accept. Dear Skylar had gone off and joined the military three years ago, and Dad had moved out. Mom was right, but I wasn't ready. I wouldn't be leaving home for years. *I'm only fourteen!*

It was all beginning to feel way too real. "Why does that mean we have to go away for a whole year?!" I nearly cried all over again, unable to grasp that length of time. *A year is all the time between one birthday and another, the entire time from one Christmas to the next!!* The wait between those events already seemed to take forever. I couldn't even imagine how it would feel to be away from home SO LONG, pining to come back every single day.

"Because if I'm going to go to all the effort of selling everything, any less time just wouldn't be worth it. If you're going to go see it, you may as well REALLY see it," she explained.

"See what!?"

"The WORLD, Savannah! There's so much out there we can't even imagine." My mouth hung open as I tried to form words, but nothing came out. It was one of the most eye-opening days I'd ever experienced – the day I realized how completely unpredictable life can be. One day it's going this way and the next, it's spiralling off in a semicircle, taking a blind leap from atop a sheer cliff. And I'm in the back seat, unsure if we'll somehow magically soar off into a regal sky or suffer what I figured was the far more likely outcome, the one where gravity kicks in and causes us all to be ripped to shreds on the jagged rocks below. That is essentially what it was: a blind leap of faith – faith in one's self, in one's ability, happiness, strength, endurance – the list could go on and on.

Completely drained by the day's emotional toll, I sobbed myself to sleep. The whole giant disaster began forming into nightmares. Harrison always slept at the end of the bed and kept my feet warm, but I was grateful to him for staying close and letting me cuddle him in my arms that night, at least until I fell asleep. It was as if he could sense my pain and knew I needed him.

Itinerary
3

A few days passed but, unfortunately, Mom's sanity level did not change. She had disciplined me for bad behaviour in the past, but I always knew I'd crossed the line when she threatened to take my pets away. She once literally let my hamsters loose in the yard. But this, THIS, was more devastating than my puny little mind could absorb. *She didn't even consult me about it first. And then it hit me. This wasn't about me. There's nothing to complain about because she wasn't doing it to punish me, so it wasn't something I could beg or cry my way out of. I had to try to reason with her.*

I walked casually into her room, Harrison's nails clicking gently on the hardwood floor behind me. Standing at the end of the bed where she lay, I tilted my head sideways to see what she was reading. *Hrmph! Just as I suspected.* She seemed unmoved by my presence, so I grabbed her foot and bit her toe.

"Yoweeee!" she yelped, slamming the book down. I chuckled, and she returned to her book. I jumped onto the three-and-a-half-foot-high bed and crawled down the length of her body, disturbing her completely. I then shoved her book away so she was forced to look at me.

"STOP planning this!" I said in a typically theatrical tone, grabbing the something-or-other Asian book from her hands "Errrr" I growled at her and reinforced it with a crazy, wagging head movement and clenched teeth. Adding a second, more forceful "eerrrgggg," I did my best to intimidate her.

"Savannah! For goodness sake!" She lifted her blankets in a self-defensive stance, trying hard not to giggle in discomfort.

Dropping to her belly, I bit her hips and shook her, imitating a disgruntled animal's wild mauling behaviour, then looked up pleadingly, "But a whole year, Mom? Really?" I buried my head again. "We could just stay here, nice and cozy by the fireplace," I said, smiling to emphasize how attractive that would be. "We don't need the Asian sun to keep us warm. And why couldn't we just use a tanning bed? And hey, we can buy those straw hats here, too, I'm sure. Heck, we've got Discovery Channel for your little warrior guys. Plus, you know how much I HATE rice."

"Oh, Savannah, that's not the same at all," she said. "It's a bit too late to talk me out of this, and you'll learn to like it, I promise."

"Like what? The trip or rice? I doubt I'll ever like either." With a sudden jolt, I remembered another argument, this time a strong one. *She can't just leave the family business.*

"What about the tour business!? We can still run it as a family without Dad," I pressured desperately. My own powers of persuasion were failing to convince her, so I began putting a lot of this on his shoulders and became a little less jocular.

"Yah, I thought about that at first, but it's a heck of a lot of work to run it all, you know." My parents had built their tour business from scratch. What started out as a favour, driving our hosted Japanese students to Seattle, turned into a multi-bus company offering adventure tours on weekends for Vancouver's ESL (English as a Second Language) students. We highlighted main attractions around B.C. and parts of the U.S., including all the major attractions as well as activities such as skiing, river rafting, sky diving, and bungee jumping.

"But we've done it for all this time!" I waved one hand around, leaning the rest of my weight on the other arm. "And it's doing so well. How can you just stop now?"

"Oowwww! Your boney hips are killing me!" she whined.

Adjusting myself to relieve her now that I finally had her attention, I added, "Mom, you basically run it all anyway."

"Without your Dad, though, it's going to be a lot harder. It won't be the same anymore," she told me.

"It's not like Dad did a whole lot anyway," I spat out venomously. *If it weren't for him leaving, Mom never would have had this stupid idea of selling everything. Live out of a bag! Good Grief!* "You'll still have Ammon and everyone else helping, and soon I'll be old enough to work for you, too."

I couldn't understand why this didn't seem to register with her. Our family had worked so hard on this business. We'd made a pretty good living, and now that our only competitors were relocating to Toronto, there was more potential than ever. How could she turn her back on it when, after ten years of hard work, legalities, paperwork, and overcoming all sorts of other obstacles, the company finally verged on real success?

"I don't know *what* your dad is going to do if I take over the business. I could run him right out of town, of course, but it's just not worth it. Who needs that kind of negativity? Life is too short for that."

"How is he ever going to do it without us? He *can't* do it without us," I stated. This was a fact.

"I'm going to have to teach him what I know before we leave. After that, he'll just have to figure it out for himself. It's the best I can do," she said, realistically.

"Don't tell me you feel sorry for him!? You're just going to give him everything??" I simply couldn't believe it.

"No, no. Not at all! He'll have to buy me out of the business. Plus, when I was talking to Pam---"

"You mean *she* told you to do this!?" I jumped in, trying to comprehend my wealthy aunt coming up with the idea of backpacking. Dad's sister-in-law was my well-to-do Aunt Pam who lived in Seattle, three hours south of us. I had always respected and loved her dearly.

"No, no. Of course not. But when I told her I was going to take over the business, she asked me if that was what I really wanted to do. 'Don't just do what you think you *have* to do to meet other peoples' expectations,' she said. She just planted that little bit of doubt in my mind, and then I started thinking, 'Yah. What *do* I want to do?' That's when it hit me very strongly that I need to take you guys and go see the world."

"But how are we going to support ourselves? What are you going to do for work?" Finally, more pressing concerns began to surface. I just looked at her, desperately seeking answers.

"My whole life, things have always worked out. I've never been without food, never without shelter. One way or another, things have always worked out for me, and I've always had what I needed," she replied, her faith in the universe's inherent bounty shining through, as always.

She'd given neither a solid, nor a comforting answer. I didn't share her confidence, but I had never yet seen her doubt herself. If she ever did, it never showed. She excelled at holding her head high and comforting others with her presence, never seeming to feel pressured by hard times. But her confidence still somehow managed to surprise me this time.

"So, when are you planning to go!?"

"Well, I'd leave immediately, but Ammon still has a few months left at university. If we wait for him, Bree'll basically be finished high school by then, too."

"And me?! What about me?" I nearly shouted, "What about my schooling!?"

"You're smart. You'll have no problem catching up. It's only a year. I made an appointment for two o'clock next Tuesday with your counsellor." I shook my head as it slowly sank in. She was actually going to implement this crazy scheme! I felt trapped, cornered, out of air, and tears welled up again. I realized then that, despite my stuttering, incoherent cries, nothing would come between her and this opportunity – she'd made up her mind.

After studying the world's seasons, temperatures, and main attractions, it was decided that we should start in Hong Kong. From there, we could travel north to Beijing, stopping en route at main attractions such as the Terra Cotta Warriors and the Great Wall of China, proceeding to Mongolia, Russia, Kazakhstan, and Kyrgyzstan. We could then re-enter China at a western border crossing and pass through

Tibet to reach Nepal in time for the trekking season to see the one and only Mount Everest! This was the six-month outline that was presented to Bree and me. After that we would head to India, Southeast Asia and finally Australia. Nothing I did or would try to do in the next five months could alter this, *but something had to,* I thought cynically. *I had to find some way to stop this madness!*

My Brother's Battles
4

*L*ight streamed in after a one-week absence where humid, almost steamy air lingered as Mom began carefully pulling back the edges of the blood-caked bandages from Ammon's scalp. Squeamish, she hesitantly peeked in before exclaiming, "It's … it's … it's an EAR!" the way someone else might announce the sex of a newborn baby after peeking at its privates. It seemed quite reasonable she would find a reconstructed ear; after all, that's what the plastic surgeon was for. Still, she had envisioned the worst, despite his earlier assurances that he'd done his best to make it look like an ear. He'd gently added, though, that it wouldn't be as nice as the one she'd made him. She had secretly confided her fear that it might look like someone had come by with scissors and chopped it off.

"Ammon, did you hear that! It's really cute, even," she said, quickly moving in front of him to see his face. He forced a stiff smile. The past few weeks had been an intensely difficult period for him. Now we at least knew he'd still have an ear, noticeably smaller than the original, but an ear nonetheless. He'd envisioned all sorts of outcomes throughout the days of sitting around in bandages, feeling nauseous. But the waiting was only just beginning.

It was only pure chance that Ammon had gone to the doctor to check a slightly irritating mole on the back of his ear, whereupon it was promptly removed. The tiny mole could so easily have been ignored or overlooked, given how much he had on his plate: He guided and drove the family's tour bus, was a teaching assistant at Simon Fraser University, juggled his studies to complete his final honours project, and planned the trip of his dreams.

A few days after the removal and subsequent biopsy of the dark mole, Ammon had returned to the doctor's office to have the stitches removed. But when he got there, he was greeted with what he'd feared most.

"I did a most precise job on your stitches to ensure the faintest of scars, but unfortunately, it was all for nothing," the surgeon had said as he broke the news to him. "I'm very sorry to have to tell you that we're going to have to remove a larger part of your ear. The biopsy revealed the mole was carrying an aggressive malignant melanoma cancer. You're going to have to come in for a more extensive operation to ensure the entire cancerous area is gone. We can't take any chances with this."

As Ammon left the doctor's office, his teary eyes blurred his vision and the road ahead. He had never felt so vulnerable in his life. He pulled over and hit the steering wheel hard with the palms of his hands, gripping it rigidly as he sat stiff and straight for what seemed like forever. Even when he began to drive again, his emotions in check, he didn't yet feel able to face us. At a red light, he had to choose whether to turn left to go home or to head right to Simon Fraser. Crossing three lanes of traffic, he sped up the mountain to the school. It was quiet and the halls echoed, but he was grateful to see she was still there, long past regular office hours. He knocked on the door that was just slightly ajar, and Doctor Northwood opened it.

"What are you doing here, you twerp? Get out of my sight!" she shouted, in keeping with her reputation as the big bad wolf of the department, the one professor everyone feared. Sticking her head out, she looked both ways down the hall before pulling him in by his collar. Over the years, Ammon's banter and his witty attitude had propelled him past her wicked-witch facade. When he didn't laugh at her charade, she asked, "What's wrong?" in a gentler tone than he'd ever heard her use. He broke down and told her the bad news first.

When he'd finally made it home and announced the unexpected news, the word cancer set off a red alert in my mind, but I stopped dead in my tracks when I heard him translate his particular diagnosis into non-scientific English. "It's the most *lethal* form of skin cancer, causing seventy-seven percent of all skin cancer related deaths." Or perhaps it was Mom's terrified face, frozen with confusion, that frightened me most. His cancer was potentially on the move and being the knowledge sponge he is, Ammon didn't need to be told what the consequences could be. If the cancerous cells decided to get up and travel around their little Ammon world, it would be the end of him. They were like a bomb's detonation timer counting down the days, and they had to be fought as aggressively as possible.

Prior to the actual surgery, thick green dye was injected into the cartilage of his outer ear. With evident sympathy, the doctors had warned him, "We're so sorry. We're not going to lie to you. This procedure is going to be nothing less than excruciating." But that wasn't the end of it. In addition to removing the required portion of the ear, they also had to slice into his neck to determine whether or not the cancer had spread to his lymph nodes. While we waited for the results of the lymph node biopsy, the trip planning was put on hold. And we waited.

We found it really hard to watch a healthy, twenty-five year old man face some of the harsher realities of life. Ammon had far fewer answers than he had stitches. The first day and night after his surgery were tremendously difficult, especially for someone who was always in tip-top condition. Watching Ammon deal with this terrifying, painful disruption to the life he had planned made me realize I wasn't the only person learning the life lesson of how abruptly the ground can fall out from beneath you.

Even the short journey to the bathroom was painful for him and a struggle for Mom and me. We first transferred him from the couch in

Mom's bedroom to the computer chair and then wheeled him across the wood floor to the bathroom, Harrison following dutifully to show his support. He paced from side to side wanting to help and make his presence known, even though the last thing Ammon wanted was a dog hanging around.

"Not now, Harrison," I had to tell him every time. Head low, he sulked over to the corner where he could sit out of the way but still keep a watchful eye.

Giving Ammon some privacy in the bathroom, we waited for him to shout, "Ok." On each return trip, despite our best efforts, clearing the bump at the doorway made him groan miserably.

"Oops, sorry," was about all we could say about that as we wheeled the pale-green, almost corpse-like patient back into Mom's room, parked him next to the fireplace, and tucked him up in a blanket.

Regardless of all the drugs, surgery, and stress, he was utterly determined not to vomit. It was simply mind over matter for him. Have I mentioned what a strong will Ammon always demonstrated? Even unbalanced and physically weak, he was devoted to maintaining his resolve not to puke. I always thought it strange what boys will do and the bizarre games they play, but he actually managed to come out of this ongoing competition without breaking his personal record of eight years.

Thankfully, the trip was put on the backburner until we felt that our designated leader would be, not only still alive, but healthy enough to survive a year on the road. *We don't want him to drop dead in the middle of the world and leave us as live bait for the locals! With my luck, they'd be related to the heart-eating tribe from Indiana Jones. It wouldn't take long before we'd wind up in the same state as him. DEAD! They'd gobble us up in pieces.* The days of waiting seemed to take weeks, and I felt somehow responsible for Ammon's condition because of all the negativity I'd been putting out. I felt guilty because, on a very basic level, I was torn between the conflict of losing my brother or losing everything else.

The house was silent, a rare state of affairs with three children still living at home, not to mention hosting varying numbers of home-stay students and the ever-intrusive business phones ringing off the hook. With the fluffy duvet tucked snuggly under her chin, Maggie-the-Mom sat contentedly with her arms folded across her tummy. It was here, nestled in her warm bed, that she took advantage of the precious quiet. A few minutes were wisely spent in calmly pondering the many arrangements involved with making a smooth exit from this stage of her life. There was so much to be done, so many nagging concerns. She didn't know how she would manage everything in her set time frame, especially with the preparation time Ammon's cancer had lost her, but she was taking it day by day and doing her best to ensure she would not be overwhelmed.

The only sound she heard was the soothing hum of the minibar fridge she used as a bedside table. Sensing that rhythmic vibration, she promptly reached down, opened the door and picked out one of many Dr. Peppers. Sitting back, the "spisss" of the can opening brought her a calm release, like a smoker's first puff after a long, red-eye flight. One or two soft drinks a day was the only addiction she had developed in her forty-five years.

Mom looked across the empty bed, big enough to host her six-member family in a pinch. Gathering together at the end of the day to chat one-on-one with her was something of a nightly ritual, but these days it happened less and less. Unaccustomed to the luxury of space to herself, she inched towards the centre. She rarely had any personal time and, like most mothers, sacrificed herself for the benefit of her loved ones. Reaching over to what had been "his" side of the bed, she took an extra pillow and, laughing to herself, she inwardly noted that he certainly wouldn't be using it anymore! That simple act epitomized a whole new concept to her as she slowly began to identify the first signs of selfhood – If she wanted a pillow, she'd take a pillow, dam-mit! Sitting back with her fizzy drink, she thought, *Maybe I can get used to this solitude. It might be nice.* She was always hopeful there was a way to get past the hardships, and this realization was the first step towards mending her heart.

Everyone was out of the house. Now that he was cleared of cancer, Ammon was once again busy writing exams, I was off with friends trying to escape the trip's fast-approaching reality, and Bree spent every waking hour with Fernando. Her mood changed abruptly. It began to seem very lonesome as she imagined getting old alone in that bed, the kids grown with families and homes of their own. She flinched slightly from that thought, and her heart fluttered as she instinctively thought of Skylar, her second oldest child and the first to leave home.

The only offspring born in his father's homeland, he felt his country calling and had unexpectedly declared that the U.S. Marine Corps was the place for him. When he and his father had first walked into the enlistment hall three years earlier after visiting other branches of the military and learning about their various signing incentives, he'd been asked who had recruited him. His sincere explanation that no one had actually approached him and that the challenge of becoming one of the toughest and joining the best of the best was incentive enough for him, surprised them. It may also have got him off on a positive note with the Marines, as the recruiting agents rarely had people walk in on their own accord. The day after his twenty-first birthday, he left for boot camp at the MCRD (Marine Corps Recruit Depot) in San Diego, California. Within six months, he graduated as one of the few recruits who were able to survive the gruelling marine training.

As if in recognition of that train of thought, her reverie was broken by a phone call from Sky. Shortly after our parents' separation and the announcement of Mom's plans to travel the world, Sky was being deployed to Iraq for his first tour of duty, so he would not be joining his family on the trip.

"Oh Sky!!! It's so good to hear your voice. How are you? Where are you? North Carolina?"

"Yep, just in my barracks at Cherry Point. I'm … I'm ok, I guess."

"You guess?"

"Well, I'm just trying … I need your help, Mom. I just can't do this," he broke down, "I'm trying to fill out a form."

"Well, what are you doing?" she asked gently.

"I gotta make my will and fill out funeral forms," he said, trying to sound calm.

"What? Your funeral? You've got to make funeral plans? How awful. Why would they make you do that?"

"Yah, I know. The military just doesn't want any worries for us or you if something happens to me in Iraq, but it's really hard."

"Oh, lovely! That's *so* good of them," she said sarcastically.

"We have some things to fill out."

"Like what?"

"We have to choose our songs and our pall bearers, a whole bunch of stuff like that."

"I can't believe you have to do that. No wonder you're having a hard time!" she sympathized.

"We have to get everything in order before we go away," he paused, reluctant to upset her but needing her help to do what was required of him, he continued, "in case we don't come back." And there it was. The awful, stark reality of it all. Her son may not return home alive to her, and they both knew it all too well.

Mom's throat tightened. Her chest was burning, but she wouldn't let that affect him any more than it had to. He needed her to be strong. He needed her guidance and support, so she could not let herself crumble. And she wouldn't. The most important thing was making sure she made it as easy as possible for him. Tears would not help the situation, so she struggled to ignore the excruciating dread.

"So, I need your help 'cause I can't get through this. It's just too darn real."

"Okay, Sky. We'll do it together. Let's start at the top."

"I've already been working on it a bit."

"What part are you stuck on?"

"Ummm …" She could hear papers rustling at the other end of the line, "What kind of casket should I get?"

"Well, yikes, what do you like?" her lips tightened before the words were forced out in a calm tone.

"I don't like any of it! I don't know if I want to be buried at all," he confessed.

Since he was an impressionable kid, he'd had his mind set on having his bones dipped in adamantium (regardless of the fact that it's a fictional metal from the Wolverine/X-Men comic books) so his indestructible skeleton could be displayed in a glass cabinet, like the also fictional Terminator, for all his future kids and grandkids to see. That way he could "live on" forever. She thought this might explain why he didn't want to be buried and his inability to choose a coffin.

"I have this ridiculous fear of being buried alive, you know? Like in that movie, what was it called? Oh yah, *The Serpent and the Rainbow*. What if they put me in before I'm really dead?" Surprised that this could be his biggest worry with all the more likely challenges he was about to face, she could sense his emotions faltering. Instead of drilling him about the unlikelihood of such an eventuality, she sought to allay the fear he'd given voice to. If this was his biggest concern, she was determined to help him work through it.

"Ok, then, let's just see what we can do," she started. Putting herself in his place, fearful of being trapped underground, she instinctively chose her approach, "We'll just have to make sure that you have a way to get out if you wake up. 'Cause the worst that could happen is you can't get out, right?" She paused to give him time to acknowledge this. "So you'll need an axe in there with you so you can escape."

"Can you really do that?!?!" he asked.

"Of course! We can do whatever we want. It's *your* funeral. And if they won't do it, I will."

"Aw, thanks Mom. I guess I'll only have a short time to get out, I mean, the air supply will be limited."

"Then you'll need a small oxygen tank in there, too. That will give you some time to break your way out."

"Yah, yah. That's a good idea," he agreed, oddly beginning to calm down. Like Bree, Sky was always up for a "mission." "And an axe seems a bit bulky and heavy, I think I'll just keep my Marine K-Bar. I want to have that with me," he added.

Mom felt his mood lightening as it became a game of logistics, even breaking into some unexpected laughter as potential scenarios unfolded.

"But you'll have to make sure it's a pretty thin coffin so it's easy to get out of."

"Oh, yah. For sure! That's important, so I'll tell them I want a soft pine one."

"So you've got your knife and an oxygen tank, and I'll put in a flashlight, too, so you can see what you're doing."

"Can you do that for me, Mom?" he said, back on a more serious note now.

"I'll absolutely put it in there. I promise. If you want it, I will put it in," she vowed, fully intending to follow through with that if the time came. With one problem solved and out of the way, they continued to fill out the form.

"Well, I put you in as my beneficiary for the insurance. It's doubled if I get killed in combat," he informed her.

"Thanks, but I'll take you instead," she said unhesitatingly.

"And I need a number for someone if anything goes wrong. I already have Aunt Pam and Grandma on here, but what about you? How am I going to reach you if you're all out travelling?"

"I'm going to take a phone with me for emergencies and for if you need to call me," she said. She was not entirely sure how she would manage it, but she had every intention of figuring out the billing, SIM cards, and reception abroad so she would be available to him if he needed comfort through the hard times coming.

"Oh, that's good. I'm really glad," Sky said. "And for songs, I like this one. Do you know it, Mom? It's by Mariah Carey and Boyz II Men, "One Sweet Day." Do you think you could play it?" he asked. Mom quickly found it, and they sat together listening to the lyrics over the phone – "Shining down on me from heaven like so many friends we've lost along the way."

Her eyes closed as a single tear trickled down her cheek. At the same time, she strongly felt the song would not be necessary – that he was going to come back. In one piece or not, he would return home to her and the family. She would take him up in her arms as she so often had when he was small and helpless. He was still her baby, a part of her being.

"Don't you worry. We are *not* going to need this song," she said firmly.

"I really hope not, Mom. I miss you."

"I miss you too. We all miss you. When do you leave?"

"In a few months. How is everything up there? How is Ammon doing?"

"Yah, he's okay. Everything is alright. It was pretty scary for a bit, but the results came back and it looks like he's good to go. Nothing spread. He's lucky he found it in time, but he'll definitely need to have follow-ups."

"Ok, good. Are you sure? 'Cause I'm so worried about him. I'd die if anything happened to him!" Sky said sincerely.

"I'm sure. Don't you worry about that! You just make sure you take care of yourself. We are going to be fine. Do we get to see you before you go?"

"Well, I wanted to surprise you, but I'll be home to say goodbye just before we ship out."

"Oh, that's so exciting!! I can't wait to see you. I love you, Sky."

"I love you too, Mom. Thanks for your help. I've got to get in to the mess hall for lunch in a minute, so OUT from Cherry Point!"

"OUT from Vancouver," she replied, reaching for tissues as she placed the receiver back on the hook.

The Shells of Life
5

*O*ver the hum of sizzling bacon, a ringing startled me into cracking the eggshell in my hand. The sound echoed into the empty spaces of the high ceiling. Glancing down, I saw the devilish white remnants marring the beautiful yellow egg in the centre of my pan. Frustrated, I swirled them around with my much-too-fat spatula without gaining any headway. I'd need a better tool.

"Hey, it's for you," Terri said, grabbing my attention away from the stove.

Spinning around, spatula held out at my side like a wing, I saw what she meant. Though only a banal, solid object in her hand, it was more than just the black mass she held. To me, the telephone was now usually the bearer of bad news. Giving her a childish glare, my expression said it all. *Can't I just not be here for once, for heaven's sake?* Preoccupied, I turned back to my task. I was certainly not going to let my newly complicated life get in the way of enjoying my breakfast; I was determined not to let that little bit of shell ruin my morning. A snapshot of my dad's absolutely debilitating fear of crunching egg shells flashed into my mind. A giggle worked its way up into my throat only to be cut off abruptly by the reality of the past few months, a reality that cast a shadow over that image and everything else these days, for that matter.

I hope every egg he eats for the rest of his life is filled with eggshells. How could he just walk out on us and start this whole travel mess? A gentle "Eerr, hhrrmmm" from behind me interrupted my thoughts as I poked and prodded at the little pieces of shell. With the sympathetic lift of a delicate brow and her characteristic, gentle persistence, Terri held the phone out to me.

"Nuh uh!" I grunted, shaking my head at her. My lips were tightly sealed to show I wasn't there. To make sure she understood, I added a peevish demonstration of wide eyes to demonstrate how deadly serious I was. She inhaled a slow, unnervingly quiet breath and tightened her full lips together as if to say, *Don't you make me!* She shook the phone at me.

Unwilling to budge are the best words to describe the girl – the most stubborn kind of the most stubborn breed there is. That is Terri, and she is proud of it. Had I ever won a "fight" with her in the entire history of our friendship, I might have stood my ground, but this was Terri I was challenging. Muted argument or not, she would eventually overpower me. I had a vision of us in a tangled mess on the floor, with her holding me down with one hand and tightly gripping the phone in the other as she prepared to tie it to the side of my head, like Steve Irwin might tackle a wild croc. Given she was my best friend and all, I selflessly thought perhaps I shouldn't put her through all that hassle. I smiled feebly at my food one last time.

"Just take it," she directed, holding the phone out. Throwing my shoulders back in the most proper posture I could assume, I took it like a lady in a weak attempt to preserve my own dignity. Conveying an outward air of disinterest, I jumped up onto the kitchen counter and handed responsibility for breakfast over to Terri, along with the fork and spatula. It could have been my inner turmoil or simply the step back from the stove, but the phone felt chillingly cold. As I put the receiver to my ear, tremors resulting from the stress of the past weeks rushed through me again.

I'd been spending every moment I could away from home, seeking refuge in the comfort and ease of Terri's house. Her place was the exact opposite of the recent chaos at home. Home – the word lingered in my mind. There were only a few short months left to call it "home." After that came a mind-numbing fog, graying the road ahead of me. Here at Terri's, it was quiet. I could more easily pretend everything was normal – there were no boxes, no maps, no ringing telephones, and most of all, no tears.

Mom's voice snapped me back to the present. "Somebody found Harrison!" she said the moment she heard me come on the phone. I exhaled deeply, releasing the tension I'd been holding in. I looked over at Terri, who by now was wondering what I was smiling about. "Harrison," I whispered as I bit down on my lower lip. That was the only news that could possibly have brought me happiness. My dog, the love of my life, was safe! I jumped down from the counter as Terri dished out the food.

Up until now, Christmas had been my favourite season, but this year it was when we had to sell our four female Maltese to another breeder and say goodbye. Christmas Eve should've been a day where the hearth glowed as red as the lights gleaming through the frosted windows, bringing warmth and security to the home. Instead, it was the day Harrison had gone looking for his family alone. The joyful season had not brought warmth or happiness or laughter as it had in the past. As I sat in front of the rain-streaked window, it was like looking out from the inside of a glass fountain. I could only imagine the worst for my helpless, little blue dog, out there in the rain, searching in vain.

Unable to keep most of our stuff now that we were leaving, we first had to find homes for all our pets. People always said our house was like a zoo. At the time we had a peach-faced lovebird who, ironically, talked more than Verbal, our African Grey parrot; a tortoise; a pair of king snakes; two very large, salt-water fish tanks; and five Maltese dogs. I had also personally bred rabbits, hamsters and lizards then sold the babies to local pet stores in order to earn my own money. Now I had to hand each one over, giving them up in order to do something I never wanted in the first place. Not only did I not want it, I resented the heck out of it! This was by far the hardest step of the process, but it was at least some comfort to know that we found a home where all the female dogs were able to stay together under one roof. It was truly all just too much to bear.

Harrison had lost his family because of this trip, too. It was miserably wet the night he'd disappeared. He did not flee to avoid the negative energy flying around at home, though I wouldn't have blamed him if he had. I'd have run away right alongside him, were that the case, but he had not run away. He had gone on a desperate, heroic hunt to find his lost harem. He was a dog on a mission, a mission I knew to be doomed because Hazel, Hope, Hayley, and Hiccup were already on their way to another breeder in Alberta, an entire province away. *Surely he had to give up some time. Surely he had to come home to sleep, to eat, to reassure me.* I'd mentally repeated this mantra for the past few days. *So why wasn't he back?!!!*

"When is he coming home?" I exploded, hounding Mom for an answer.

"A woman named Kathy says she found him," she explained as I sat down at the round glass table with my freshly cooked meal. Oh, it smelled so good! My fork stopped midway to my gaping mouth at what I heard next. "But listen, this woman, she's really fallen in love with Harrison. She wants to keep him." My fork slowly returned to the plate, but I was rendered speechless. This was a direct blow that sent my mind spinning and tears flowing. As swiftly as it had come, the joy of Harrison's return was gone again, unwelcomed and unfamiliar to the disheartened soul I'd become. Days had passed without any sign of the little guy, and I finally knew why. He was being held captive, and if he had been *able*, he would have come home. *At least she had found him instead of a cat-eating coyote, or an awful bear that had uncharacteristically stirred from a winter's slumber.*

"Kathy has another dog that Harrison gets along really well with. I told her about our trip and how you still had to find a home for him."

"But Uncle Gord already said he'd take him!" I protested. I knew if my uncle took him I'd always be able to see him, but now a complete stranger wanted to take him.

"Just listen for a minute, Savannah. She really wants to keep him, and she only lives one street up from us. You'll be able to go over and see him whenever you want. She seems like a really nice lady, and she's become really attached to him," Mom continued. "Plus, Gordon doesn't *really* want him. He's just trying to help."

Pushing my now lukewarm eggs round and round on my plate, I sighed. I didn't have an appetite anyway. This kind of stress always threw me off my food, no matter how good it smelled. I was really being put on the spot. I had to make this heart-breaking choice for both Harrison, who had no voice but mine, and for me. I felt like a peach weighted down by an oversized pit balanced precariously upon the branches of an olive tree. I hit unfathomable emotional lows and plummeted dizzyingly towards the stones below.

"He's your dog, so it's your decision. I'm not going to make it for you. You don't have to if you don't want to, but I think it would be the best thing for everyone, and it's the grown-up thing to do." Once again, Terri was there to comfort me when I got off the phone.

"Savannah, this is stupid! You don't have to give her your dog. They have no right to guilt trip you like this. Just don't do it," she advised. She could clearly see I didn't want to lose my dog but I didn't like the thought of Harrison unnecessarily breaking two hearts instead of one, and he'd clearly won this Kathy woman's heart. I choked back tears, torn by the apparent reality that Mom was probably right. Making one last desperate attempt to enjoy what was left of my morning, I forced a bit of breakfast into my mouth and looked up at Terri in complete despair as I felt the distinct crunch of an egg shell.

The absence of Harrison's nails clinking on the tiles and hardwood floors behind me was deafening and depressed me even more.

"What's up with her?" Ammon asked as he entered the front hallway.

"She's upset about Harrison," Mom informed him.

"You mean 'Dumb Harry One Ball'?" Ammon corrected to his satisfaction, implying the dog was only half a man for more than just wearing ribbons and being dyed pink or blue half the time. "Well, it does seem a bit messed up," Ammon added.

Being the only person I know who truly dislikes dogs, I was actually taken aback by Ammon's empathy. Even he did not feel right about it. Meanwhile, I paced anxiously by the door, waiting for Kathy to bring him back. I missed him so much.

"I'm not just giving him away. You promise she's going to let me see him, right?" I asked Mom again before she arrived.

"Yes, that's what she said. She even kind of implied that you could have him back after the year."

"Because I don't want to give him away. If she isn't going to let me see him, I'm not letting him go," I clarified for the umpteenth time. Then, before I knew it, I was on the floor in Mom's sitting room with my back against the wall, discussing conditions and agreements regarding Harrison. Across the room, Kathy stood in front of the fireplace with him in her arms, a sight that made my heart twist. She was a middle-aged woman, divorced with two children, friendly and very average, from what I could tell. She had the kind of face you wouldn't remember or recognize in a crowd. Kathy's other dog, Charlie, pranced in circles at her feet. His eyes bulged severely from his squished Shiatsu face as his neck cranked back further to look up at Harrison jealously. Setting Harrison down, she spoke adoringly of him and their week together.

"I'm going to take really good care of him. You don't need to worry about a thing, darling," she continued, not noticing as Harrison secretly made his way across the wood floor to duck his head beneath my bent knees. He looked out from beneath my legs, his big, sad eyes prompting the most gut-wrenching sense of guilt I'd ever experienced. *But what more can I do to make this right? It's not permanent. Don't make this any harder on us!* My nostrils flared as I took a shaky breath and reached down to scratch the top of his head. While I took a few more minutes to comfort Harrison, Mom did the talking.

"Oh, of course! Savannah can call me anytime." Kathy smiled as she turned to me. "If you want to see him, we'll arrange a date. You don't have to worry about a thing. You can even have him come over for sleepovers. We live just up the street." Turning back to Mom, she continued, "And I gave you my address. You know where that is, right?"

"Yes, yes. It's really close, only a block," Mom confirmed. With everything apparently having been said, not much remained to be done.

"Ok, so I guess we'll be keeping in touch and seeing you soon," Mom gestured her towards the door.

"Oh wait, I need to get a few things first," I said, running off to my bedroom. Harrison dashed behind me as I raced upstairs to collect the few items lying around which I knew would be useless to me now. Grabbing his few coats in one hand, bundling his booties, brush, spare collars, and a leash in the other, I glanced around my room. Everything I could think of, every trace of him, was gone. I had to take a moment to regroup, but I couldn't think too much about what was happening.

As I approached the living room to face the hardest challenge of all, I heard her telling Mom, "When you get back from your trip, just make sure you give me a call. We'll keep in touch." Seeing me slide in, Harrison in tow, she reached for him at the same time I leaned down to pick him off the floor. Nearly bumping heads, I hesitated with my open hands in mid-grab. I lowered them and stood up, letting her take him. I had to fight this natural instinct. Attaching my favourite leash to his collar, I reached over and kissed the top of his head, gripping his ears in my hands. Just as he had sensed my sadness before, I deeply feared that he was confused and didn't understand a thing about what was happening. I saw the question in his big brown eyes. *I just got here. Why am I going back with this person?* He wasn't the type who bonded with just any human – he was very selective, like me. He had been such a loyal companion. I couldn't believe I was sending him away after missing him so much already. *How could I do this to him? How can I make him understand when I'm not sure if I understand it myself?*

Holding the door open, Kathy turned back one last time to reassure me, "Call me any time and we'll arrange a date. We'll come by and say hello when I take him on walks." I smiled, but I didn't dare try to choke a word out. Harrison paused and looked over his shoulder as he walked. Unsure, he needed a tug or two to get him to follow. Shutting the door, I spun on my heels and didn't stop running until I had collapsed on Mom's bed, whereupon I immediately burst into yet another flood of tears. Marshalling every last bit of strength I had to keep from running after him, I buried my face into a pillow, clenching it so hard it nearly split at the seams. I just wanted to evaporate into that pillow as I stifled my cries; there was no point in upsetting everyone else.

I can't do this. I can't do this! It was the only way to anchor myself to the earth. *Oh please Heavenly Father,* I begged in silence, *Please. Please.*

Please. I didn't know what I was asking for, exactly; "please" was all I could think of. Then I heard a loud voice, rough and direct.

"SAVANNAH!" Perhaps I was expecting God or some heavenly guidance, but what I got was Bree. "Do you want me to get him back? You don't HAVE to do this." She could hardly stand to see me in this state.

Completely spastic by this time, I could not respond, but I felt her green eyes on me. The mere task of breathing was too much of a struggle between gasps and chokes. Unwilling to act without my approval, she became frustrated. Being somewhat claustrophobic with her own emotions, she reverted to anger, her usual way of dealing with pain.

"I'm going to go get him," Bree decided, enraged by my evident distress. I rolled onto my back, the pillow still attached to my face.

"No, no, no," I whispered through quivering lips. My mind spoke over my heart. I couldn't rationalize getting him back so I couldn't *take* him back. From the corner of my watery eyes, I could see that Mom was crying, too, but I quickly clenched them shut again. I had to reassure myself I hadn't lost him forever, that it shouldn't be as painful as it felt because I would see him soon. A part of me even felt stupid over the level of my grief, but I couldn't avoid the gnawing pain. *I did the right thing. I'm going to see him soon. He'll be back soon. I did the right thing.* I told myself over and over.

"Just tell me if you made the right decision or *not.* Did you make the right decision!!?" Bree demanded, her words ringing in my already throbbing head.

"I don't know!" I screamed at her before once again weeping myself into a stupor. My gasping cries finally died down to nothing more than occasional whimpers before I fell into an exhausted slumber. *I should have seen in those helpless eyes that he was telling me to hold him close and protect him.* Had I known that was the last time I would *ever* see him, I'd have run out that door myself.

Shots
6

*M*om was consumed with buying backpacks and supplies, packing, having business meetings with Dad and arranging everything else that has to be done before you shut your life down. Our landlord miraculously allowed us to back out of the five-year lease agreement she'd signed only months before, when Dad moved out. Understandably amazed by Mom's plan, he generously offered nothing but good wishes for us on our travels. Everything was falling perfectly into place, giving her even more blind-faith-driven confirmation that she was doing the right thing.

Ammon, the devil's commander-in-chief, was busy researching the most effective vaccines for tropical diseases I'd never even heard of, applying for visas, and planning the safest, most convenient travel routes. Bree was, well, Bree! She was still spending every last waking moment with Fernando who was making his own preparations for his two-year religious mission. I, on the other hand, was working my butt off to finish a few grade eight/nine correspondence courses.

We were in the midst of getting a series of about twelve inoculations to protect us from all sorts of different viruses and illnesses – meningococcal meningitis, for example. *Like, seriously, what the heck is that?!* The four of us headed downtown to the health and travel clinic for yet another vaccination. I didn't feel like talking during the drive or when the doctor came into the room where we waited; my heart still ached over Harrison's loss to Kathy/Cruella de Vil (who had thus far ignored every one of my calls). Comparing her records against Ammon's travel health log-book, the doctor brought us up to date. "Okay, so you've had the Japanese B encephalitis, typhoid, and hepatitis A and B. That was all of them?"

"So far, yup," Ammon responded.

"You must be so excited about this big trip!" I looked away at this. "I'd love to get out of the office and get on the road again," she continued with a sigh. I hadn't ever realized how many people wanted to travel, and that awareness still amazed me. *What could be so phenomenal about running around other peoples' countries?*

"The nurse will be back in with the yellow fever and diphtheria vaccines shortly. You can pay at the front desk on your way out. I wish you guys the best of luck on your adventure."

Bree jumped up to grab more suckers before the door closed. She ended up with one in each hand and a few more in each pocket. I'd be raiding her stash later, but right now, she needed them more than I did.

"Dip a theory? Diaper-ia? What did she say this one was?" Bree asked, her cheeks bulging like a chipmunk.

"Diphtheria," Ammon corrected patiently.

"Seriously, that's bizarre. What's it for?" I asked.

"It's---" he began but then the nurse came in to prepare our inoculations, interrupting our conversation.

Bree had, as usual, wrapped her ankles around her chair legs in anxious anticipation. Her white-knuckled fist grasped the now soggy stick of her second lollipop as she sucked even more frantically. I had actually been banking on her almost desperate fear of needles to save us from this crazy expedition, now that Ammon was apparently determined to keep on living. I was sure she would chicken out and run out of the office, sealing the deal and forcing us to stay put. But nooooo! Not this time. Where was her fear when I needed it? She was sitting there with arm extended, her pits sweating but present nonetheless. Her eyes rolled back as the white surgical gloves snapped into place around the nurse's wrists and the wet cotton ball encased in her gloved hand swabbed Bree's goose-bumped flesh clean.

Bree came by her fear naturally enough. Mom was an avid needle hater too, so for her to be taking this step meant my hopes were truly shattered. *This harebrained idea of hers is only going forward from here, not backwards.* I mused, finally recognizing defeat, *I'm really gonna have to find a way to survive this next year.*

I was not used to being at this end of the needle. Usually it was Mom and me giving our puppies the necessary shots and inserting microchips before they left for their new homes while Bree ran to hide at the other end of the house and get beyond audible range. She'd literally go flying up the staircase with her hands suction-cupped to the side of her head. I caught myself smiling cruelly as I saw the sharp end of a tiny needle puncture Bree's upper right arm and watched her face turn white for the fifth time. At least it made *me* feel better.

Shortly afterwards, we were all standing in the office, well, all except Bree, who'd collapsed into the nearest chair, exhausted from her ordeal.

"OK. That's two hundred and fifty-eight dollars for the three girls, and yours will be eighty-six dollars," the receptionist told Ammon. "The diphtheria combo is covered."

Collecting the money from Mom, who continued to complain quietly about the price, and then putting the bills on the desk, Ammon said, "And I guess we'll still need a few more appointments for rabies, tetanus, and the rest. As soon as possible, I'd think. We still have a few left to do and we should get the rabies started if it's a triple series." As the heavy, wooden door closed behind us, Ammon said almost to himself. "At least we don't need anything for tuberculosis. But, oh right, I was explaining what diphtheria---"

Bree whipped around, cut him off and said, "A Tubular Colossus? What now?! That sounds like some huge, peanut-butter-tube shot! The kind you get in the arse," she said, freaking herself out once again.

"No! You don't need a shot! Tuberculosis, it's---" Ammon began what would only have been a long, drawn-out, scientific explanation.

"AND rabies shots?! What kind of trip are you taking me on?" I demanded.

"Yah!" Bree backed me up, "I don't want that one! I'm not taking anything involving a triple whammy!!"

"You're going to have to. You don't want to risk getting rabies, believe me," Mom said.

"Well, actually," Ammon explained in a way which only meant bad news, "those ones won't prevent it or even save you from it. It's not something that's preventable with a vaccine."

"Then there's no freaking way I'm getting it! Why would I want to do that if I'm just going to get it anyway!?" Bree concluded, crossing her arms with a loud and final-sounding "hrmph!"

"'Cause it buys you more time to get to a hospital and THAT is where they'll hopefully be able to give you an anti-rabies shot. But if you're out in the boonies, you're right. You're probably doomed anyway."

"Wonderful," I said simply, stepping from the elevator.

Packrat Rehabilitation
7

*T*he walls inside the house were now stripped bare and seemingly shamed by their nudity, though our pictures hadn't even been up long enough to leave their faded outlines behind. The halls echoed, and what had once been the most popular and heavily visited driveway in the "hood" lay naked and exposed in the sun. *It's as though we never even lived here.*

Whispers started and rumours spread as we'd condensed what was left from a seven-bedroom house, load after load, into a nine-by-twelve foot storage unit. Some considered it running away from our troubles, while others deemed it to be pure nonsense. With a heavy heart, I co-operated in giving and throwing away, selling and packing up everything I owned at the time. Only a few people we knew believed we could pull it off. I understood how hard it was for family and friends to understand how we could just drop everything and give up our secure, relatively luxurious life for the unpredictable road ahead, challenging the world and backpacking through places most considered dangerous! I had never thought about China that way, but then, all I really knew about China was that I was supposed to get there through my backyard, something that had never held any particular appeal. I found myself learning all sorts of new things from my helpful peers and relatives, mainly how "smelly," "dirty," and "uncouth" the country was. "They will kidnap you for your hair," and "Just don't let them see your retainer; braces are a sign of wealth," and other stuff like that. But now the last of our remains were being consolidated into green Rubbermaid buckets, and we'd soon be closing the door behind us forever.

"Bree, get down here!" I heard Mom shout from the bottom of the stairs for what seemed to be the umpteenth time.

"You can't have all these buckets," Mom explained when Bree reluctantly appeared. "Look how many the rest of us have," she said, stepping aside so Bree could count the tubs stacked against the stairwell. "Ammon's got three, Savannah has five. You have *eighteen*! We're only saving the most important things."

"But it's ALL important," Bree insisted. Reaching into one of the dozen boxes Mom grabbed a half-eaten stuffed animal that must've been lost in storage and smelled like it had been used as a rat's toilet.

Pinching only a tiny corner to hold it up, Mom grimaced almost sympathetically. "This?" "How did you ever get THIS past our last move?" I smiled and had to work hard to hold back a snorting laugh. The tone in her voice clearly said, *You poor thing. You are so confused.*

"But Mom, I made that in my grade eight sewing class!!"

"That was four years ago," I informed her righteously.

"Bree, this is disgusting. I'm sure it was lovely at the time, but what are you going to do with it? It stinks!" Mom insisted, crinkling her nose to demonstrate her distaste. "Most of this stuff is garbage! It isn't even good enough to donate to the Salvation Army. Heaven forbid, I would ever let you try and sell this stuff at the garage sale." Searching another box she continued, "And these!! Where have you been hiding THESE all those years?" Mom was astounded.

"I love my binkies!" she whined, snatching them from Mom's hands and pressing the baby pacifiers to her chest. Bree was consumed with savouring these childhood treasures in her muscular hands before she put them, one by one, on each of her fingers. She had to have had at least nine of them.

"Bree! Are you listening to me?" Mom demanded.

"Yes," she said, furrowing her brows and turning a shoulder to Mom to protect the precious goods she clung to.

"You simply can't keep all of this. They can't be that important. I bet you can't even remember where half of it came from."

"Of course I can!" she defended, and that was probably true. Bree, like Ammon, has the most incredible memory when she chooses to use it. The problem is that she often has selective, biased hearing; she remembers every single time she's been deceived, like the time she didn't get the ice cream she was promised at the park when she was three years old – that kind of stuff. Basically, you don't ever want to get on her bad side because she will never forget it.

Piece by piece, shred by shred, Mom held her hand as she chucked odd socks, already filled in colouring books, cap guns, and crumpled up notes passed in class from years before.

"You have got to stop being a pack rat. This is ridiculous," Mom said, waving a Popsicle stick in her face.

"But it's about the memories," Bree insisted, her now stormy green eyes set on the next sacrificial item.

A derisive laugh escaped me just as the phone rang, and Mom grumbled a frustrated response. Having grown up with five brothers and raised four children, she had, over the course of her life, unknowingly perfected Marge Simpson's famous groan of disapproval.

"Just give me a sec," Mom said as she put down another one of Bree's hoarded treasures. "When I get back, you better have at least half a bucket emptied." She used the calm, consoling tone all mothers develop as a last resort. "You can do this, Bree. Just take this stuff, go through it once more really well, and only keep what you *need*." And she left to answer the phone in her bedroom.

Momentarily escaping Mom's oversight, Bree only managed to collect the things she wanted to keep, rather than what she could throw away, which was everything she had got her hands on. Sitting on the floor to better pick things out and collect a bigger pile in her lap, she sifted through her first box, all the while inventing reasons to justify each worthless item.

"Oh, ok, have to keep this. Can't chuck this. Definitely, this has to stay. Mmmhrmmpphh, yep, yep, mmmm, yep! Uh huh! Oh no, no, no. This one's a keeper for sure."

"It was Gordon," Mom announced as she came down the hall. "He's giving us six months," she laughed. Geez, I hoped he was right. Of my nine uncles, he had given us the best odds. They had formed a betting pool, and the odds were that it would take three months, maximum, before Bree and I would crumble in the third world, forcing the family's return. My "Aunt Plastic" had avidly expressed her opinion that she would rather have her arms and legs slowly severed than go on a trip like ours while flipping her expensive, bottled-blonde hairdo in our faces. Being nothing less than gorgeous to begin with, she spent her energy and time perfecting the art of femininity, and boy, did it show! Batting the luxurious lashes that framed her stunning blue eyes, her extra-white teeth blinded me as she bid us an early farewell. *So I guess I'm not the only person who thinks this plan is crazy. Not everyone wants to take my place!* Although I was finally not alone in my opinion, the knowledge that I was in good company somehow just didn't settle my stomach the way I'd hoped. In fact, it only confirmed my fears and made it worse.

Bree's begging brought me back from my contemplation. Every other item Mom pulled out – be it one of a dozen decks of playing cards, a bouncy ball of any shade or size, or old candy – was getting tossed. Bree was hysterical. Her junk is her life.

"And half of these clothes will be too small for you by the time you get home. The same goes for you, Savannah." Mom was sitting cross-legged on the floor as she unpacked. "When was the last time you used this?" Mom kept impatiently repeating the typical questions you would pose to a compulsive hoarder, finishing on a resigned note. "I can't believe I didn't check what you were storing sooner!"

Ammon arrived home and stepped right into the middle of the bucket battle spread across the front entryway. He raised an eyebrow, but knew better than to ask. A gust of wind played with the ends of his long trench coat as he stepped through the doorway like some sort of dark lord of the manor, his black boots depositing splotches of mud everywhere he stepped.

"Choke, choke. Cough, cough," he began preparing us for his speech, "Hey, okay, so guys …" getting our attention as he manoeuvred his way through the maze of buckets. I ignored the sight of Bree stealing back a deck of cards to slip it down the side of a bucket. *Well, if it's that important to her …*

"I found our tickets. We're flying out of SeaTac International Airport," he said, pausing afterwards to extract the full effect. "It saves us at least a hundred bucks each on the fare. And that way it works for Aunt Pam, since she wanted to arrange a farewell party. We stopover in Seoul, and arrive in Hong Kong May 5th. That's the cheapest day, and get this – it's 05/05/05!"

"Oh that's so cool, I love the number five," Mom said joyfully. You could just see fives dancing in her eyes.

"Let's just hope that's good luck," Ammon said.

"Of course it is!" she insisted. In numerology, the number five represents freedom. It fit so appropriately with her freshly kindled sense of adventure that nothing could hold her back now. She had the freedom she'd never experienced before and the newly discovered courage to act on it.

"That's a week after I finish my Bachelor of Science degree," Ammon finished, but there was a slight mix of joy and sadness in his voice. He'd hoped that the scholarships he'd always earned would allow him to continue studying for the rest of his life, having no greater love than the pure pursuit of knowledge, but Fate was preparing to close that door. As each of us faced closing doors, an even bigger one was opening up, and we would all step through it together. I, more reluctant than the rest, was frantically clinging to the nearest symbolic doorframe and the familiar comforts it represented. There I hung in suspense until a family team member came back to collect and shove me forward into the unknown.

Arrival
8

*T*hroughout the nearly forty-hour transit to Hong Kong, I had expected to hear myself screaming hysterically at any moment – *Get me out of here. Get me off this plane now!* But there was never any peak of panic or specific moment when I knew I'd crossed over to the "other" side. I was still just me. It's possible I was still waiting for my numb senses to thaw.

After my first overseas flight, I drooped like the branches of a dying plant. All that strange airplane food did nothing for either my stomach or my breath, and I knew that my hair was frazzled beyond belief just by looking at the state of the hair on my fellow travellers.

When we finally got through security, baggage pick-up, and customs, the last set of glass doors slid open and I saw the wave of people waiting on the other side. Family, friends, and lovers greeted one another warmly, but I knew nobody would be there to greet me. My head hung low as I entered this new world, wanting nothing more than to have my old one back. *Just a normal door, with normal people, with normal shops. This is okay so far,* I told myself. *Just take it one step at a time.*

"Well, we might as well get comfy," I heard Ammon advise. "We'll pack up and leave in the morning." As he dug through his big backpack and started unraveling his sleeping bag, my jaw nearly dropped right off.

"What!? You're telling me we're sleeping HERE!? Where and how do you suppose we do that?" I asked, looking around at the airport's shiny hallways lined with trash bins, benches, and the now closed shops.

"Find a good bench and claim it quick," he said, as if the answer were obvious to all. *When they said we'd be sleeping in the airport, I assumed they meant a hotel close by, not literally IN the airport!* I didn't yet know that this was but the first of many sleepless nights I would spend tossing and turning in less than ideal conditions.

I woke to a loud, automated, "Ding. Ding. Ding. Thai Airways flight TG 603 to Bangkok is now boarding at gate 44." Peeking out of one eye, I noticed all sorts of shuffling movements around me. Shiny, black dress shoes were nearly stepping on my nose where I lay. The airport was much busier in the early morning hours. The floor was no harder than the benches, and it had offered more room to stretch out after that long, cramped flight. *What time is it?* I thought, searching for a clock as I tried to casually sit up.

My morning ritual began in a public bathroom, where I brushed my teeth and hair. *Man, I look like something that's been washed up by the sea,* I thought when I leaned over the sink for a closer look. Feeling out of place, I wished someone would come along and throw me right back in.

"Oh, don't do that," Mom said, with a quick tilt of her head.

Facing her in the mirror next to me, I demanded, "Do what?"

"And don't do that, either!"

"What?" I growled, brushing my excessively foamy mouth and creating ever more bubbles. "It doesn't matter. I'm just a bum anyway!"

"You are not. Lots of people travel like this. That's why you're allowed to sleep on the floor. And I was talking about that face."

"What face?" I said, snarling at myself in the mirror again.

"It isn't the end of the world. You haven't even given it a chance. Maybe you're really going to like it here. At least save your complaining until we get out of the airport, for heaven's sake."

"I don't have to wait until I'm out there. What do you call sleeping on a public floor!? Fun?"

"It's a beautiful airport," she said, "and it's my first time, too. I see it as an adventure." *Can she honestly think that? Is that enthusiasm I hear in her voice?*

"Especially with that thunderstorm last night!" Bree added, her own toothbrush dangling from one corner of her mouth. She may have enjoyed the gushing waterfall on the big glass windows. I, on the other hand, had mistaken the thundering of the tropical storm for the panicked reaction of my surging heart.

"Fun. Right," I began sarcastically. "I came all the way here to sleep on a *floor* to see a rainstorm that I could just as easily have seen at home."

"Well, it was a very clean floor," Mom said, pointing out the obvious. *Heaven forbid it had been anything but!* "Clean! How is that supposed to make me feel? Enthusiastic? You can't be serious," I said, affirming my misgivings. "Pft! And Ammon says this is a good place."

"Oh, that's just Ammon. You don't have to listen to everything he says. He just wants to break us in quickly," she said, casually dismissing him. *Now at least she's talking some common sense,* I thought, but I still struggled to follow her advice.

Meeting back at the benches near our so-called beds, we used the free Internet on available computers and wrote a quick note on the blog to let our family know we'd arrived safely.

> ** *We have finally arrived (though we have yet to*
> *get out of the airport). Wicked thunderstorm here*
> *to welcome us to Hong Kong last night. Very muggy*
> *and overcast. Well, let's go see what we can find …*
> *Ammon*

> *Well guys,*
> *Yesterday was officially the first day of the*
> *"New Beginning" – The start of our long and*
> *prosperous "journey." The day all hell breaks loose*
> *and we become open targets for adventure. Only*
> *time will reveal the secrets that lay ahead …*
> *Savannah*

That was the longest freakin flight I've
ever had to deal with.
Breanna

We all look the way you would imagine after
37 hours in airports and planes. And yes, we did
sleep/rest in the airport last night as planned.
Maggie **

And with that task taken care of, we loaded our packs and walked out of the airport, keeping in mind our newly devised Travel Rule #3: The Buddy System. The sun shone brightly as I took my first timid steps onto Chinese soil.

"Oh, Lord! Stop it! Seriously, you look retarded," Ammon said as we made our way to the bus station.

Holding the collar of my shirt up to protect my mouth and nose, I shook my head violently, muttering under my breath, "not yet, but it'll come, it'll come." They were all looking at me strangely, but I didn't care. Terri's final, farewell warning echoed in my subconscious. *You're going to keel over and die!* she had joked in a feeble attempt to lighten the mood. It was the only time I didn't crack even a smile at hearing one of our most commonly used expressions. And now, I was deathly afraid of what everyone who "knew so well" had shared with me – that rancid, putrid smells would wash over me the instant my nostril hairs tingled in the Chinese air.

"You can come out now," Bree laughed, demonstrating how safe it was with a big gulp of seemingly harmless air. Flaring her nostrils, she inhaled deeply again to prove it was stink-free.

"Yah, right! This, coming from the girl who loves the smell of horse manure in the morning!" I said, hesitant to trust her judgement. But the air didn't seem to have the same *Total Recall* effect that I anticipated. She was indeed, still her normal, Bree self, happy and joking and ready to take on a challenge. She didn't even seemed bothered by her new single state. *Maybe she's being practical for the first time in her life. Nah!!* I thought, glaring over my covered nose at her.

Bree's cheery attitude began to irritate me later on the bus. *Look at her, all happy in her little world. Why is she glued to the window like she gives a darn? Since when did she want to go to Asia?* I played with my little zebra stuffy hanging on my bag in a moment of contemplation. *What could she possibly be so excited about?*

Scrambling off the bus, I tripped on the last step and was unceremoniously spat out into the spinning world around me. Men and women zipped by on foot or bicycles, and I immediately felt lost in the throng. My fairer features stood out in stark contrast with the hordes of miniature working clones with black hair and dark eyes. *Actually, they all kind of look like my manicurist. I guess she was from China after all,* I thought, taking my eyes off the road to look at my freshly done nails and promptly stumbled from the unaccustomed weight on my back.

As I recovered, I somehow inadvertently let my guard down and removed my hand from tightly clenching at my collar. I waited and waited for the dreaded smell to hit me, expecting to fall over, or at the very least, gag. *So where is this awful smell hiding?* Maybe I'd have to admit defeat and say I was wrong – but only to myself, of course. That was one nagging fear out of the way. Now, on to the next.

I was being bounced around like a pinball in the massive crowds, my pack steering me rather than the other way around as it sagged awkwardly on my butt. *What the heck is in this bag?* I wondered as I waddled down the street like an obese duck, constantly reaching behind my back trying to adjust my drooping pants.

What looked like routine havoc wreaked the streets. No one noticed me amid the rush of downtown Hong Kong. No one, that is, except for the few red taxis and their female drivers. Slowing down, they tried to tempt us to climb in, get the bags off our backs, and take a restful seat in the air conditioning. *I swear as soon as I get this wretched thing off me, I'm chucking half of whatever the bleep-jeeps they put in it.* Sensing that we were fading in the heat and noise, Ammon promptly reminded us about Travel Rule #2: No Taxis, and then quickened his pace without a single backward glance. I certainly did not want to be left behind so I reluctantly picked up my pace to match his. *I'd rather go with these loonies than be lost here,* I reasoned quickly. *How on earth would I ever find them again? Phone call? No, who would I phone? Grandma? What could she do to help from Vancouver? She doesn't know where I'm going either. I know. I'd just find an Internet café! I'd just email Mom, and then wait. But how would I know how to tell her where I was? And I've never even seen one of those before. How would I know what one looks like?* I panicked, looking at the glowing shop signs and advertisements and searching vainly for recognizable street names. *How do you pronounce THAT? They don't even have an alphabet I can read. How will I know where they are if I don't even know where I am!? I don't have any local currency. I've got some American money hidden in there somewhere, but what am I going to do with that here? What if they never came back? How would I get home?*

"Have you ever seen so many?" Bree asked out loud, disrupting my endless string of worries.

"Yah, but only when I was in London. It was exactly like this," Mom replied, as we crossed onto a less crowded street.

"Seriously?" I asked, glancing down the road which was still flooded with red double-decker buses, a sight which caught me completely off guard. *It really looks like this! Maybe I am in England – now that wouldn't be so bad.* "So it really is like the movies there, eh? Wow. I can't imagine this being normal."

"It was a British colony until just eight years ago, so the buses make sense," Ammon added, looking up from his map for a split second.

The whole street seemed to be full of screaming "Pick me!!! Pick me!!!" florescent signs. Each vender was yelling louder than the last and competing with the shop next door as to whose wares could be bigger and brighter. There were *Hello Kitties* on all forms of merchandise to both my right and my left, along with just about anything else you could possibly imagine. The vendors sold it all.

"Whoa, this is a lot like Vegas," Bree chirped, beaming at the variety of lights radiating from the city streets.

"Minus all the chicken scratch," I pointed out. "Plus, there's no English. I feel like I took a wrong turn in Chinatown and we're gonna be lost forever." *Forever.* It was a daunting word these days. Why was it that a year felt like a lifetime? I knew it was only one of nearly a hundred. It was nothing, only one percent of my ENTIRE life. But this was only the first of three-hundred-and-sixty-five days, and that seemed like an eternity.

I yanked at Mom's pack as she stepped off the sidewalk, nearly getting herself shmucked by a little motorcycle darting through the early morning rush hour. This was immediately followed by a fierce glare from Ammon on my left, silently reminding us about Travel Rule #1: DON'T GET DEAD! *We'll see how long that rule lasts.* There was no time to stop or think. We had to continue. We were as ready as we were likely to be now that we'd affirmed the wisdom of our top three rules under real live circumstances.

"Okay, then" I said to the world, only somewhat prepared to take on this madness as I stepped down from the curb.

My feet were on fire and yet felt icy at the same time as I lifted each one separately to scratch imaginary itches. Cramped in the small box they called an elevator that dripped with its own form of sticky sweat, my legs were weak and hot. I pushed my way out the moment the door opened, desperate for cooler air.

The man with the keys, groggy from being wakened from his post downstairs, twisted the knob and presented our room, if you could call it that. It was as small as a "Harry Potter" closet under the stairs and it contained nothing more than a bed, which was all that could physically fit in the space. My eyes widened involuntarily as I took in the sad sight. *So, this is my new life.*

"Oh, don't be so dramatic, Savannah," Mom yawned. I tossed my pack onto the bed and watched it roll off and get stuck between the bed and the wall. I directed the most irritated, disbelieving face I could muster at the light blue and black, sixty-litre backpack. *I hate you already,* I thought with the fiercest passion I'd yet experienced. And then I laughed with a touch of hysteria.

"Hey, you better enjoy it. This'll be one of the best rooms you'll get," Ammon said, peeking around the doorway beside where I was still transfixed by our accommodations.

"What's your guys' room like?" I asked.

"The same." With no space to walk, I crawled from the door onto the bed next to Mom.

"Can you believe this place?" In disbelief, I looked around at the room which held all of one door, one bed, and a crooked mirror on one wall.

"Ammon booked the best he could find for a reasonable price. Even this costs fifty dollars a night. Hong Kong is a big city; nothing is cheap here."

"How can they charge that much for this?" I asked, baffled. "You can hardly even fit a bag in here!" I tilted my head towards our two packs which consumed the entire floor space.

For us, fifty bucks was a lot. Whenever we went on a family road trip, we'd either camp or all stay in a single, forty-dollar-a-night room in a Motel 6. That was another deep, dark secret that not even Terri knew. I always felt ashamed that I could only imagine the five-star hotels my friends stayed in on holidays.

"Yes, I know, Savannah. But it's clean, and you don't actually NEED any more than this," she emphasized. *Yah, and you don't actually NEED underwear either, but it's still nice to have them,* I thought bitterly.

"Doesn't it make you wonder how they ever got the bed in here in the first place?" I asked, too tired to argue. I was too tired for anything but the simplest complaints. I had no strength left to stage one of my usual, more dramatic performances. *So this is their plan, is it? Tire me out so much I can't complain. Keep me quiet. How could I let them take over like this? Those sneaky devils!* A frightening realization hit me. *No wonder my – they must've – I'll bet they planted weights in my bag!!!* I sprang to check my pack.

"What are you doing?" Mom jumped at my sudden movements.

"What the heck on earth," I rambled, completely ignoring her as I flipped back the top of my big backpack and loosened the string to get into the main section, "could possi---BOOKS!?!?!" I exclaimed as I felt the hard flat surface and the bundled pages.

"Yes, books. Lots of them," Mom said without flinching. "What about it?"

"That's horrible. How could you do this to me?" I asked, too flabbergasted to be angry.

"I told you before we left that everyone is going to keep a journal, too," she added.

"Yah, yah. A journal. Okay, I can see that. But you didn't mention the rest of the library that comes with it!" I said, feeling deceived as I continued to pull them out one-by-one like a magician might pull rabbits from a hat.

I had only found a notebook and pen at the very last minute for a journal because of Mom's insistence, but I never thought she'd actually try to enforce reading, particularly if we had to lug the books around with us! It was a family tradition, I guess. When Bree and I visited our relatives at their summer house on Lake Chelan, Washington, Aunt Pam expected us to read for an hour each day. But we'd spent our entire summer vacation time boating, wakeboarding, and Seadoo-ing with our cousins. I couldn't recall ever seeing, let alone opening, a single book, so it didn't really follow that reading and writing would actually happen on this trip of our own volition.

"You're cruel," I said, pulling the last of five books out and placing it on the bed.

"It's good for you," she said.

"I'm already carrying all my school work!" I reminded her.

"That was your choice, not mine." *When they asked if I packed my own bag at the airport I should have said "Certainly NOT!"*

"Yah, so?" Before the trip, I had been enrolled in self-taught correspondence courses, an optional form of home-schooling that replaces a traditional school using either the Internet or the postal system to send assignments and other materials back and forth. Each of my siblings had done this type of schooling at one point in their lives, though we had different reasons. I decided on my last visit to the school where my instructors were based that I would take a couple of courses with me on the road.

"You aren't going to have time for school, Savannah. It seems a bit pointless for you to be carrying all that around."

"Are you kidding me? At least there's a point to this, an end in sight, but to read and write with no ultimate goal is pointless," I retaliated. "Do you have any idea how heavy this bag is?"

"You can catch up with your coursework when you get back," she said calmly.

"NO! 'Cause I don't want to be behind. I already told you that!" *Geez, is that really too much to ask?*

"They said you can just skip some of the work," Mom added.

"I don't believe it. That's so stupid. You can't just *skip*!"

"You heard what they said as well as I did," she said, mentally backing me into a corner.

I thought back to the meetings we'd had with school personnel. Some said it was ridiculous and too much of a risk to take me out of school. Others thought it was brilliant, that the lessons I would learn abroad would provide a better education than they could ever offer in the school system. Bree's counsellor had voiced the opinion I heard far more often than I cared to. "After all, what better way to prepare yourself for the real world than to experience it firsthand?" I personally had yet to see the advantages.

Bree vehemently objected to bringing any schooling materials along, preferring to fool herself into thinking she had already graduated instead. My counsellor assured me that there were alternatives and showed me independent projects kids had done to catch up in similar situations, but I was determined not to fall behind. *So what if I HAD insisted on doing all the work? Shouldn't I be rewarded for that rather than punished!?* "But still, I'm already carrying the school work," I reminded her again.

"Books are great because you can just take them out and read them any time. Your school work is too bulky, plus you'll need an Internet connection that won't often be available. Trust me, you should just leave it behind and catch up later. Your brain will be engaged in lots of other ways."

Bree came crashing in at that point, nearly slamming into the door when it hit the end of the bed and stopped abruptly in mid-swing.

I was sure she would share my outrage, and burst out, "These criminals put BOOKS in my bag!!"

"Have you seen the bathroom?" she asked, completely ignoring my protest. Her famous selective hearing had kicked in again.

"Oh no! It's a squatty, isn't it!?" I bolted upright in a panic. The state of the toilets we would be using was a far more pressing issue.

"No, you're lucky this time," Ammon said, coming in behind her.

"Phew," I exhaled, leaning back. *I'm safe for one more day, at least.*

"You gotta see it, though," she said urgently, as if I was somehow going to miss it during our four-day stay. "Like, the shower and sink and toilet are all together in a tiny room, with nothing separating them. So weird!"

"Why don't I find that hard to believe?" I asked, glancing around me.

"The toilet is in the middle of the shower. You can just sit there and do your thing and get clean at the same time!" she laughed.

"Oh hey, you've got *The Count of Monte Cristo*?" Ammon commented when he saw the small pile of unwanted books scattered on the bed. "Can I borrow that one?"

"Be my guest," I said, standing up to go check out Bree's bathroom.

"Trust me, you'll want them," Ammon noted starkly, expecting everyone to be as nerdy as he.

"No, no. Trust me, I won't," I said, walking away and waving my hand above my head, "Take them all. Go nuts!"

The Conqueror
9

*S*andra was one of Ammon's closest friends, though he often refused to admit he had any. They had worked in the same lab at Simon Fraser University for almost a year before we finally met her for the first time in Hong Kong. She was referred to as The Chocolate Chick because she brought a candy bar to work every day in an attempt to fatten him up. This act of generosity was strongly influenced by his study of the health benefits of chocolate, but also because of the way his ribcage protruded from his slender frame.

We learned quickly how friendly and positive Sandra was – the kind of person who celebrates her birthday by buying you lunch. She happened to be visiting her hometown when we arrived May 5th, 2005, and she was gracious enough to show us around for a few days. Sandra fit right in with what I perceived to be the millions of little clones marching the streets with their black hair and round cheeks, and we eagerly followed our bubbly new friend around the city as the days raced by, on foot and riding the occasional water ferry and double-decker city buses. We were introduced to a wide range of traditional songs and food as well as to Mr. Buddha in my very first incense-permeated monastery. We did everything from tracing the Avenue of Stars, to hiking, to exploring little caves in Macau, the former Portuguese colony across the bay.

Sandra, my new four-day-old best friend, was like an angel from heaven, a piece of home. *Couldn't we just call it a deal already and let her take me home with her? Haven't I put in enough travel time?* When we had completed her four-day, introductory crash course to the marvels of her birth city, the five of us said goodbye at the front entrance of the subway station. I gave her one last hug and then faced the dark escalator which would lower me down to my very first underground metro. I only turned around once and, as the rest of the early morning rush hour swallowed her up, I saw a tiny hand waving. Oh, how I longed to stay by her side, but Ammon was pressing forward so confidently and it never once occurred to me that he, too, might feel a tinge of apprehension.

From a distance, the city looked a lot like Vancouver, with its high-rises, busy streets and waterfront activities. Its "Hongcouver" moniker and its incredible diversity partially explained why I felt as comfortable as I did there. The daily markets crammed between tiny alleys bursting with goods of all kinds amazed me, but we were being set free now, underway with all sails set, strong winds blowing, and a whole world of possibilities opening up to us.

I felt I was teetering on the edge of my last chance to escape. I knew that the farther we travelled inland, the farther we'd get from an airport and civilization. All along, I had been expecting some kind of Big Bang type of reaction. I resented the trip so deeply and yet, despite the months of foreboding, it had not yet "hit" me. I was still waiting for some sort of physical manifestation of my ambivalence about this trip, like a quake in my knees that would send me toppling to the ground, or something – anything! *I wanted to be shocked! To be surprised! Where were my fireworks?!* I almost began to feel ripped off about the lack of a significant personal breakdown of any kind, though we did, by sheer happenstance, see the nightly firework and laser lightshow from Hong Kong's seawall on our last night in the city.

The subway was nearly empty when we got on, but it got busier and busier as we passed more stops. *What else did I expect in the most populous country in the world – 1.3 billion people had to get where they were going somehow, obviously!?* A man sat and shoved me and my pack over because we were taking up part of his seat. *How rude!* I thought, glaring cynically in his direction while trying to balance a single, numb, buttcheek on the hard plastic. To avoid having to stand, I leaned forward awkwardly, only just managing to squeeze half of my pack onto the seat. I struggled to make enough room for both of us on the seat, the straps of my pack coming up over my ears like a kid swimming with an oversized lifejacket. I had to sacrifice most of my bum space for the darn thing. *This isn't my bloody child*, I thought, refusing to be abused. *It's just a dumb bag. I'd sit it on my lap if my daypack wasn't already occupying that space. Nope, that isn't going to work, either.* I was getting more and more annoyed. *Is it getting hotter in here?* I wondered as still more people poured in, but it was likely my face flushing from rage and embarrassment. *Can't you see this is awkward for me?* Returning the stare an older couple was giving me, I wanted to shout at them instead. *It's not my fault. Can't you see how much I don't WANT to be here!!?*

After crossing the border into Shenzhen on mainland China, we were drenched by a tropical storm as we transferred from the subway to a bus. I squinted through the droplets to study my new surroundings. Rain flooded the streets and the open shopping mall we passed. It felt warm, like a fresh breath on an early summer day, and the palm trees were shining and blowing in the wind. Shenzhen was another city seemingly made up of lots of people in heels and business suits walking briskly, but typically, they still seemed to find time to gawp at the spectacle our foreign parade evidently presented.

Why does everyone have to stare at me? This being only the second time I'd ever carried my pack, I felt self-conscious and paranoid that people were staring and snickering behind my back. It was like a high-school drama where everyone hides behind lockers and spreads the newest rumours – I had always hated that kind of thing.

"This is the biggest city you've been to," Ammon told us. "More than ten million people live here. Do you realize that's almost a third the population of all of Canada just in this one city?!" And it felt like every one of those ten million citizens were staring right at me. As if to confirm my insecurity, a random woman approached us speaking in Mandarin, and her friends started laughing. I understood nothing, and again felt like the new kid at school – like a stupid outcast who was oblivious to the latest fashions and the "hottest" new quotes and phrases. I continued to revel in my humiliation. *I'm so glad no one from home sees me looking like the laughing stock of the entire world!* After my long

walk of shame, Ammon lead us through the markets towards the
bus station area. Women merchants loudly accosted us, attempting to
make a sale as we neared their stalls.

We passed a humming refrigerator, and Mom started dragging her
feet and drooling, "Oooh, Peeeppssii." I pushed her along as she began to crumble from the inside out.

"C'mon Mom, you're not allowed," I reminded her. We had made
Mom agree to quit drinking pop on the basis that we were all starting a new life, healthy and fresh. We knew the trip would consist of
a lot more exercise and organic food than we had ever before experienced, not to mention that we would be on the skinniest shoestring
budget anyone had ever heard of; Travel Rule # something-or-other
was that Coca-Cola and Pepsi are unnecessary delights. That was only
one of many scary laws in Ammon's self-made, budget rulebook. But
of course, no such book ever existed in written form, otherwise he
wouldn't have been able to invent and change the rules whenever the
occasion called for it.

"No, I didn't say I was going to stop drinking pop. I said I wouldn't
drink Dr. Pepper. I didn't say anything about Pepsi," she said in a val-
iant attempt to convince herself.

"Oh Mom---" I started just before I was distracted by the sight of
what could only be considered a godsend – a magnetic force calling
my name. He was tall with golden twine upon his crown, and he displayed the most prominent nose I'd ever seen, at least in the last week.
He spoke Chinese but was definitely not from around here. He had
a backpack, too. I felt like shouting, "Yeah! We're saved!" and rushing over to him to have him sort out our next meal, hotel, and bus.
Checking side-to-side to scout his territory, Ammon finally came to
a halt, pulled one strap over his shoulder, and said, "Okay, just drop
your bags here." He calmly jaunted over to the foreign man in his "I
am an experienced traveller" mode. This was the preferable course of
action, of course, 'cause if I had just run up and clung to his leg like
a blood-thirsty savage like I wanted to, we'd have lost him for sure. I
would've scared just about anybody away in my current unstable state.

Ammon stood next to the man and nonchalantly asked, "Where
are you headed?"

"Yangshuo," came the equally cool reply. He was tall and lanky, like Ammon. *Maybe it's not a coincidence that he looks so much like Ammon. Maybe after a while all backpackers start to develop that same appearance.* I began to wonder how I would look as a six-foot-two chick with a bristly jaw. *At least I could keep my ponytail,* I thought, putting a positive spin on it.

"Same as us, then. Do you happen to know which bus it is?" Ammon asked to save himself the trouble of consulting his complicated guidebooks yet again.

"Sure, it's that one over there, the one that says Yangshuo," he said, pointing down the station at one of the dozens of buses with a big white sign in the front window. Easing in behind Ammon, I looked at the bus, then at Mom.

"THAT says Yangshuo?!" I whispered incredulously.

"How the heck would I know?!" Mom whispered back, peering down the rows and feeling just as clueless regarding which bus they meant.

"Unbelievable. That's what he just said. I don't think I could ever read Chinese. How can they tell one letter from the next?!!" I asked under my breath, completely baffled and unable to discern any differences in the writing.

"Okay, great. Thanks a lot. We'll see you there, I guess," Ammon said, before giving us the only bit of information he remembered. "The bus leaves in about forty-five minutes. You'll need a bathroom before you go. You never know when these guys will stop for a break. It could be all night, or it could be every twenty minutes, so you have to be prepared for anything. There's a good place in that hotel just through the shops. You'll see a big golden sign with lions in front of it," he instructed. Mom began practically pulling my arm off in the direction he pointed.

"Do you have to go that badly?" I whispered out of the side of my mouth.

"Yes," she lied.

"Okay, okay. Bree, Mom and I will be back in a minute," I told her. "Ammon's obviously still busy, so you stay here and guard our bags while we scout it out." I turned to tell Ammon the same, but he had resumed his conversation with the tall, golden-haired backpacker.

"Are you guys new at this?" the man was asking, looking down at our scuff-free boots.

"Actually, it's our first overnighter bus," was all I heard before the other noises of the station drowned out their voices.

I paced along behind Mom, re-entering the shopping strip and looking everywhere for the golden signs. In my concentrated attempt to skirt the dozens of Chinese men and women peddling or shopping in the station, I took my eyes off Mom for a split second. When I didn't see her little red shirt five steps ahead of me, I almost had a heart attack. *Where the heck did she go?* I began to panic, my head twisting frantically like a lost chicken. I finally spotted her inside a shop. *What on earth is she doing?* I thought angrily to cover my relief. Approaching her from behind, I quickly saw her strategy.

"What on earth?"

"Well, we're going to need snacks for the trip," she rushed to explain. By hanging over the counter and pointing and waving her arms, she had managed to collect an assortment of cookies, chips, and water for the twelve hours we'd be on the bus, but one thing in particular had drawn her into this store, the one item that shouldn't have been in her pile.

Shaking the antique glass Coca-Cola bottle, I asked her, "And what's this?"

"Oh, but I'm so thirsty, Savannah." I glared at her as she continued, "and I haven't had one in days! Couldn't we just share it?" she proposed with a co-conspirators' smile.

I thought hard about her suggestion. Splotches of sweat were soaking through my shirt from the long walk to the bus station. Still holding the cold bottle in my hot hand, I gave in to her devious wiles. Creeping around the nearest corner, we passed the drink back and forth like junkies in a doorway, savouring each sip while also keeping a sharp eye out for Ammon. After indulging in our guilty pleasure, Mom and I found the toilets and quickly ran back to collect Bree.

"It's a squatty!" I lamented once we'd entered the building, "but we've looked everywhere, and didn't see anything else." During our first few days, we had ingeniously managed to avoid using them by taking refuge in the occasional McDonalds. They were the only places we knew that had western toilets. There hadn't been anything more shocking in my first week than the length of the line-up for the squatty toilet in the women's bathroom while the western-style facilities right next to it stood empty, even though there was no "out of order" sign attached. *Why and how could ANYONE in their right mind – how could they – let alone want to use it – ever?!* But then, maybe it was just me. After months of dreading this, I finally had to face my worst nightmare. There was no escape, no way out. It was now or it would be later, all over myself in a crowded bus. As tempting as a burst bladder sounded, which seemed to be my only alternative at the time, I opted to overcome my fear.

Mom and Bree each took a step and disappeared into two of the three stalls. Looking around wildly for an escape and seeing none, I finally stepped into mine. I knew what I had to do, but how!?!

"Wow, you went that fast?" Mom asked with a hint of congratulations and surprise as we all stepped out at the same time. But it wasn't going to be that simple. I hadn't even unbuckled my pants, and my silence was answer enough.

"Savannah! Get back in there right now!"

"I can't! I simply cannot do that," I insisted, but they pushed me back in.

"Yes, you can. Now just go! There's nobody here. Just do it, you dingbat."

Okay, so I admit my fear of the squatties was irrational. Like most such phobias, this one started when I was about six years old. A lengthy camping trip across the United States brought us to the Florida everglades. Uninterested in swamps or crocs, I was desperately tapping my feet on the bottom of a wooden canoe, urgently wiggling and holding it in. Finally allowed to climb from the boat onto a high bank, I found my spot in the tall grass.

I was a typical kid, the kind who pulls their pants right down to their ankles, jumps on the toilet, and swings their feet around as they go. Well, it must've been the first time I'd had to negotiate the more natural style, because I didn't factor in the part where the facilities were a bit lacking. Toilet was toilet to my way of thinking, so away I went, pulling my pants down as I always had. Soon, a yellow stream completely soaked the pile of underwear and pants neatly pooled around my feet! I was absolutely horrified. I had just reached the age of awareness and embarrassment. Thankfully, the memory blurs after that point, to what I can only imagine was a long day spent in soggy pants trying to pretend that nothing happened.

So there I was. My unconquered fear had finally caught up with me. Or had I caught up with it? I did a double take upon seeing the flat, rectangular porcelain bowl embedded in the tile floor with a spot on either side to put my feet. I still didn't know what to make of it. *Well, for starters, I guess I'll put my feet on these weird looking footprints. Good. Now what? Pull my pants down to my knees? That seems about right.* I stood completely baffled for a good few minutes before whining aloud to anyone who cared, "How the heck do you do this?!" Crouched down and teetering on my tippy toes, I let out one last cry for help. "I'm going to pee on my pants if I don't fall over first."

The only response I got was Mom insisting, "Just do it! It's really not that bad."

"You guys!! I can't!! Breeee!" I called for support.

"Oh, let me in then!" The bang on the door almost knocked me backwards onto my bare butt.

"Bree, come back here! She needs to figure this out for herself," Mom said, stopping her from entering.

"It's not that easy, ya know," I shouted back, regaining my balance.

"But it is just that easy, Savannah. We both did it!" Mom continued.

I kept grumbling as I gathered my courage and concentrated. *Okay, now for the hard part. Squat and aim. Aim for what? That doesn't matter, you idiot. All I want is to get it in this toilet instead of in my shoes!!!* I was sure I would miss the bowl as I shuffled back a little and then forward again. *Okay, here goes.* Keeping one eye closed to focus, I finally released, knowing that if I did it wrong, there would be no way to hide my mistake. *I'm quite getting the hang of this!* I thought triumphantly. Opening my closed eye, I watched my fears wash away. My face was beaming as a smile grew to laughter and I stepped out of that bathroom having accomplished a good deal more than just flushing.

Mr. Toad's Wild Ride
10

Forty-five minutes passed much too quickly, and we proceeded to where our bus was boarding. It was a big coach with long mirrors hanging down over the front windshield like the antennae of an adorable insect. I was thrilled to part with the burden of our big backpacks when we finally loaded them into the under-carriage of the shiny bus, knowing I wouldn't have to worry about the damn thing for the next twelve hours. As we climbed aboard, the plump driver stood up from his seat and stopped us in our tracks, shaking a handful of plastic bags at us. I was intimidated by his incoherent sputters and took a step backwards, understanding absolutely nothing. Ahead of me, Mom cautiously took a bag from him. Observing the white, sterile interior of the bus and reacting to the man's insistent, downward hand gestures, she eventually put the puzzle pieces together. Balancing in the stairwell, she removed each of her shoes and placed them in the bag. Noting no further frantic demonstrations from the driver, she proceeded to the back of the empty bus. We all followed, shoe bags in hand.

"Have you ever seen something like this, Ammon? On any of your travels?" Mom asked.

"No, this is definitely a first for me," he said before dropping onto one of the bottom bunks in the back which was raised a few inches off the ground. There were three rows of bunk beds separated by two narrow aisles that were just wide enough for skinny Ammon to squeeze by.

"This is like a hospital on wheels," I exclaimed, looking down the aisle of bunk beds that reminded me of military barracks with their crisp, tightly folded, white linen.

"Holy! This is awesome!" Bree said, creeping in to pass us. "Sleeper bus. You can say that again. Hah, Hah, this is SO awesome."

"See, it's not that bad," Mom said, "I thought we'd be sitting up all night."

"Well, it's way better than a reclining chair," Ammon said, wiggling his feet which were awkwardly hanging over the end of his bed rail, "even if they are a bit short."

"I call top," Bree shouted, leaping onto her claimed bunk. "I could sleep all night on one of these things."

"Good. I'd say take advantage of it, because we're going to be up all day tomorrow exploring. No slacking," Ammon reminded us.

"Can't we just take tomorrow off? We've been going without a break for days, and walking so much," I said, climbing up onto the bed above Ammon so I was head to head with Bree, my black daypack over one shoulder. "I've already got blisters!"

I tried a different tactic as I awkwardly fastened the bulging daypack around my ankle. "I want to know when we get to ride the horses."

"Not for a while. The horse riding is in Songpan, a town in the mountains," Ammon explained.

It felt a bit worrying and a bit scary to be heading further inland and thus further from civilization. In fact, as soon as we left Hong Kong, there was no English whatsoever to be heard – none. The man at the hotel the night before barely even understood when we'd asked for Internet, one of the few universal terms we'd thought we could count on. But no matter what came our way, we'd have to sort the problem; apparently, quitting wasn't an option.

"Yah, but how long until we're there," I pressed, visualizing the wind in my hair as I galloped across an open valley. In his bed below me, Ammon picked the guidebook out of his small green daypack and stood up.

Opening up the map on my lap, he pointed and said, "Okay, here. This is the map and it's right about here!"

"And we're here now? But how long 'til we're there?" I repeated.

"Hmmm," he said, just slowly enough to leave me in suspense, "first we are staying in Yangshuo," pointing to it on the map, "for about four days, then we take a train which is just about---"

I cut him off briefly. "A train!? I've never been on a train before!"

"Yah, most of the world uses trains, Savannah. You're just used to the North American way, where everyone has a car. Can you imagine the chaos if everyone here had one? It would be ridiculous. That's why public transport is usually a lot better in other parts of the world. But anyway, let's not get side-tracked," he said. "The first train should be roughly twenty-two hours."

"Oh, ONLY twenty-two hours?" I said sarcastically, more to myself than anyone else, 'cause by now, they had all mostly tuned out my complaints.

Looking up briefly from his book to glare at me, he continued, "Then we do the Tiger Leaping Gorge, after Mom's birthday in Dali, then yadda, yadda, yadda. It should take about two weeks before we're in Songpan," and he abruptly shut the book on my nose.

"Two weeks?! Seriously? Man, and it has barely been a week. That means double what we've already done!" I collapsed flat on my back.

The tall, blond man Ammon had met earlier was coming down the aisle to join us, saying, "The name's Kent. Sorry, I never properly introduced myself." He was an English teacher who'd lived in China for a few years. After falling in love and marrying a Chinese girl, he'd decided to stay. His words were like a soothing lullaby to my ears, like childhood songs. I leaned back on my bed and thought about home as Chinese locals of all ages filed in and began to settle, their own shoe bags in hand. It was night-time, and the station was brightly lit under its concrete cover. The bus engine roared up and blared its horn in final warning and we started to roll as the chubby driver dressed in a bright, striped shirt nestled into his chair and released the brakes. The lights from the station disappeared behind us and night took over. The streets were unlit and dark.

"It's like a *mental* hospital with these seatbelts," Bree joked, grabbing her belt and holding it up. "Strap her down before she escapes," she quoted from some movie or another. There was an ancient Jackie Chan film playing on a TV suspended from the roof in the centre of the bus. The flashing blues and whites of the TV were enough to light our faces dimly. I was surprised Bree wasn't glued to it until I realized it was all in Chinese.

"They make you wear seatbelts on a bus? Why would they have seatbelts?" I was confused until I realized that Mom, lying in her bunk just across the aisle, had the horizontal window slid open half the length of her body. "You could fall right out that window! You'd better be wearing that seatbelt," I warned as we went around the first harsh bend in the rapidly deteriorating paved road. The ride became progressively wilder, and I quickly learned that the coach's beautiful appearance didn't extend to the condition of the roads around here.

"And I wouldn't even know what hit me," she joked, laughing at how different it all was. Seemingly unbothered and unafraid, she nonetheless buckled herself in and closed the window to ease my mind.

Our driver turned into a wild man with a lead foot, as if he were playing some kind of Dodge-the-cow video game. We were thrown around like cargo as the driver constantly slammed on the brakes, honking non-stop to avoid who knows what on the road. We couldn't see what the commotion was about, so all I could do was try to sleep and just ignore the chaos. We'd either make it or we wouldn't. I'd just have to wait to find out our fate, but I did think it would be a shame to come this far only to die on this stupid bus.

Roughly four hours later the erratic rocking and bouncing came to a halt as the driver made the first potty stop. It was dark out, except for a few dimly lit stalls in the gravelly bus pit stop. Some wooden stands with canvas covers had single light bulbs suspended by thin electrical wires over piles of fruits and vegetables. Mom, Bree, and I rushed past them to follow the crowd to the toilet.

I quickly became aware that the phrase "it can only get better" could very quickly turn into "it could always be worse," because it was. Now that I had achieved a bit of perspective, I grew ever more appreciative of what I'd had back home (which is, after all, one of the major benefits of travel). I had thought myself quite the conquering hero and that with my newly acquired skill of squatting that I could pee in any situation I encountered but my imagination couldn't possibly foresee what was coming. There was no preparation or crash course for what I was about to experience. Yup, I thought I was invincible until I walked in to that bathroom.

Forget locks. Forget doors. There were only two-foot-high, concrete separators. Forget worrying that it wouldn't flush. There was only a bucket of water and a tiny scoop sitting next to the brown, stained porcelain for that. A scoop I did not intend to use, as it appeared no one else had. The place looked as though nothing had been cleaned in just under a million years. Looking around wildly for non-existent tissue holders, I realized that toilet paper was another luxury not provided.

"They don't even give you toilet paper? How crazy is that?"

"But we know they use it," Mom said, eyeing the garbage can full of brown papers next to the toilet. "I guess we can't flush paper here."

"I saw someone out there selling tissues. I'll go grab some," Bree offered. And that was all it took to start her newest pack-rat addiction.

"Mom, I'm not doing it," I tried.

"You have to. Now stop fussing and go before the bus leaves," and that was that. Under duress, I did what would have been unthinkable even two days ago.

Back on the bus, the driver took off at the same pace he'd been maintaining all night. I swung a hand up to make a grab for the belt, but I missed and had to grab onto the side rails of my bed with clenched, bloodless knuckles to keep myself grounded. I waited a moment between bumps. Sensing a smooth patch, I reached again and felt the tightly woven strap of a belt. Securing my weight with this one, I bravely took my other hand and snatched at the remaining strap. In one clean, quick motion, I slammed my fists together and heard the click. I couldn't help but squeal with delight. It was actually just a bit thrilling! *Mom is so lucky. If it weren't for me, she'd have fallen out that window five times over by now, open or not!* Safely secured, I checked on Bree, who was being tossed about crazily and laughing out loud. We braced ourselves against the next huge bash before resuming our chatter about the American guy. We'd been watching him bounce wildly around in his bed.

"How can he possibly sleep?" I whispered to Bree, who was trying desperately not to howl. "I swear he's going to fall out!"

We kept a keen eye on Mr. Kent as we rode the road's tidal waves. In one particularly massive collision, he was abruptly ejected from his bed, just as we'd predicted! His long, blond hair seemed to linger in slow motion in mid-air before he landed with a loud thud. We face-planted our heads into our pillows to stifle snorts of laughter. Stumbling sleepily from the floor, he clambered back into his top bunk, this time finding his belt and securing himself in for the rest of the night.

A Moment in Time
11

*T*he mattress beneath me rumbled from the engine as the tires grabbed the dewy pavement. My eyes slowly blinked open. It had to have been about four-thirty in the morning. The sun had not quite risen, but it was gently making itself known. The view was hazy so I drowsily clenched my hands into fists and rubbed my eyes, wrists twisting back and forth. Reopening them, nothing had changed. I was unable to tell if I was awake or still dreaming as my previous world collided with what I saw through the eerie morning fog.

Images dripping with mystery and wonder flew by. The earth swelled up into monstrous snails that had lain petrified for so long that vegetation had found refuge on their backs. Mist swirled around the base of the lush mounds of earth, wandering magically and time-lessly above the fields of rice and around the ankles of water buffalo hauling wooden ploughs. Small silhouettes of men with loose shirts and conical straw hats trailed behind their gentle beasts of burden.

The night had whisked me into another dimension completely. There was no trace of the city's technology or machinery here. The land lay undiscovered, as if it were reserved for dinosaurs to nest and graze amidst its beauty. I felt I could dream endlessly in this modern-day time capsule where birds were taking flight, suspended between earth and sky with outstretched wings. *This is going to be my very own Never Ending Story,* I thought, *but if it looks anything like this, I may never want to leave.*

As the sun came up, the silhouettes in the smoky charcoal painting were transformed into a vivid masterpiece etched in brilliant shades of green. Foot trails skipped deviously through the fields. The keepers of this land tromped barefoot through the sticky mud, pant legs rolled up to their knees as the fields of rice began to glow from the reflection in the water pools.

The beauty of the scene before me caught me completely off guard, and goose bumps worked their way up and down my arms. Till now, I had assumed that my angst about this trip would manifest itself in the form of something terrible or shocking, like the sky falling down on me. Instead, in my half-asleep state, something within me awakened, and I felt the most calming form of peace imaginable. For just an instant, I let go and peered curiously through that doorway of exciting possibilities, but it was one I was not yet ready to step through. I lost it just as quickly as it had appeared, but a tiny seed of joyful anticipation was planted before I fell back to sleep.

Reality Check
12

"**W**ell, so long! And have a good trip," Kent said as he walked away with what looked like a hint of a limp. As he was swallowed up by the throngs in the Yangshuo market, I knew we wouldn't be seeing him again. We headed off in our own direction to find a place to stay. Just as we'd hoped, one of few locals trying to get commissions found us. He wore thin-brimmed, wire glasses and as a bonus, he spoke English. I was surprised to find someone who did, and he seemed just as surprised to find us.

"Yes, yes. Come. Good place for you," and he waved us on. Ammon, shrugging his fully-loaded shoulders, decided to follow him and check the place out.

Yangshuo was supposed to be a quieter, less populated town, but it appeared to be just as fast-paced as anywhere else we'd seen. The streets were buzzing but in a different way. Briefcases and shiny shoes had apparently been traded in for rakes and sandals. Double-decker buses became wagons loaded with bundles of hay that towered threateningly over bustling pedestrians. Flashing city lights were transformed into shirts and underwear billowing from balconies and windows. Though a little more tanned and weathered than city folk, little about the inhabitants' physical attributes had changed. The men were uniformly clean shaven with short, well-groomed hair and soft features, and the women all looked like our friend Sandra.

The gawking continued, but it was here that a new, less-biased awareness finally sank in: it was not me the inhabitants were staring at, but Ammon! I was not alone in having to crane my neck to look up at him. He was a full foot taller than everyone else! Our five-foot-three height had miraculously become average sized, and we were like three little ducklings trailing in a row behind our brown-haired leader. He stood out like a flamingo in a flock of geese, a feature that often came in handy when we were chasing him in a crowd.

I would react the same way if I saw a purple-headed space giant walking down my street, I realized. *If I saw a long, stringy hair dangling from someone's mole, I'd be tempted to stare, too.* In fact, I had sent out some pretty inquisitive looks myself in the last few days! And it was not just his relative size that drew attention. Ammon's short brown ringlets and five hooped earrings looked like something from the age of pirates. *They must think he's a woman. No wonder they're confused and curious.* Here, women wore only simple earrings and men would never be seen with such feminine accessories. Long hair on a male was completely unthinkable.

Leaping over a puddle, I was cautious to gauge the hectic speed of approaching motorbikes and bicycles that could potentially swipe me off my feet.

"Was that a chicken?!" I bellowed, staring at another bicycle passing by, this one with four hens strapped upside down by their feet to the handle bars. Another went by shortly with a load of fresh eggs stacked high in wooden crates teetering on the back fender. Clothes danced above us on lines strung from the windows as we made our way down the small, dirt streets of the residential areas, causing Bree to wonder aloud at the apparent lack of dryers.

"They probably don't have washers either," Mom piped in, looking up.

"I'm sure they don't. It's called haaand waassshhhing," Ammon said, arrogantly sounding it out for us.

Waddling up alongside Ammon, I expressed my disbelief, "Noooo, they don't! You've gotta be kidding me."

"You would have said the same about the way they work their fields. People just don't have all the modern appliances you're used to. It's not necessary."

"Hand washing, huh? Is this the slum area?" I asked, cautiously surveying the rickety buildings.

"No! It is not the *slums*. You're going to be doing it too, ya know," he warned in what I took to be an ominous fashion. I hadn't thought that far ahead and suddenly regretted the clumsy smudge of chocolate I'd gotten on my pink shirt. I began helplessly searching my memory for any Laundromats I might've seen along the way, but I couldn't recall a single one. Only a few weeks earlier, my head would've exploded at even the prospect of using coins in a machine to do my laundry. Never once in my cushy life had hand washing crossed my mind.

The majority of the buildings were concrete blocks with white tiled fronts and grey tile roofing. Wet, brick-strewn alleyways led us to our hotel at last. Shiny, golden gates encased the doorway where two large, captivating lions stood guard in typical Chinese style. Their round heads featured snarling red smiles.

"If you need anything, you ask for me. My name is Larry," our escort said before letting us go.

Sneaking up behind Ammon at the small reception desk, I asked the question that was always foremost in my mind when it came to our accommodations, "Do they have Internet?" A man came out from behind the desk to show us that the Internet was at the bottom of the stairs. My heart leapt with joy at the news that guests were allowed one free hour a day per person. This was one bit of happiness I felt I could freely show. This would be the first time, aside from the quick note on our family blog at the airport, that we'd get to read and send emails, and I had so much to share. It had been one very long week, and I'd often wished that Terri and the others could have been there. My mind couldn't stop spinning words around, trying to pick the ones that would best describe our experiences thus far. *Not that I wouldn't have traded them in a heartbeat to be back in my room at home with my friends, but brilliant, stunning, and gorgeous were the words that came immediately to mind.*

We were shown to our room on the fifth floor. I sure would've appreciated an elevator, and felt just a tiny bit irritated at how effortlessly the little reception man climbed all those stairs. My preoccupation with the prospect of Internet access dulled the pain surging through my body a bit. My jellied legs were wobbling under the heavy, book-weighted backpack; they felt as if they'd been carrying two libraries. But our room was big enough to give me some hope that maybe, just maybe, I wouldn't be sleeping partly on my backpack for the whole year! In comparison to Hong Kong, I was totally impressed.

Ammon saw the surprise on my face and had a good laugh at my expense, "Hey I didn't say anything. I just let you draw your own conclusions."

"Oh you did not! You purposely let me believe the rooms were going to get smaller! I don't know how I could've fallen for that."

Our room had three beds with a bathroom and was less than half the price of Hong Kong's closet, but of course, it was I who would be sleeping on the floor. Now I knew for sure they were out to get me as, once again, the dubious benefits of being the youngest were hammered home. *Why should I be the one to go bedless? Surely my whining had caused them enough pain to have earned some comfort for a change!*

Had I bothered to voice that argument, Mom would surely have responded, "And that's exactly why YOU got the floor!"

Suddenly, I noticed Bree's absence. "Where the devil?" and then it hit me. Mom was already busy claiming first shower, and that was fine by me; all I wanted was the Internet! I was halfway down the staircase before she'd even opened the bathroom door and caught sight of Bree's long ponytail around a corner of the open stairwell. She was already two flights closer to the computer, but I was gaining on her!

"You can NOT do this to me," I commanded, flying in right behind her on the main floor.

"Hey, first one gets dibs. I won it fair and square."

"You are such a loser!"

"Oh poooor baaby," she rubbed it in gleefully.

"Please Breeeeeee?" I begged, using my helpless baby sister voice and bouncing anxiously.

"Oh, okaaayyy," she laughed and scooted over to make room for me on the rudimentary, wooden chair. "You write down what you want to say before you do it while I'm checking and then while I'm planning how to respond, you can type what you wrote."

Our hour was nearly over and one side of my boney butt was asleep when Bree complained that she couldn't get on to the blog.

"What do you mean, you can't get on the blog?"

"Well, I mean, I did. I wrote my thing and posted it, but I can't open the site up to read it or see anyone's comments."

"Wow. That's weird."

We turned simultaneously towards Ammon, who had just found us. "It must be censored. Somebody said something about that before. But that's a huge bummer."

"Why would they do that?" I asked.

"I guess they don't want the influence of the outside world. I didn't realize the blog would be blocked, but it makes sense. They don't know what we're saying, so they don't want their people to read it." We couldn't think of much to say to that which would change anything, so we moved on. Noticing that Ammon had his daypack slung over his shoulder, Bree asked where he was going.

"*We* are going out. I know it's sort of cheating, but I just booked two days of activities with the hotel. So get off the computer, we're going. One of you run up and get your mother."

With my Internet fix only partially satisfied, Ammon was back on his feet and ready to *start* the day when I was ready to end it. It wasn't even noon and I'd already exhausted myself visually and physically. Of course, no one cared what I thought about anything, so it wasn't long before we set off on our next expedition.

Eye to Eye
13

I didn't know what was in store for the day and just followed along as usual as we were whisked away by a local lady who spoke little, if any, English. Setting eyes on the simple bicycles that we rented for the day, my first thought was, *Oh, yay! I haven't ridden in, geez, forever. This should be fun!* But not here so much. Despite the familiar phrase, "you never forget how to ride a bike," riding became surprisingly complicated by the sheer number of obstacles ahead. Bree and I turned to each other with pinched expressions; hers, eager and ebullient, and mine, worried and intimidated.

Two lanes were being used as a four-lane highway. Chaotic didn't begin to describe the scene we witnessed. Imagine something akin to a bus passing a worn-out tractor that was passing an ox squeezing by the biker who was pedalling slightly faster than the oriental dude chasing a cat with a butcher's knife! Women balanced feather-spewing boxes of chirping chicks and basins of sloshing fish in their arms as they dashed across alleys and streets. I tried to visualize how on earth I could break into that thread and weave myself into the pattern.

And this is supposed to be fun?!? I've been hoaxed into their little games of amusing ways to commit suicide once again! Given no options, I stepped on my pedals, mentally preparing myself for take-off. The puffs of smoke escaping cracked mufflers made me cough. I wobbled all over the place, and I was clipped by oncoming bicycles and cut off by three-wheeled trucks, not to mention nearly crashing several times into piles of crates and a few caged, singing birds. Constantly check-ing side-to-side, the most peculiar sights flashed around me. I could hardly make out any single images. Shifting shapes whorled by, caus-ing my brain to spin round and round like a rotating glass door. *This must be another test of "travelhood." Don't I get some sort of Scouts' badge for this?! Badge #1 – Foreign toilets. Badge #2 – Foreign roads.* As I gradually gained my bearings, though, I had to admit that I was passing this test with flying colours. Literally!

Dodging my share of quadrupeds and motorized vehicles, I raced behind our darting guide, fearing how quickly she might vanish amidst the bedlam. This was no time for second guessing; I had to be alert and move instinctively. Soon there was just one last stretch before we reached the arched pathway of greenery. I kept on peddling towards the clearing. A truck was coming at me on the left and a pair of bikers on my right as I swerved around a herd of goats. I could only close my eyes and hope for the best.

Barely escaping the havoc, I was suddenly encased in a bubble of silence in the fields on the outskirts of town. I heard Bree comment, "I don't know why they even have lines on the roads. No one uses them! Everyone just honks at each other to get the heck out of the way."

"Tell me about it! I thought I was a goner back there," I respond-ed. My ears were still ringing, but I was inordinately surprised by my own delight in having made it through.

The rumbling chokes of broken mufflers dissolved into power-ful commands directed at water buffalo as we rode single file along dauntingly narrow, elevated dirt paths with ever-present mud on ei-ther side. Farmers weeded and worked their land, stomping barefoot in the rich, wet soil that stretched as far as the eye could see. My pale face was warmed by the soft sun, while my exposed legs were cooled by the gentle breeze. The light caught my waist-long hair as the wind wrapped its fingers around every strand.

Back roads led us deeper and deeper into the heart of the Yulong River Valley where we delighted in the river's glistening waters. The dirt track opened up as we approached the green banks of the river, and our guide slowed to a halt before jumping off her bike where two simple rafts waited for us. The rafts were each only eight bamboo poles wide and tied tightly together with rough rope. They were barely wide enough for the two bamboo chairs that were perched side-by-side on what served as the deck. The colourful umbrellas exceeded the width of the entire raft.

We were handed over to the care of our two captains who helpfully put our bicycles in the small space behind the chairs, making for an even heavier load. Mom and Ammon were already on their raft when my captain held out a hand to assist me. I checked his baggy shorts and vertically striped t-shirt before noticing the wet plastic sandals he wore onboard. I hesitated before I cautiously stepped on with one foot, questioning whether what looked for all the world like a young schoolboy's woodwork project could really support our collective weight.

Bree and I pushed off from shore as the young captain steered from the back with his long, thin, bamboo pole. Enjoying virtually complete solitude, with only birds and the gentle splashes created by the bobbing rafts for company, we slowly floated downstream.

"Welcome to the Chinese version of Venice," Ammon said, floating beside us on the river.

"What's a Venice?" asked Bree.

After a long, disbelieving pause, Ammon gently explained, "The famous place in Italy where they have all the long, skinny boats in canals." Anticipating that she might also ask what a canal was, he quickly continued, "You know, where the guys stand on the back with the long poles in black and white striped shirts."

"Oooh, yah, *that* place! Why didn't you say so? Yah, it is like that!! This totally beats being in school!" she squealed joyfully. The sun was bright and there was not a cloud in the sky. Now that Bree had brought it up, maybe I could see the downside of sitting behind a desk all day under fluorescent lights. This felt so much freer and was just so beautiful.

And yet, the stress of taking an entire year away from my studies and friends kept threatening my enjoyment of this tranquil, relaxing experience. *All this fun and play is going to catch up and bite you in the butt. You're gonna pay later when everyone else is free while you're the one sitting alone doing homework to catch up and graduate.* Slamming the imaginary door to my thoughts, I retaliated with the practical notion that I HAD to put any future cost out of my mind before it ruined this amazing present. *I may as well enjoy it now if I'm going to have to pay for it later.* My rationalization didn't last forever, but it bought me some time until my negative thoughts inevitably returned.

The volcano-like figures towering over us reinforced the fairy-tale-like setting that surrounded us. It seemed as if some sort of mythical creature controlled these lands, and we were tiny pixies dancing on the glistening ripples. I dreamt of a dragon lord swooping down to take me away to the top of one of these fascinating, natural towers.

"What are these strange things anyway?" Mom asked, as if reading my thoughts.

"It's called a karst peak; they're typically made of limestone or other carbonate rock shaped by the dissolution of layers of soluble bedrock," Ammon read out from the guidebook.

"Limestone, huh?" I repeated as I looked up. They were everywhere around us and were no less magical at closer range. The vibrant greens shone as brightly as the reflecting waters. Waterfalls spraying misty clouds off to the left caught my eye.

"This is INCREDIBLE!" Bree announced. I was afraid she was about to stand up and lead us in a cheerleading routine, for heaven's sake. Pointing to one of the bigger waterfalls we saw ahead of us in the river, she launched into the "what if" game we'd always play. "Look at that! What would you do if we had to go down THAT one?!"

"I'd be scared," I said bluntly.

Moments later, reality intruded and we turned instinctively towards each other, blank-faced, before Bree stuttered, "Wait a sec. What's going on here?"

I caught on quick and cried out, "We ARE going down it! Aaaah!!!!" From a closer vantage point, it became clear that the single fall was one giant, river-wide semicircle pouring over a rather steep edge. Totally unprepared, we screamed in unison as the whole front half of the raft dipped under the churning foam, soaking our sandaled feet before the raft popped back up and sloshing water poured through the cracks.

The trip that was somehow both idyllic and terrifying inevitably came to an end, and we slipped onto grassy shores with our wet feet. In a small village near the soft banks of the meandering river, we were dropped off at one of few open-faced wood huts. Upon entering one of the larger huts that posed as a restaurant, my eyes focused upwards on the thick, dusty cobwebs hanging from the sooty wooden ceiling beams. Unfortunately, it was dark, or perhaps that was a stroke of luck? It was the last place I'd usually want to associate with food.

Aside from what looked to be the chef and his various family members, we were the only people in the place. There was no menu on the table, but thankfully, it was a set meal, so we wouldn't have to decipher each Chinese symbol with our guidebook.

As we waited, a younger girl offered us a bush with orange fruit dangling from the branches. She placed the bundle on the wooden table before showing us how to peel the thin skin and eat the juicy middle part.

"Seriously, this is so yummy!" Bree said, picking a bit of thin peal from her tongue with sticky fingers. She enthusiastically plopped another one in her mouth, then spat out the few big seeds left over. The loquat was citrusy and sweet and had the same sort of texture as a kiwi.

While we discussed the new fruit, a couple of the ladies and a man cooked in the back, while two girls entertained an infant at one of the outermost tables. The baby's sex was clear from the exposure of his nether regions through the open slit in his pants, and he was definitely going commando. His red one-piece was designed to be bottomless, a style worn by children and babies in China.

"At least people won't ask a thousand times, "Aaww, is it a girl or a boy?"" Reminiscing about her own child-rearing experiences, Mom joked, "Like DUH! Can't you see she's dressed in pink, is wearing ribbons, and has her ears pierced?! Could I have made it any more obvious?"

"Or maybe Bree was just always kind of manly," Ammon teased.

"Hey! You shut up!" Bree barked.

Mom's Marge Simpson glare made him laugh and pull back a bit, anticipating a whack. Just as we were discussing the downside of crotchless infant clothing, the goo-goo/ga-ga sounds and kiss-smacking coming from their direction turned into hysterical squeals. The younger of the two girls was flapping her arms, standing stunned and wide eyed, as if someone had just--- *Oh wait!* I thought, just as the irregular spray caught the sunlight. His tiny penis was erect and flying, as was she, directly into the sanctuary of the garden.

"EEEW! That is just nasty!" Bree said, her general distaste for kids showing.

The girls' hysterical shrieks moved the baby to tears, and his weepy eyes became large and pouty.

"I can imagine they learn quickly not to do that. See how scared the little guy looks?" Mom said, expressing a tiny smile. "Poor thing, he looks so confused!" I felt more sympathy for the young lady running in circles around the garden, trying to somehow escape her own skin. Her friend had finished pacifying the traumatized infant and was giggling at her suffering pal's comical plight.

Outside was very bright in contrast to our dark corner of the wooden shack. A dog swiftly snuck by the unsuspecting cook. My eyes traced his steps as he scavenged in the garden, circling ever closer towards the kitchen where he eventually found his prize. Snatching up a freshly slaughtered chicken, he began contentedly gnawing its neck with the limp body strewn across his front paws.

"See? Now that is when you know your food is fresh," Ammon said, admiring the beauty of the scene, despite his inherent dislike for dogs. Just then, a man came over with a steaming, soot-smeared pot and shooed the dog away to retake possession of his chicken. Picking up the dead bird, he dropped it with a splash into the hot water and put the pot back on the stove. The dog took momentary refuge in the shade of a bush before sneaking back. Though he cautiously observed the boney, yellow feet sticking out of the pot, hot steam prevented the dog from making a second attempt. He scampered off on his way, seeing no fresh opportunities for more lunch. Minutes later, the cook returned to finish his task. He began harshly stroking the chicken's skin, which by now had the texture of a newborn mouse, until it was completely bare. Grabbing its ankles in one hand, he took it to the kitchen.

"Mmm, chicken!" Bree drooled. Just as we were getting excited about enjoying organic meat for lunch, our completely vegetarian meal arrived.

"Eggs?! Where's our chicken?" I said, disappointed when the free range chicken "babies" were laid before us instead. Nonetheless, I was elated by the dishes set before us, so full of new and exotic flavours, including my first taste of eggplant and that wonderful orange fruit, loquat, that is indigenous to Southeast China. It wasn't the Chinese food I knew from home that's dry and crunchy in places it shouldn't be. It was WAY better than that; in fact, it was delicious! Several different vegetable dishes were placed on the table along with one very large bowl of plain rice. Everything was steaming and succulent. This impressive gourmet meal, with more food than we could possibly consume, came to the equivalent of just a couple of dollars, though the setting certainly did not match the exquisite quality of the four-person meal, which would have cost more than a hundred dollars in Vancouver.

Our last real local meal in Hong Kong had consisted of soggy, lukewarm noodles that tasted like they'd been bathing in a bucket of fish remains, and I hate fish. I'd had a terrible time trying to stomach the dish and had characteristically assumed that such would be my new diet and that I'd starve to death before the end of the year. I was so relieved that this meal was not only downright edible, but even delicious.

"Oh, poor Ammon. You hate tomatoes," Mom said, sincerely.

"Yes, I'm very aware of that," he said, frowning at the juicy red dish.

"But of course," I quipped as I dug into the delightful dish, "this comes from the guy who will happily eat ants!" As one of his many scare tactics before we'd left home, he'd enlightened us with tales of his noodle soup experiences in Southeast Asia. Having anticipated the worst and concluding that the whole of Asia would most likely be suffering an ant infestation by the time I arrived, I'd had frequent nightmares where noodles came to life like in Donald Duck's stolen picnic cartoon. I'd envisioned my entire bowl walking off the table with an army of ants scurrying beneath it.

"Oh, you can learn to just eat around them," Mom had said, trying to soothe the innocuous sibling rivalry. *Not me, boy. I'd rather starve!*

"But by the end," he'd grinned as he finished his horror story, "you start to overlook them completely and treat them like little flakes of pepper."

"Oh, no. I most certainly will not!" I'd told him, foreseeing absolutely no possibility whatsoever of ever failing to notice that my "seasoning" was little walking bugs.

Aunt Plastic's warning, "… rather have my arms and legs slowly severed …" echoed in my ears.

Tomatoes, for my taste, were much more appetizing, though in this dull lighting, ants *could* conceivably be overlooked. Glancing subtly under the food I'd lifted with my fork, I checked one last time before putting the next bite in my mouth.

The blur began once more as we stepped out from the dark restaurant into the light and bicycled to the enchanted Moon Water Cave. We had been told about the restorative mud bath hidden deep within the cave that extended three kilometres beneath three mountains. I reluctantly looked over at Bree, whose eyes lit up in anticipation of the opportunity to get dirty. I knew what I was in for.

"C'mon, Savannah. You have to go!" she said.

"I don't have a suit," I insisted.

"But he said you can get them just over there in that hut."

"Used suits? Gross! Seriously, no!"

"Well, I'm going," she said, making her way towards the thatch hut to choose her rental suit. I chased after her to try to change her mind, but her will overpowered mine once again.

"It's a once-in-a-lifetime opportunity," she said as she sorted through the bucket weaved from blue plastic that contained mismatched, partially disfigured bikinis. "Where are you *ever* gonna find an underground mud bath again!?" she argued, using her wide, expressive eyes to convince me before adding triumphantly, "Only in CHINA, that's where!" Always the braver, fiercer sister, she took charge and I once again crumbled under the force of her conviction.

"You girls are going to be all gross and dirty. Think about the bike ride back. You'll be all muddy and wet," Mom scowled and tried to save at least one of us, but Bree would have none of it. Mom didn't need to voice the rest of the worries that were already crowding my brain, but as much as I didn't want to be cold and wet in a swimsuit that had been worn by who knows how many people, I was even more afraid of being left out of something spectacular. I could probably live with the regret of not going, but I knew I could not deal with Bree having the best time of her life without me.

"Okay, I'll at least get a suit on so I can decide later," I said, swiping one from the bucket.

"Wicked!" Bree said. She already knew my submission on that point meant I was in the process of convincing myself, though I still denied it.

We floated into the darkness of the cave in a little wooden rowboat. The low, flowing river was too narrow for oars, so we relied on muscle power to pull ourselves through the entrance using a thick, wet rope attached to a rock somewhere in the cave's inner shadows.

"Here's an interesting fact, guys. The local villagers from around here used this cave to hide out from the invading Japanese army in World War II," Ammon gravely informed us.

"See? Now I just think that is so great!" Mom said, her eyes taking in every inch of the experience. "I love learning new things."

With no more light than what was provided by a dimly lit path and the headlamps on our hardhats, we approached the innards of the underworld. Despite having plummeted into the depths of Mammoth Cave in Kentucky, recognized as the longest, most thoroughly mapped cave system discovered in the world, the Carlsbad Caverns in New Mexico, and many other cave systems, I was nonetheless impressed. From the look on Mom's face, I'd say she was, too.

"Wow, this is great. I just love caves!" Mom said, for probably the tenth time since we'd heard we were going there. We found only minimal modifications within the cave with only some simple garden lights attached to very, very long extension cords along already existing pathways.

"This is really great. You can just wander around and go anywhere you want. There are no fenced-off parts or cement walkways. It feels so natural! North America has so many safety regulations that prevent you from doing anything," Mom said, typically disagreeing with such patronizing precautions.

"That's just because they are so paranoid about being sued. I almost don't blame them. If you can be sued for making hot coffee too hot, then they pretty much have to treat you like a disabled child so they can't be held liable for anything," Ammon commented.

"Yah, it's a shame, though, because a lot of the time it ruins the natural beauty of it. But," Mom added, "I am grateful for these helmets, 'cause I've been bumping my head everywhere." With the help of rope ladders we climbed like Gollum up rocky, slippery slopes and crossed over wooden bridges within the caves. Some of the stalagmites rang with music and hummed with the vibration of even a gentle smack. Stalactites hung overhead, dripping with upside-down bats hanging in every crevice. Every now and again, one would release its death-like grip and drop from its perch. The sound of its flicking wings echoed down jagged corridors until the bat nestled itself back into a cozy spot, disappearing completely.

We discovered our main attraction, the large pool of oozing, brown mud, after a long trek that involved following the underground river, crawling through puddles, and squeezing between bizarre and curious shapes.

"I can't believe you're going to swim in that. How disgusting!" was Ammon's first comment, "Cowabunga!!!" was Bree's, and Mom offered a persuasive remark or two as she attempted to convince us to reconsider.

After Bree's shallow but graceful dive, I kind of duck-flopped in behind her. On the far rock wall, we climbed to the top of a natural slide where we could once again slip back into the dark pit. It was completely relaxing. I floated weightlessly in what felt like smooth, chocolate icing, swimming as if in an underworld cloud, swiping my hands through the mud beneath my bare belly and feeling the whooshing movement on my tingling skin. Although I knew my friends back home would be having the traditional massages, facials, and saunas along with their mud baths, I was sure this was far more enjoyable. *I wouldn't give up this experience for anything. Oh, if only Terri could have--- I'm going to bring her here one day,* I decided, turning a sad thought into something more positive. *She will love this!*

Although we'd been to bigger and "better" caves in the United States on family road trips, it somehow didn't compare to the experience that day. It was very personal and hands on. I almost felt as though I was a little kid again, making up stories to match these adventures. I was an explorer. Every corner and every rock was something newly discovered, and I'd made my first imprint. I wandered aimlessly for what seemed like hours, sneaking around with the monsters on my tail, jumping and hiding in small tunnels. Aside from our guide, we had the place to ourselves. I imagined the lives of the local people during World War II when they'd come to hide from the invading Japanese. Not much would have changed since that time. I crouched down and crept slyly, checking my back as if it were me evading the enemy. Covered from head to toe in dry reddish mud as I was, I blended into the earth and stones, becoming nearly invisible. I picked up a small, crumbly stone and wondered who else had passed by here in this fashion. *Whose stories could that rock share? How long would they have gone without food, hiding like serpents in the dark? Days? Weeks? Who had they lost along the way?* Given that the cave had only opened up to tourism ten years before, I felt even more like an explorer. I wondered how long it had existed with only the chirping echoes of bats and critters for company. *Did the Japanese ever find it?* These thoughts continued until my mind hurt from the novelty of considering historical issues. History was always my least favourite class in school. The dry textbooks full of dates just never caught my attention, and I had never before really considered war from a personal perspective. Yet here, I found myself totally captivated by the little bits of information I'd just learned about World War II.

Making our way further along, we rinsed our new layer of red-chocolate skin in the unusually warm waters of the underground river we'd been following. Bree and I wallowed in it as we dunked, swam, and scrubbed each other's backs. Crawling on hands and knees upstream, I watched the reddish cloud wash downstream, looking for all the world like blood.

Traces of crusty mud remained around our jaw lines and in behind our ears to remind us of our adventure. We climbed for a long time towards the top of the cave where we could see a gaping opening into an endless blue sky. We bathed in the clearest, purest light which streamed in on particles of dust as we re-emerged from the wet belly of the earth.

Whet Your Appetite
14

*S*mall, smothered fires choked desperately beneath brewing stews and meats. My outstretched fingers slid through the ashy smoke as I reached forward to try to clear a visual path. The long and seemingly endless day of activities was wrapping up. All we needed now was FOOD, so we'd gone off to the local market.

It presented a flurry of hanging lights under awnings strung up with ropes and sticks, and we felt like we had been transported back to some ancient, mythical era. That illusion was heightened by the reactions of the locals, who stared at the sight of our unusual, foreign appearance and attire.

The frequent, sudden squawks coming from baskets of fighting, pecking chickens at my ankles made me jump. Their flapping wings protruded awkwardly from their cages and stirred up dust and feathers as we passed by. Women seemed to shout from all directions. Bucket after bucket, stained and dented in various places, lined the narrow alleys. Cages upon cages stuffed with big eyed creatures were stacked high and threatened to collapse at any moment. Snakes coiled together in rusted cages. Turtles grown to be sold and made into delicious soups struggled in only inches of water. Long lobster legs wiggled like spiders as they pinched each other in a desperate dance. Fish panicked in shallow tubs, only half covered by the minimal amount of water; one would occasionally spring out and bounce around on its side making a mud puddle under the wood stalls before a nearby granny would get up from her three-legged stool to toss the escapee back into the rubber tub with the rest. *This is no pet shop,* I reminded myself as I looked helplessly at the twitching noses of white bunnies; *this is the grocery store.*

The whacked-out reality of it jangled my nerves. I followed the yearning, upwards stare of a caged dove. There must have been stars out that night, beautiful sparkly stars, but it was hard to see the night sky through the haze of the burning fires' dense smoke. I watched as a woman examined a sack of four big frogs, put it back down, and then picked up the next one, comparing their relative size. Their springy feet hung awkwardly through the open spaces in the woven orange sacks. I almost expected her to squeeze their bellies to test for ripeness. In the midst of the startling sights around me, I flashed back to the childhood story of Hansel and Gretel, which came to life as the woman progressively pinched their dangling green legs to decide which were the meatiest.

Catching myself in the middle of a long, drawn-out stare, I surprised myself as much as anyone by saying, "I'm starved. Seriously, these frogs are starting to look good."

"And what better way to dress a home-cooked meal than with some rich, pungent spices," Ammon said jokingly as we entered the next section of the market. Sour, sweet, bitter, and salty flavours blurred into one overwhelming waft.

"Careful what you wish for," Mom cautioned wisely.

Merchants, mainly women, sat cross-legged on tarps or on short stools in front of three-foot, burlap sacks. The thick smell of various spices soaked into my moist skin. Big, overflowing bags presented an assortment of dried animal parts and herbs. Threads of crimson saffron were dried and sold by the scoop. Shrivelled mushrooms, sea horses, and other exotic bits and pieces were weighed and wrapped. Even in death, long, tangled tentacles appeared to reach out towards an unknowing sky. The merchants reminded me of Shakespeare's witches, and I chanted quietly to myself the classic phrase, "Eye of newt, leg of frog." Add to that one barb of salty sea urchin and these innocent little Chinese women could be Macbeth's witches.

Heading back empty-handed in the direction of our accommodations, we ran into Larry, the hotel's guest recruiter. As nothing in the marketplace had seemed even remotely edible, we were driven by desperation and hunger. We needed to eat, NOW!

"So Larry, could you recommend a good place for dinner?" Ammon asked coolly, as if he were merely in search of a snack. I twitched in my place. My approach to the situation would have been, *Gosh dang it! Where's the food at! Give it to me. Now!*

"Ah, yes, yes. I know good place. Come with me," he said brightly, anxious to show off his town and culture, and off we went through yet more alleys and puddles. Darkness had long since fallen, and we'd been awake for days if you count the restless journey on the overnight bus. We were led up the back stairs of a relatively dank, two-story building where we found ourselves in a secluded room with grey walls. A large round table in the room was covered with a white tarp. Larry spoke quickly and efficiently in Mandarin as we wondered what we would be eating.

The first course came in a steaming pot accompanied by five empty bowls and a big ladle so we could serve ourselves.

"Oh, soup. Nice," Bree said, leaning in over the pot. I dug right in to the cloudy, white liquid and found chunks of different vegetables and pieces of boney pork and a few mystery body parts.

"Mom, this is like pig artery. One of those big fat tubes that goes into your heart!" I said out of the side of my mouth. I searched desperately for a napkin to ditch it in. *I'm getting rid of whatever the heck this is.* One way or the other, I was sure of that.

"Don't think about it, just keep chewing," she said, keeping a smile on her face and talking through her teeth so as not to draw unwanted attention.

"You like? Very good!" Larry said, causing Mom to jump and nod overly enthusiastically. I rolled my eyes at her and continued chewing to no avail. The tubular chunk of pig artery was as rubbery as a balloon, and it squirted fatty juices with each bite. Fed up and tired of chewing the unchewable, I swallowed the throat-stretching lump whole because I couldn't figure out how else to get rid of it. Before I could choke it down, a train of male servers placed four main courses in front of us. It was by now quite apparent that food came in communal dishes rather than as individual dishes.

Oh my gosh! That was only the starter! I thought, gulping once more to force it all to keep going down.

"What is it?" Mom asked politely, leaning in over the steaming plates. I was pretty sure I'd rather not know. Having visited the markets, how could I be surprised to see what was served to us? The first dish came with lots of little legs that had once belonged to hopping swamp creatures. The skin was very thin and peeled off in dangly threads of speckled green.

"Is very nice! This frog. The leg. Leg. You know? And this, rabbit. Last one, duck. Is very nice!" Larry said, nodding his head robustly.

"Well, there you go, Savannah," Ammon said smugly, as if he had cooked it himself.

"Yah, well. Pft! They're tiny," I mumbled, feeling a bit short-changed because they were nowhere near as big and meaty as the ones I'd seen outside for sale.

"After all, if it's on your plate, it should have some edible parts! Or is this just a garnish?" I whispered to Bree, who was sitting next to me.

"Well, *he* certainly found something edible," she replied, nodding towards Larry who was already busy with his chopsticks.

"Well, that's not hard to do when you eat the whole dang thing at once!" I exclaimed, as I continued to watch him from across the table. He was crunching on a frog leg, bone and all, as he picked through the other dishes. To my left, Mom was delicately nibbling on a leg of her own.

"Think of all the little froggies that had to die for us – don't waste them," she said with a pout, as she forced herself to eat more. Every dish was soaked in Szechuan spices, preventing spicy-food haters like Bree and Mom from eating as much as they'd like. The duck meat came still attached to sharp shards of bone. The rabbit was also boney, as if it had simply been hacked at with a butcher's cleaver instead of precisely cut. I spent a lot more time and effort sifting out cartilage and bone chips with my tongue, similar to the way you might work grape seeds out, than actually swallowing, but Larry seemed to have no such problems.

"I think you forgot one key word in that request, Ammon! Normal. *Normal* food!" I said.

"Well, sweetheart, you ain't gonna *find* 'normal' here," he growled at me with his mouth full.

"Ok seriously, let's not do that again," I said as we climbed the five flights of stairs, the very last obstacle before I could finally collapse onto my lumpy mattress on the ground, though even this inadequate bed grew more appealing every day.

"Yah, that was scary," Mom puffed as we climbed.

"Tell me about it. Did you see the price of it?" Ammon shuddered, "We *can't* do that again."

"How much?" Bree turned to ask.

"Like, fifteen bucks!!"

"Seriously? Isn't that, like, pretty reasonable?" I asked, stopping to massage the kinks out of my thighs.

"Hell no! We've been averaging five bucks a day for *all* of us!" he retorted.

"What?! Really??? Wow!!" Bree exclaimed.

"If we want to make this year last, we really can't do that anymore," Mom agreed.

"I think we should. It was SO delicious," I teased, thinking that an annihilated food budget would drain our funds and get us home sooner. *Furthermore, if what I just saw was the high end of the available food selection, I am scared to death to imagine what a low-budget meal could include. What next? Grass-stuffed intestines?!* I didn't doubt the others would willingly subject themselves to something like that just to stay the full year.

Back to School
15

*T*he sun and all its servants were well on their way to another successful day. We were up early, but it was late by Chinese standards. The rhythmic thud of hand tools banging on cement framing disturbed our sleep every morning at five. Labourers' muscular arms swinging repetitively just across the alley were silhouetted behind our window's drab curtains. The equivalent of a few baseball teams' worth of players was working on a new, five-story building. At home, the same job would take five men using modern cranes and machinery. Here, where they didn't have access to contemporary equipment, they counted on manpower to do the job, and the constant pounding never seemed to stop.

As I was slowly peeking out between heavy lids and wondering for a few moments where the heck I was, the locals had already thrown back their blankets, brushed their teeth, had a cup of tea or two, eaten two dozen dumplings with sauce, and long since biked or carted their way to work. Finally crawling over to the window, I observed the narrow alleyway between the new construction and our hotel. The workers were scattered like ants, crawling and hanging from the elegant scaffolding made of bound bamboo stocks. Once again I was amazed by the strength of these plants, which were clearly used for more than just panda-bear food and making rafts.

"Yah, bamboo's one of the strongest plants in the world. Harder than red oak. It's like nature's form of steel. And it's one of the fastest growing, too," Ammon had told us back on the Yulong River.

"Some varieties grow as much as three feet a day!" Mom had added.

"You can practically sit and watch them grow," Ammon agreed.

Although bamboo was clearly up to the job, I couldn't even count how many western-style "safety regulations" were being broken. Not a single worker wore a hardhat or safety harness.

"I'm not going," I said, turning away from the window.

"Oh yes you are!" Mom said definitively, leaving me with little choice.

The night before had ended with a surprise invitation to visit Larry's high school a few villages away, where he made a living as an English teacher. I had secretly wished that we wouldn't take him up on his invitation, that we could just make up an excuse not to go. I really wanted to spend my only free day sleeping in, but my resolve crumbled when I heard Larry's final words, "Is honour, is honour." *It clearly meant a lot to him.* By the time morning came, though, I didn't care as much about Larry anymore.

"Well, if you don't want to go, just think of it as volunteer work," was Mom's encouragement for the start of the day. *Oh joy!!! Just what I need at six o'clock! – Volunteer work! Pft! What I need is my pillow, some earplugs, and some more sleep.* So of course, twenty minutes later we met Larry downstairs with nothing more than a few yuan, the clothes on our backs, and the one thing we had to offer: our native tongues. We travelled an hour down the road in a minibus to an even smaller village than Yangshuo. Students on foot and riding bicycles lined the small road.

"This is my school!" he announced proudly once we'd walked a few blocks and turned the corner where a white, four-story building with bold Chinese writing stood.

"So when does school start?" Ammon asked, observing the hundreds of kids still pouring in from all directions.

"School start every day from seven-forty in morning until five. Is like this six times of week. And Sunday, they go study on homeworks," Larry told us.

"Really? Wow! In Canada we only go five days a week, and it ends at three o'clock. And school doesn't start until nine in the morning," Ammon told a surprised Larry. The students' stares, smiles, and giggles overwhelmed us as we stood in the crowded schoolyard. We would not go unnoticed, that was for sure.

"My class there. See window?" he proudly pointed up to one on the second floor where the balcony wrapped around the building.

"And how often do you teach?" Mom asked him.

"Every day I teach two hours English. I have two classes."

"What age group do you teach?"

"My students are thirteen to sixteen. So sweet kids." It was obvious how fond he was of them. The wide age range reminded me of the *Little House on the Prairie* series, where the school was just one big room with only one teacher for all of the kids. I had always thought that was strange.

"Oh, really? Our schools teach one age. Sometimes they have split classes where they have two ages, but mostly, kids the same age are in a single classroom. How many students do you generally have in each class?"

"About," he stopped to calculate, "I have about fifty students each class. Forty-five to fifty kids in one class. Oh, my students will be so excited!" he continued. "They had never guest like this before. They will be so happy. So best surprise for them."

"Really? They've never had a native English speaker visit before?" Bree asked.

"No, no. Never. Never they see white person. You know, they living out in small village, no tourist come, they don't travel. I meet foreigner sometime, from hotel I meet, but never they have time. Never they want come."

I began to get nervous and the butterflies in my stomach took flight. I didn't like school presentations at the best of times, and that was in my own schools, where I would generally be forgotten and overlooked. With each curious stare, I came to realize more and more that I was about to get up in front of fifty students around my age who were not likely to ever forget my face. I thought about something that Shean, Mom's long-time childhood friend who was once an

RCMP officer and was now an anaesthesiologist, had emailed only a few days earlier. While sharing our family tales in his operating room, one of his colleagues, who was born in a small town in China, said he could still remember the first white tourists he had ever seen some thirty years before. *I'm not qualified for this. I've never done anything like it!* I thought, stressed by the thought that in this case, *I* would be that first tourist.

"Well, we are excited to meet your class," Mom assured him.

We saw the orderly field where bikes of the approximately two thousand students were stored for the day. Hundreds of them were neatly lined up in covered rows. The main extra-curricular activities available to the kids were football (aka soccer) and ping pong.

"Asians and their table tennis!" Ammon laughed, recalling the many rambunctious matches he'd played with ESL students at home. But these were not the flimsy green tables with folding metal legs we were accustomed to using. Instead, theirs were just big blocks of cement. A line of stones gathered from the fields was piled across the middle and used as a net. My first thought upon seeing their tables was, *Heaven only knows what they use for the ball and paddles.*

"My kids very young, and only short time they have each week English learn. They know small English, but very smart!" I could imagine that they would have very few, if any, opportunities to practice, living in a remote village with no English exposure.

We made our way to the first classroom on the second floor. The bell had already rung, and the school grounds were much quieter now that the students were waiting in their classrooms. Larry had asked us to stay outside so he could first explain our presence and settle the students. From what I could see from peeking in the windows, they were already mostly sitting quietly at their desks. *Settle the students? Dude! You're not even in there and they're just sitting at their desks. Is this a joke?! They totally knew we were coming! But they couldn't have known, because we only arranged this visit the night before. They must be this well behaved all the time!* He first greeted the students, and the class simultaneously responded with a roaring "good morning" that made me take a step back. This was obviously their regular morning routine. To prepare them for their lesson, he gave a little speech about a special surprise, and then invited us in.

By the time I got into the room (being at the end of the line, as usual), they were all wide-eyed and looking alternately at us and then at their classmates. Some flashed big smiles, while others hid their faces behind their hands. A few had probably seen us in the school-yard, but all looked equally surprised and excited.

The building appeared larger and more impressive from the out-side than I'd expected, but the interior was much more like what I'd anticipated. The students sat behind beaten-up wooden desks, and the ceiling showed various signs of green and yellow leakage. The floor was unfinished, rough cement, and the once-white walls were brown and stained, but surprisingly clean for all that.

I stood at the front of the class feeling a bit dizzy from having all those kids watching me. Larry sputtered a few things in Chinese and then asked us to start introducing ourselves, conveniently handing the class over to us. *As if that's not intimidating; how do we even know where to begin?*

"Hello," Ammon blurted out with a smile. *Well, I guess that's a good start.*

"Hello," one or two responded. They must have been the brave, outspoken members of the group, but it didn't take much for them to shy away when they realized no one else had spoken. One smothered his face in folded arms on top of his desk to hide his flushed cheeks. My presence was as intimidating to them as theirs was to me, and I realized that *they* felt more uncomfortable than I did.

While I observed this brief interaction, Ammon picked up a piece of chalk and began writing on the blackboard so all could see. *How does he even know they can read our alphabet? But, hey, we're improvising!* As he finished writing his name on the board, he said very slowly, "My name is Ammon, and this is my mother." With that, he handed it off to her. They understood at least that much because they reacted with surprise, unable to fathom how she could be the mother of this prominent man who stood almost a foot taller than her. Then Mom picked up another small piece of chalk. She, too, began very slowly, having had lots of practice with ESL students in Vancouver.

"My name is Maggie. We are from Canada. These are my daugh-ters," she said, gesturing towards us.

"Hi. My name is Breanna."

"And my name is Savannah."

An awkward pause ensued as we desperately wondered what our next trick should be. Flustered, but clearly on the same brainwave, we simultaneously pointed at each other and jinxed, "She is my sister," as if we'd been rehearsing. The class joined in with our giggles.

"I am twenty-five years old," Ammon said as he again picked up his piece of chalk. I studied the students as he wrote it on the board for them all to see. They were not being disruptive or rolling their eyes, as I had seen so often in other schools. *Why couldn't the idiots at home have been a bit more like this?* It was obvious that these kids really wanted to be there. Remembering the construction workers who had woken me with their hammering the past few mornings, I thought it must have something to do with their culture. They were naturally hard workers who were raised to be obedient and respectful, qualities that were seriously lacking in the schools I had attended.

Larry made his way back to the front and told us, "If anyone wants ask a question, you answer. Or maybe you ask, too?" He translated every word for those who couldn't understand. A few raised their hands, and Larry signalled for them to speak.

"Is ... you ..." one boy tried, a deepening blush creeping in from behind his ears and beginning to show in his cheeks. He quickly turned towards Larry for reassurance before continuing in Mandarin. They spoke briefly before Larry turned to us, saying, "Twins. He wants to know, are you twins?" Bree and I smiled at each other; it wasn't the first time we'd been asked this question.

"No. She is three years younger," Bree responded. The entire class simultaneously said, "Ooohhh" when Larry translated that. "I am seventeen. She is fourteen." Upon hearing this, the students were unable to contain themselves. They swiftly threw off their sedate, serious manner and reacted like jittery little monkeys. Heads turned and several chattered with Larry in their native tongue as he nodded to them proudly.

"They do not believe that you are fourteen. They think you are much older than them." I could relate. It was hard to believe they were around my age. *In fact they looked nothing like my peers at home.* Some were even a couple years older than me, I knew, but I'd never be able to pick them out. I tried to pinpoint what it was that made them look so young. It wasn't just that they were small with chubby cheeks; it was also the way they dressed. They wore simple t-shirts and jeans, far less provocative attire than I was used to seeing. No one wore jewellery or hid under makeup either. They were really there to learn, not to play games. *So perhaps they don't look young, they just look their age. At home, we obsess over trying to grow up and look more mature. Would life be easier without all that competition?*

Ammon asked a boy from the front row who looked to be about ten how old he was. He was sitting with his head tucked in, speaking more to the pencil he fiddled in his hands than to us.

"I am five," He shook his head to get it right. "No. Fifteen." His correction came out strong.

"You really fourteen?" a little girl beside him asked me.

"Yes."

This created another minor shock wave. *And I'm not even dressed up. They would fall over in astonishment if they walked into Sentinel or West Van and saw the difference! I hated the way people in my school were so rude and disruptive or skipped class altogether. If they had been as respectful as these kids, maybe I would have stayed in high school longer than two months and not opted to take correspondence courses instead!* There were a few reasons I didn't like public school. Leaving elementary school felt liberating at first. I loved upgrading to my own locker and being able to eat in the hallways and stay indoors during lunch on rainy days. I thought high school was light years better than a confined elementary school, but it was the slack behaviour and the disrespectful way kids treated teachers, not to mention each other, that I didn't like. My absolute loathing for early mornings also contributed to my decision to leave, of course.

Following a few more courteous questions, Larry separated us into four smaller groups so we could work one-on-one and talk with those students willing to try. As I got up close and personal with the ten students assigned to my group, I became ever more impressed with their attempts to learn English in this little village. They were so sweet and innocent as they playfully smacked and teased each other. Sometimes they'd switch back into Chinese without noticing to seek confirmation about a word or to get reassurance from their friends. With my chin on my fists, I just watched them and their banter for a moment. My heart tensed slightly at the sight, and a nagging homesickness came over me. I'd been gone just over a week but I knew this was only the beginning. There were fifty-one more to go before I would see my friends again, and I already missed them so much.

"You are beautiful," a boy told me, his statement causing the rest to burst into helpless giggles. He blushed at that, but I think it had more to do with speaking English than what he actually said. He had a friendly face and reminded me so much of Terri's twin brother, Tyee. This boy was the smallest in the class; maybe that was what made me think of him – that or his deep set dimples.

"Thank you," I said.

"You welcome," he tried earnestly.

"You *are* welcome," I corrected, returning his sweet smile.

I found a stack of thin text books inside when I opened the top of a desk. I slid one out, closed the lid, and opened the book. I found a world map. *Oh this'll be a good place to start,* I thought, *I'll just point out Canada and show them where we live so they can see how far away our "village" is.* Before I could show them, I looked instinctively at the top left side of the page and did a double take. Where was my world? Canada was not where I expected it to be. In its place was China. I struggled to get my bearings as I realized the map was backwards. China and Russia were on the top left side of the page, and the Americas on the right.

Sincerely confused, I tried whisper/shouting to Ammon, "Hey! Don't our maps come from China?!!" but I failed to get his attention from across the room. He was sitting in a chair that was so tiny it accentuated his size. I had to laugh as I watched all the children hovering around him like bees surrounding a honeycomb. They were busying themselves practicing such words as "blue," "eye," "hair," "ear," and "tall" as they played with his soft brown hair and golden earrings. They even held his eyelids open to get a closer look at their deep blue colouring. Clearly, he was too absorbed with their antics to hear me. His group was growing as a few kids crept over from other groups to join his. They were twisting and pulling his curls down to watch the novelty of how they'd spring back into a nice ringlet. He was definitely a treasured novelty.

I glanced over at the other groups. Bree was busy impressing hers with her gymnastics, doing simple cartwheels and back handsprings. Mom was in the middle of a small crowd leaning over one of the books she was explaining. Larry leaned against a desk in a corner with his arms crossed, a beaming smile covering his face.

"What is, what is mouth? In," one of my students came in closer to get my attention.

"In, in! What, what?" another said, pointing at my mouth.

"Oh that. It's a retainer." I repeated it a couple of times slowly for them. They all tried to say the word, but it came out more like "letinel" as they struggled to pronounce the two Rs. Two of the girls tried to help each other by looking in each other's mouths to see why the L was happening.

I couldn't help but wonder how they'd have reacted to my entire mouth being full of shiny, metal braces, plus the strange head gear I had worn for three years. If it weren't for the trip forcing us to have them removed prematurely, I'd have had them for at least another year! There was at least one happy and immediate result.

The year before, a couple of brackets had broken off my bottom teeth. Given my typical "know it all" attitude, I ripped what was left of them off one-by-one using scissors and pliers. The disappointment on my orthodontist's face when he saw what I had done caused me more pain than the act itself had. Though he was reluctant to speed up my carefully planned treatment, he did supply a retainer to hold my teeth in place during our trip.

The children's curiosity wasn't the first I'd experienced since we got to China. I'd been approached by random men on buses and women in shops; complete strangers questioned me about my retainer by pointing and staring into my mouth, even interrupting conversations to point it out. Their questions prompted questions of my own. *I wonder if they have braces in China? Are there even any orthodontists? Would they have telephone books? What would it be called in Chinese?* It hadn't escaped my notice how terrible people's teeth were. Many older generations displayed huge gaps between rotted teeth or flashed only a gummy smile. Middle-aged people's teeth tended to have dark stains and an occasional tooth missing, while the younger generation, such as those in this class, often had very overcrowded and crooked teeth. *I guess I was pretty lucky to be able to have mine fixed,* I thought, fully aware of how horribly buck-toothed and overlapping mine had once been. Absent western technology, my teeth would no doubt have come to the same fate as those of the average middle-aged person here. Most Chinese citizens were unable to clean between their crowded teeth or afford regular visits to the dentist, so it was no surprise that teeth were generally in pretty poor condition by our standards. That also explained why people were so surprised by Mom's age. Some had actually used a form of charades along with bits of broken English to convey that she could not possibly be forty-six because she still had all of her teeth.

If only Bree would show them her tooth! Now that would give them a laugh! Bree's teeth were straight enough, but the poor girl was missing FIVE of her permanent teeth. Braces had pulled her teeth together enough that she only had to have one fake tooth attached to her retainer.

"See? See?" the kids were demanding, still not quite understanding *why* I had a metal strip called a "letinel" in my mouth. For both hygienic and social reasons, I never take my retainer out in public, but I figured this was a special occasion. I wanted to show them something advanced and different from another culture, so I suctioned it out with my tongue and dropped it down from the top of my mouth. They couldn't have been more amazed if I'd just removed my whole mouth. One girl's shriek made me laugh out loud.

An hour went by far too quickly, and our time with the first class was coming to an end. Just before we left, everyone got up to have a photo taken. One young girl snuck in behind Ammon when she thought no one was looking and measured herself against him. Unable to believe that she only reached the bottom of his shoulder blades, she tried a second time. She straightened her shirt, stretched her neck, and stood as tall and erect as possible before placing her hand at the top of her head to measure. The second results were just as shocking as the first, and she scampered back to the group before any of her peers could see.

After we'd finished with the autographs and photos, we said our goodbyes before heading to the next class to do it all over again. As we turned to leave, I heard "thank you, thank you, thank you" from all around me and I couldn't help but smile and be glad we'd come. I knew there was nothing to be afraid of.

Dragon Spine
16

*A*nother early-morning adventure sent us bumping down the road in a minibus for three-and-a-half hours. Time and time again on that trip, locals scrambled over each other as they stumbled in or out of the bus. They'd waddle off with big cloth sacks of vegetables as others carrying upturned chickens by their legs climbed in. Warm wind tickled my face through the big open windows as the seat beneath me rattled like a grater over gravel. My hair fell weightlessly from my braid, lioness style, contributing to an overall sensation of feeling rather cat-like. My narrowed eyes peered out at the world as I wondered how I could ever capture this for the people back home. My mind playfully tossed and twisted words and descriptors around. I felt inspired to use them like colours on an old, black and white television screen, but I was frustrated at the same time by my inability to generate the perfect expressions to express the uniqueness of what we were experiencing. I felt that way far too often for my liking as we continued our travels.

The driver finally turned around in his seat and pointed at the open door to show us that we had arrived at our stop. "What was this village called again?" I asked Ammon as I ducked out the door behind him.

"Longji," he told me.

"Ahh, Longji" The word rolled off my tongue and took flight in the wind as I soaked up the calmness of the setting around me. The sun shone down in bright rays between wispy, early clouds.

Having been dropped off at the edge of the village, we had to walk the rest of the way. Aside from British Columbia's Whistler Village that was lined with glossy, four star hotels packed with tourists and skiers, I had never seen a village prior to this trip. Tucked away in the foothills, today's destination exactly replicated an authentic "village" straight out of my childhood fantasies or from the movies, a place where grassy trails are explored only by horseback or on foot. It matched my impression of Tolkien's famous hobbit Shire. Wooden cottages with black, shingled roofs stood on stilts, and bundles of yellow corn cobs dried as they hung from wooden balconies. Each bend took me deeper still into favourite, long-held fantasies.

"We're going to be hiking pretty far to get a view of this place. Longji means Dragon's Spine in Chinese," Ammon said, sharing his facts for the day. "The terraces you've been seeing – you know, the rice fields everywhere? Well, Longji is, like, the ultimate terracing creation. It began back in the days when …" Ammon droned on as he led us through the sleepy village.

An older man who was about my size was leaning over a trough by the road holding a bluish bird resembling a turkey in his fist. His other hand displayed a menacing knife.

"… and the villagers still, to this day …" I honestly tried to listen to Ammon. I tried to hear his words, but I could not take my eyes off the man and his bird. With one stroke, he sliced into its flimsy neck, folding it back nearly in half. Both bird and knife now glistened a bright red in the sunlight, and I felt my chin quivering slightly.

"… ancient ways, and they make their living that way," Ammon continued.

"They certainly do," I said.

"Do what?" Bree asked, looking around at me questioningly, but we had already passed the scene that was forever burned into my memory.

"Live off the land the same way they did in ancient days. Can you imagine, Bree?" I said, "This is how they LIVE! It's not all staged for us. This is home for them. They've probably never seen a shopping mall, EVER!"

"Yah. That's really something," she agreed.

"But that's what's so great about it, see? It's not the olden days!" Ammon stated, pleased that we were finally getting it. But Bree had already wandered off into her own mental world, as had I. All I could see was my last glimpse of that helpless bird. The man had been squatting over the feathery, almost dead creature. The image of a few spurts of blood accompanying its final twitches lingered, leaving me weak in the stomach. I'd had surprisingly little previous exposure to death. *But death is a natural part of life,* I told myself as I tried to take control of my impractical emotions. *A normal cycle. A normal reality, but it's impacting me so much. I eat meat almost every day, but I guess I've never stopped to think that something bled out and suffered and died before it got to my plate. Of course, I always knew that, but it's different when you actually see it.* I eventually began to wonder exactly who I was trying to convince.

"Savannah!" Ammon called from ahead. "Where are you at? Were you listening?"

"Yah, yah. Six-hundred years old," I managed to spit out, indicating that I had been listening, at least on one level. We had already trudged through the weathered trails and up past the moss-shingled homes, tripping over chickens that bolted out from behind wood stacks and bushes. The air was filled with the wholesome sounds of children's laughter, cocky roosters crowing, and the faint wisps of horsetails swatting flies. A babbling brook trickled right through the steep village, and knotted wood bridges exhibited gnarled faces as they sprawled across whispering streams. Ducks were held captive in barred cages placed in the shallow, gently flowing waters. It was a clean, easy way to store the birds, which were also undoubtedly being fattened up so they could be eaten or sold. We continued to hike ever higher, and we'd fallen into a thirty-minute spell of silence before I finally gave in to my thirst.

"Whoa, Bree! Wait up," I called, desperately. "Give us the water before you run ahead."

"Seriously, why am I carrying all this stuff?" she demanded. Her athletic training had primed her nicely for this kind of work out, and she was nowhere near as red-faced or breathless as me.

"'Cause you're the one with the bag," Mom said.

"I was wondering why you even took it to begin with," I said bending over and placing my hands on my thighs to catch my breath. "Damn! I feel like a bloody old man."

"Hey! Language!" Mom snapped.

"Ammon has a bag, too," Bree pointed out.

"Yah, but you're the tough one. Remember?" Ammon said, conveniently taking advantage of her competitive nature.

"Fine, I'll take a hit for the team," she said proudly. "I never go anywhere without my bag! This thing is my life! I have everything in here!" She reached behind her to pat it reassuringly.

"After what I saw coming out of your storage buckets at home, I don't doubt you do," I said. Swinging her bag over her right shoulder, she opened it and grabbed the bottle of water. It wasn't just since the trip that she had started carrying the heavy load on her back; she had carried a bag around for as long as I could remember to hold whatever loose ends she picked up throughout the course of her life.

"I've had this same bag for nine years. It's awesome!!" she said, passing me the bottle.

We really only needed Ammon's daypack to hold our water, playing cards and score sheet, compass, and guidebook, but Bree still insisted on bringing hers. There was no separating the girl from her carry-all. I guess, in a way, she used it as her shield and comfort in the world, the same way my "puffy jacket" had served a similar need for me when I was in school.

Tilting my head back to glug down the water, I nearly spat it out and exclaimed, "Oh gross!!! It's warm."

"Better get used to it," Ammon chuckled, grabbing it from my hand as soon as I caught up to him.

"Oh, right. Get used to it, get used to it, get used to it," I sang with a smile, waving my hand in the air. "That's your answer to everything," I grumbled, changing my tune and glaring at his back as he walked off, but I was soon distracted by the sights around me.

Some farmers were working their rice patties with bare hands. Others carried bamboo poles with buckets hanging from both ends across one shoulder. As we approached, some raised their heads enough to expose round and generally worn faces, their cone-shaped hats providing protection from the ever-present sun.

I smiled at many, finding it ironic that we were looking at them in awe while *we* were the real spectacle in this land, sporting our baseball caps and shiny new hiking boots as we did. The farmers were knee deep in the pools of water from which little sprouts of green peeked. It occurred to me that we did not touch the earth in quite the same way they did.

As the incline became steeper and more strenuous, Mom and I began to fall behind. Bree and Ammon had finally disappeared around a bend. Ammon's longer legs never seemed to stop Bree from trying to prove she was stronger and more athletic. Mom and I slowed down and occasionally stopped, hands on our hips, to gasp between sentences. It would probably take a day or two to decide if my red face was the result of sunburn or exertion.

Forty-five minutes and thousands of steps later, we reached the top where Bree and Ammon stood triumphantly. When I finally reached the edge and hung my head over, I understood their joyful expressions. Below us was a magnificent vista blending the best of humankind and nature. Balancing on that rim, I became one with history. *Maintained, cultivated, and passed down through generations.* Ammon's words echoed in my brain. *Built six-hundred years ago, it took three-hundred years to complete this riveting masterpiece.* The hundreds of tiers carved into the mountainsides looked like the ancient steps of an Aztec pyramid and added visual exhaustion to my physical fatigue. *A beautiful system engendered by some historical genius. I'm not so sure about Dragon Spine, but some mythical creature must surely be running this show.* Nonetheless, I envisioned a dragon with rippling skin and shiny green scales curling around the mountains like a guardian with one golden, burning eye keeping constant watch over his minions as they'd worked to create this functional masterpiece of balance and harmony.

Night was falling and the light was fading fast, forcing us to retreat or face a long, dark journey. My final, stunning view was of each tiered pool reflecting the dying sunlight, like a million mirrors. *I wouldn't have missed this. I would walk that walk again,* I thought, my cheeks still flushed.

Thoughts occurred to me during the strenuous descent that had never surfaced before. What we'd seen over the past few days revealed so clearly what Ammon had been trying to get across. It felt as if my text books had come to life. We had gotten a taste of what life is really like for the people in rural China. They have families, and everyone plays a role in keeping them together. Although the rituals and culture they relied on to do that were vastly different from my own, they were just *people,* living and working to provide the essentials of life. Despite my fears and prior judgments, I slowly began to see that, in the end, they were no different from us; their wants and needs were the same. Still, I couldn't imagine living their lives for one day!

Rails and Trails
17

I *was wandering endlessly and searching aimlessly when I glimpsed a tall, lumi-nous mansion hovering above a hill. A door opened high above, mysteriously welcoming me in. Could this be it? Oh how I want to be out of this cool darkness. I know this place. The wind gripped my hair, pulling me backwards as a rope lad-der was thrown down, rapidly unraveling and twisting in the breeze. I craned my neck backwards to take in the sight. There has to be a place in there where I can lay my weary head. A whirling tunnel of orange leaves appeared, rapidly changing to brown as they passed me. As I took a first, faltering step towards the house, I heard Ammon's impatient wakeup call.*

"Wharaahharg," I groaned, holding a hand out, reaching and push-ing in unison to try to salvage what was left of my dream. That restful place was still there. I could still get to it, if only he'd leave me alone.

"What is she doing?" his distant voice interrupted again, but I stubbornly held on to my semi-conscious state.

"Go whack your sister," it came again. *Oh, please, just go away,* I mentally pleaded with him. I tried to raise my legs, but they felt im-movable, like metal on a magnetic surface. I could not escape, could not move fast enough in this other world.

"We're leaving. C'mon," he said, and with that, I lost it! The dream was gone, and yet the scenario I was waking up to was no more real than the one I'd inhabited just moments before – until the worries resurrected themselves, that is.

"Nooo, no, no!" I moaned. The hotel's five flights of stairs, among other irritants, had definitely caught up with me. My legs were dead weights, and my butt felt like it must be scabbed over from miles of biking. I felt bruised everywhere. I reached behind to pat my aching bottom and then crawled off the mattress onto the tile floor to cool my burning skin.

"I hate mornings!!!" I said as I banged my head on the floor beside the pillow I'd slyly dragged with me.

"OOH, OOH, my feet," I whimpered. They felt like crushed sacks of bone.

"Well, we have a bus to catch," Mom said, a hint of compassion in her voice.

"Oohhh! I really can't," I continued, still hoping against hope that Ammon would relent, just this once.

"GET UP," he barked in a distinctly unsympathetic tone. I responded with a hate-filled look from under my pillow, but I finally caved and got up. Today, we had to travel by bus to a bigger city, Guilin, where we could catch a train to a city called Kunming. For me, this meant nothing more than hoisting our bags on and off several times and carrying them between stations and crowds, an itinerary that translated to *my body is going to kill,* which translated to *I seriously do not want to go anywhere.*

"Oh c'mon, Savannah. You don't want to miss your first train ride," Mom said with her hands on her hips.

"Yes, actually I do. Very much so," I told her bluntly.

The platform rumbled beneath me as the train drew near. The sound was enough to rattle most anything, including my teeth. Never before had I felt the roar of this massive snake, beating and breathing from the rails as it slowed to a stop. With one foot on the lower rung, I grabbed the wide metal handles on either side of the open door. Chipped green paint scratched my palms as my weight hung from my skinny arms. Bree's herculean shove from behind catapulted me and my giant backpack to the top of the metal ladder. When I popped into the crammed entryway, I saw to the left the accordion-like connector between the two carriages. To my right, two familiar backpacks were making their way down the narrow aisle. I reached back to take Bree's hand and followed them. On one side, we passed open-ended compartments with big windows. Three-tiered bunk beds hugged each wall, leaving barely enough space to squeeze in on the upper levels. On my right were bunk beds placed end to end that stretched lengthwise along the windows. Midway down the aisle, Ammon claimed one of the six available sleeping compartments.

"Here, give me your bag," he said as he reached out to help me. Squeezing into the small aisle space, I managed to turn my back towards him so he could take it off me. Doing the same for everyone, he placed the bags underneath the green vinyl benches.

"WHOA WIE!" Mom exclaimed, pointing above her head where she stood. "Everybody watch these fans. They don't have screens. If you didn't see them, you'd get your head chopped right off." Eyeing the saucer-sized fans attached to the wall on either side of the window, I was a good deal less intimidated. *Get your hair tangled, maybe, but head chopped off? I doubt it!*

"It's sooo hot," I complained wishing there were more than just the two small fans. "Oh I'm dying! I wish we had air conditioning. Next time we have to go first class!" The temperature had been running at nearly 30°C (86°F) all week, and I was still suffering from the humidity.

"Well we can't, Savannah. It'll blow our budget if we do everything first class, and then we'll never be able to afford a year of travel," Mom said.

"My point exactly. Let's make it shorter and enjoy ourselves instead," I eagerly suggested.

"Savannah," she said simply, donning her best unimpressed facial expression.

"Not even second class?" I pouted. I dragged my cheeks down as if to pull my own skin off, my tongue flopping like a dog's and my eyes rolling up in their sockets to emphasize how strongly I objected to this sort of discomfort.

"We want to get the most out of this trip," she continued, slipping her smaller pack off her front and placing it beside her as she took a seat.

"Besides, you'll get used to it," Ammon said, sitting.

There was that same old line again: get used to it. "You're crazy. There's no way!" I told him.

"You'd be surprised. Soon you won't even notice the heat anymore," he insisted.

"Not notice?! Not notice this?" I said, lifting my shirt to expose my dripping midsection. I could feel the beads of sweat rolling down into my belly button. "I'm sweating in places I didn't even KNOW I could sweat!" With that, I snuggly pulled the shirt down to my waistline.

"You don't see any of the locals suffering, do you?" Ammon stated more than asked.

"Ummm. How about this guy right over there? He looks like he's going to need a new handkerchief pretty darn quick!" I whispered. The guy across the aisle was constantly dabbing his forehead and stroking his flabby neck with his already drenched cloth.

"Okay, well, it probably doesn't help that he's so fat," Bree said out loud.

My eyes nearly popped out of my head. I was so shocked by her words that I froze and tucked in my shoulders, hoping to disappear. I didn't dare look up from the floor.

"Hah, Savannah. You're so funny. He can't understand anything we're saying. Nobody does!"

"Please just shush. Shush!" I spluttered.

"You can say anything you want," she continued to prove her point. Her next attempt, "I just farted!" sent her off into peals of laughter. *This is not normal!* I couldn't believe how easy it was for her. But I realized that she was right when I snuck a look over at the sweaty man still nonchalantly chewing his boiled egg, moist flakes falling indiscriminately from his mouth. Still, it just seemed so wrong.

"But Savannah, back to what you were saying," Mom started. I'd almost forgotten about it after Bree's outburst. "Air conditioning would cost more than twice the price, and there's no reason we need to do it that way. Imagine how much hotter it would feel coming out of that coolness and then having to walk a couple of kilometres to the guest house. And the places we're staying in won't have it, either."

"Yah, but I'd be *so* cold, it would feel great when I went outside."

"Either way you'd be complaining, so just give it up," Ammon said. "The weather's not changing so *you're* going to have to. Get used to it."

"Try to take a nap, and you won't notice it anymore," Mom suggested. I climbed to the middle bunk on the right side and lay down with my face towards the window. There were no blankets and no sheets, just the vinyl-covered bench sticking to my damp skin. It was really strange having a bed on wheels, but this trip was better than the buses had been. There was no swerving or bumping, just a consistent, side-to-side rocking. Instead of rubber tires on asphalt, it was metal on metal with squealing halts thrown in.

I tossed and turned in my own sweat, constantly checking my waterproof watch. Five minutes passed – ten–twenty-one in the morning. Another minute – ten-twenty-two. The blades of the pale green/almost grey fan above my head went round and round, humming in uneven circles. "Uughhh," I groaned and rolled back over. Time stood still. *Is this thing broken?* I thought, shaking my wrist in complete and utter frustration. Oh, ten-twenty-three. Whoopee! Lying on my stomach I stared at the wall and then rolled over to lie face-up instead, gazing blankly ahead. I laid like that as long as I could handle it. Eleven-twenty-five. A whole hour. *Twenty-one more to go?!*

"Well, that didn't work," I announced to no one in particular. How could I ignore the throbbing in my swelling feet and palms or the incurable itches you couldn't even begin to know where to scratch, all piled on top of the overwhelming heat?

"I can't sleep," I said louder, directing my comment over the edge of my bunk towards Mom, who was reading in her bunk below.

"Read your book then," was her next suggestion. Unable to sit upright in such cramped quarters, I swung my legs over and rolled and wiggled down on my belly to sit next to her.

"I am NOT reading," I told her firmly. *How could she expect me to suddenly start doing something I'd never done before in my whole life?* I'd never had any interest in reading. I was beginning to suspect that this was some form of punishment. *Isn't it enough that I came with her in the first place? Like I had a choice! Why do I have to read, too?*

"Savannah, it's not for me. It doesn't benefit me one bit. Reading is great!" she argued.

"I hate reading!! It's so stupid," Bree broke in.

"I still can't believe you haven't tried it yet. I'm already half-way through my book," Mom continued, "Once you get into it, you'll really love it. Trust me. You won't be able to put it down."

"There is no way. How can you get any emotion out of a bunch of words on a page?! I need to see what's happening. Why would anyone read when you could watch movies instead?" Bree said, getting ready to start listing more than our fill of classics.

"Not everyone has a TV," Ammon said.

"And it's way better than a movie," Mom said, sincerely.

Bree, being the person who wouldn't share the remote control with anyone in the house, sometimes even hoarding it in a secret stash of many other "missing" things, almost fell off her seat at the mere idea.

Instead, she said confidently, "That's just crazy." Suddenly uttering a loud, discouraged "Ugh," Bree rolled her eyes and unexpectedly fell back into the corner to dig in her daypack for a book, surrendering to the inevitable.

I couldn't honestly recall ever reading an entire book cover to cover, but here was Mom, reaching under the bench to open my backpack. Unpacking my load of books, she said, "You should read this one. It's a classic. It's the first book I ever read, and it got me hooked. You'll really love it, I promise!"

She chose the biggest, fattest book out of the whole stack. "What kind of big-arse, intimidating--- Why does Bree get to read that tiny book?!" I exclaimed as she took hers out. She pulled it protectively to her chest at the accusation and graced me with one of her infamous scowls.

"That's a romance. They're adult books. I'm not sure you should be reading those yet. They're pretty risqué," Mom confessed, pressing her more appropriate choice into my hands.

"Hrmph!" I protested, feeling the annoying weight of it and then promptly tossing it onto the small table beneath the open window. *The only way she would manage to trick Bree is with a risqué romance novel!*

"But yours is a romance, too," Mom urged, less than impressed by my childish behaviour. Cornered by her logic, I was not amused at all. I wasn't going to read, especially a huge, monster book that would probably take a lifetime to finish. I was sure that doing nothing would pass the time better, but about two hours later, Bree hadn't moved. She hadn't put the book down once, and I began to wonder where in the world she was. I'd expected her to fall asleep, but she was definitely still reading.

Legs stretched out on the bottom bunk on the opposite side of our compartment, Ammon sat with his back against the window as he read. I giggled at the idea of him trying to sleep that night with his big feet hanging over the end a few inches, completely vulnerable to dozy insomniacs passing in the night. *Get used to it,* I thought cynically with a smirk on my face. Somehow Bree had positioned herself at the opposite end of the bed under his feet. He kicked her book every now and then when he switched his crossed legs. She never seemed to mind or even notice. *She must think it adds a few special effects to whatever the heck is going on in that book of hers.*

"Hey, who wants to play a round of cards?" I tried to coax one of my siblings, knowing what Mom's nagging response would be. I got only an unenthusiastic wave from Ammon, and Bree just raised her book higher to cover her face.

"Oh, so that's how it's going to be, is it?"

"Just get your book and stop being stupid," Ammon said, looking up for a split second.

"The sooner you read it, the sooner you can get rid of it," Mom reasoned beside me.

"No thanks. I'll be fine." I scooted closer to the open window and crossed my arms over my belly. Shuffling my unpopular deck of cards, I glared up at the tin roof and leather straps supporting the beds. At least the landscape was pretty. I could stare at those vibrant green fields, men working, and impressive buffaloes for hours, but I'd already been gazing at the scenery for hours. Taking my eyes from the window, I saw that the dreaded book was still on the small table where I had tossed it. Its pages seemed to grow as I watched them flutter tauntingly in the breeze from the window. I felt I was somehow being lured into it, like a fish to a hook. *This is exactly what they want.* I just wanted to reach out and feel it. *I must not let it get to me!* I inched closer, eyeing it carefully. Taking a deep breath I dashed over, grabbed hold of the window's handle, and started pulling down on it frantically. Nothing happened. I pushed and pulled like one of those exaggerated cartoon characters whose feet are braced up against a wall, knees knocking from the strain of his exertion before a sudden release sends him flying. But for me, there was no burst of strength or lucky tug. The window remained most undeniably lodged in place. Falling back in defeat, I almost forgot why I so dearly wanted to close that window. No one else seemed to mind, or even notice. They were all absorbed in their books. I glanced back at the book. *There it is again! Those pages flapping relentlessly. No, no, they're dancing.* Surrendering the fight, I reluctantly snatched the book up and in an instant I, too, was *Gone with the Wind.*

Birthday Bargaining
18

O ne yuan each, about fifteen cents in Canadian money, got us on the next bus. The bad news was, it was packed beyond belief, and my backpack was stuck to my completely soaked t-shirt in the muggy 35°C (95°F) weather. If I had known it would take an hour to get there, I'd have taken my bag off, though I probably couldn't have managed to wiggle out of it in the space I had, let alone find a place to put it down. *I'm nothing but a bloody pack horse!* I'd had no peace and quiet, no time to myself, and hardly any sleep since I'd stepped off the plane in Hong Kong. And now my straps were weighing on my sunburned shoulders, rubbing them raw. The sun was shining and I'm sure there was beautiful scenery out there somewhere, had I only been able to see past all the people crowding me, whose heads were dripping with sweat. A pleasant sight, indeed, and my mood matched my distinctly uncomfortable surroundings.

Imprisoned by human walls, I clung onto the one handle I could reach. We had blitzed through the ancient stone forest in Kunming and crashed for the night after our twenty-two hour train ride. We'd barely had time to sleep before we spent another seven hours on a train that took us to the local bus station. I felt like this final hour might just be the end of me. I couldn't ignore the nagging weight at my neck and shoulders or the salty beads dripping down my butt crack (I'd like to say between my breasts, but of course, I was still waiting for them to show up!) Plus, I looked my absolute worst. Weak and tattered, I was unwillingly exposed to hundreds of people. I don't think I'd even brushed my teeth that morning, never mind the fact that my hair hadn't seen a brush for days! Everyone was staring; they might even have been sneering, but I tried to reassure myself that I was probably imagining their reactions again.

Obviously the heat was getting to me, because I heard Sky's voice warning me that you are more likely to faint if your knees are locked after standing for long periods of time. I consciously loosened mine, thankful that his military experience had served some purpose other than exempting him from keeping me company on this blasted trip.

At every stop there was an automated "Ching Chang Chow" that rendered me completely dumbstruck each time, but Bree would laugh and interrupt my self-pitying reverie.

"Listen! I can speak Chinese. 'Ching Chang Chow! Please step off the bus,'" she improvised.

"Bree, stop it!!" I urged with wide, serious eyes. "They can understand THAT," I told her, effectively admitting that she was actually speaking a bit of Chinese.

Every minute, I thought, *okay, next stop for sure,* but it never seemed to come. *Just get me outta here and get me to wherever the heck we're going.* I counted down the seconds of every minute as we went on and on and on. My bags were getting heavier and heavier, and I could hardly move. With every Ching Chang Chow, people would shove and squeeze past each other, throwing me off balance and interrupting my deliberately comatose state. With each stop I drifted further into the sea of people who got between me and the family. The unfamiliar faces blurred and became one in my exhausted vision.

Finally, a muffled, "Okay, this is it!" brought me back to the present. "Sharpen your elbows," was our fearless leader's only instruction. Raising them up, I barged my way through that sardine tin on wheels and stepped onto the curb, only to find myself in yet another crowd. As we sifted through the bystanders, a few would separate from the regular crowd and come running at the sight of us, holding up photos and poster boards of the guest houses they represented and the restaurants they wanted us to visit. Before I knew what was happening, we were following someone to #4 Guest House in Dali.

Dali waited for us as if with open arms. Here we planned to take a well-earned rest. Conveniently, Mom's birthday the next day offered a perfect excuse to sit back under a straw hut in a beautiful courtyard and relax for once. I was finally allowed to soak up some of this beauty rather than watch it whiz by me on buses, trains, or bikes. A four-bed dorm that cost three dollars per person per night was home for the next four days. I walked in and collapsed on my bed and didn't move.

A slit of light peered directly in my eye through the wooden shutters early the next morning. I first responded by burying my face under another, slightly less comfortable pillow before I remembered what day it was.

"Happy birthday, Mom," we groaned a little less enthusiastically than usual as we rolled our stiff bodies out of bed.

"You could be home right now, you know, having a nice party with a cake," I suggested.

"Are you kidding? I never liked parties. This is way more fun! I'm going to get a massage today! What more could I possibly ask for, other than maybe a Dr. Pepper? Oh well," she added in a quieter voice, "maybe a pizza. That would be lovely, too, but that's probably not possible either, even on my birthday."

"You're definitely not going to find your Dr. Pepper, and even if you could, we wouldn't let you. But we might be able to find you a pizza," Ammon offered.

"Oh, and I'm finally going to buy a jade bracelet," she added, deciding she would splurge and get herself at least one souvenir. All the buses we'd travelled on stopped at several little jade outlets. They were always glossy shops with all kinds and shapes of jade arranged in pretty glass cabinets. Even after umpteen jade store stops, the domestic Chinese tourists would still get out and ogle each display, oohing and aahing all the while.

"Is good luck. Omen. Good luck," the merchants in towns closer to bigger cities where many knew a smattering of English often told us as they bowed their heads. "Yes, yes. Is luck!"

Presenting the fifteen-dollar expense that a jade bracelet would incur gave Mom a little more leeway with Ammon if labelled as a birthday present. After some fresh, fat banana pancakes, we set off on our shopping expedition to see what kind of deals we could find.

Voices calling out a tranquil "Hallo!" came from merchants everywhere. They magically appeared from shaded spots behind stalls and from around corners in alleyways as we approached.

"Whoa, these guys are everywhere!" Bree exclaimed as one snuck up from behind her, again with the same "Hallo!"

"Country? Country you?" these persistent men and women would ask, their delicate eyes observing us closely.

"Canada," one of us would respond.

After a few puzzled looks, they would exclaim, "OH, Janada!" correcting us with big smiles on their faces.

"Okay, whatever you say!" Bree would retort shamelessly.

Merchant women ran from their shops to attack us with the gidgets and gadgets they were trying to sell. Hairclips in my hair, bracelets around my wrists – they'd squabble to adorn every part of our bodies.

Peeling the bracelets off as fast as they appeared on her wrists, Mom asked, "Where did you go?" turning to Ammon who had vanished in all the excitement.

"What? You mean, while you guys were getting mobbed? To get this," he said, holding up a bottle of water.

"How much did you pay for it?" Mom asked, while politely shaking her head at the two women on her heels trying desperately to make a sale.

"Two," he said, waving a confident hand of dismissal to the women.

"Really?" She exclaimed, and then she reconsidered for a moment. "Wait, two what?"

"Dollars. What do you think!?" He said sarcastically. "Yuan. I don't even carry dollars."

"What!!?? I paid five!" she exclaimed, as he smiled smugly and continued moving ahead. "How did he do that? Did you see what shop he went to?"

"While we were getting mobbed?" I repeated, reminding her that I'd been far too preoccupied to pay attention to where he'd gone.

Whenever Mom needed to buy something, she'd practically jump over the shop's counter, waving, pointing, and grabbing for what she wanted. The puzzled women most often laughed and just stepped out of her way, but we had a different take on her shopping behaviour. We thought her behaviour was just plain crazy.

"What? Why? I got what I wanted, and everyone's happy," she'd constantly say. She was always interested and happy to interact genially with the locals, but not when it came to bargaining. That was another story entirely.

"Three kuai?!!!!" Mom would gasp in the merchants' non-comprehending faces, exasperated. Kuai, we quickly learned, was their slang way of saying yuan. They used it the way we used bucks to mean dollars. Placing her mouth close to my ear, she would whisper in a crackly voice, "How much is that anyway?" It almost made me laugh out loud. Bree's rude demonstration on the train had revealed that attempts to be secretive were largely unnecessary.

The woman was shouting "three" in Mandarin. They often gestured with their hands to tell us the price. I was grateful that Ammon had delivered a quick lesson on numbers and the different hand gestures the Chinese used to represent numbers on the train.

"Three?" I inquired of the woman using the native hand signals I'd learned.

"Ja! Ja!" she said quickly and abruptly, hoping not to lose the sale.

Calculating and also savouring the moment, I finally turned back to Mom and, in the same secretive fashion she'd used with me, I whispered, "fifty cents."

Smiling as she raised two fingers, she said, "Oh! I'll take two then."

The woman said "Ja Ja" again, and gave Mom eight yuan in change from her ten-yuan bill. She'd thought Mom was offering to pay just two yuan, when Mom had really been trying to indicate that she wanted two at the agreed-upon price of three yuan.

"I don't get it. OH! She must have thought I meant two yuan. Oooh, yeah!" Mom gave her two yuan and indicated that she wanted another of the same item, pleased to have paid so little.

Like starving hounds, half a dozen women came rushing towards us to make another sale. They all waved their hands in our faces as they simultaneously shouted out numbers in Mandarin. They'd very skillfully done my hair up while I was still walking, and were now calling out, "forty-five, forty-five," in an attempt to sell me the same kind of hairclip they'd just put in my hair. Another came rushing from behind with a looking glass so I could see the effect. They continued to chase me with nail polish and other feminine products, and I didn't know how to handle them. I did the only thing I could think of. I ran to catch up with the rest of the family so I could try to shake some of them off onto Ammon. They certainly would have had their hands in his long hair had it not been out of their reach, but it was as if he were wearing pesticide. Somehow, they just didn't seem to bother him in the same way.

Just as we were going to cross the street, we were cut off by a donkey-drawn cart full of bamboo shoots, forcing us to stop and let my trailing friends catch up to me again. This time I was positively cornered and pinched from all sides. The determined woman with the hairclips had managed to stuff yet another one in my hand! She continued to drop her asking price. "Forty? Okay, okay. Thirty-five, thirty-five!!" I had two options: buy it or just walk away from her. I still didn't want it, and I had no money. I didn't know what to do, so I froze. *Geez, I have to stop for them, but I can't be left behind.* I'd feebly try to return the items, but the women were relentless.

"Stupid woman! If you don't take it ... Ergh, I don't want it!" I stomped. Of course she did not understand me, which made it even more frustrating. "I can't wait any longer. If you don't want it, then I'll keep it." All I knew was that I didn't want to lose the others. I kept walking away, and the one with the loudest voice kept lowering the price. The other voices seemed to blend into a babbling of numbers, but the "hairclip" gal's voice was like a shadow I couldn't escape. When her price dropped to the teens, I began to think I could actually use a hairclip. My long, flowing hair was nothing but a burden in this heat and under these circumstances. *How nice it would be to tie it up off my sweaty back.* I could already feel the cooling difference it made.

I repeated her latest offer of fifteen yuan, and then grabbed Mom's arm and asked if I could have it.

"Fifteen yuan?!!" she gasped when I told her, as if it were a fortune.

"Okay, okay. Ten. Ten," the woman said, in a reflex as natural as breathing.

"How much was that again? What was the rate?" Mom asked predictably. I looked at the woman and with raised eyebrows held out a fist which translated to ten without speaking. When she nodded, I turned back to Mom. Meanwhile Mom was having a moment of realization.

"There are six yuan to a dollar, Mom! It's less than two bucks."

"Ten, eh? How about five?" she said, cautiously flashing five confident fingers.

Sold! The woman nodded and waved at me to keep it for five.

"We'll take three of them," Mom said pointing three times.

"Three?!"

"Yah, I want one," she told me, reaching in her pocket for a few spare bills, "and Bree probably will, too."

"Wow Mom. You sure are fun to shop with. You do realize that started at forty-five!" I said, as the mob miraculously dispersed.

"Can you believe they reduced the price from forty-five to five!" Mom rushed to tell Ammon, happy to have bested his earlier success at purchasing water.

"Well, I'd say you guys learned your first lesson of bargaining today. Act like you don't want it, that's the trick. Because as soon as you look like you want it, they have the upper hand," he said wisely. Having conveniently stumbled upon this technique, Mom adopted it enthusiastically. From then on, everything was always too expensive because it could always be had for less.

After a successful day of "window" shopping and sight-seeing, we returned to the guest house with Mom, who had purchased both a full, hour-long massage and a pale green, jade bracelet. We sat in the lovely courtyard later that evening beneath the shade of the straw hut and played our ongoing card game of Daifugō, the original Japanese version of the game Asshole, infamous for requiring players to get up and change their seats according to relative rank at the end of each round. Endless flies swarmed all over our chocolate banana pancakes to ruin what would otherwise have been a perfect setting amidst the lush, inviting gardens and the warm, tropical weather.

"Two Jacks," Bree said, throwing her cards onto the pile in the middle of the stone table.

"Okay, so I read somewhere before I left that in China, people are only allowed to have one kid," Mom brought up what was a touchy subject for her, with her four kids. "Is that true, Ammon?"

"Yah. It's the Family Planning Policy, also known as the one child policy," Ammon said. "Urban people living in cities are only allowed one child, but the rural people living in the villages are allowed to have more. Ethnic minorities can, too."

"But I thought it was for all of China," Mom said, sweeping the pile and starting with a low, single four.

"Nope. Only something like thirty-five percent of the population is subject to the one-kid rule."

"It's still kind of terrible, though, isn't it?" I asked, waiting for my turn as I shook some flies off my fork.

"Well, surprisingly, they say it has prevented around two hundred and fifty to three hundred million births since 1978 when it was first implemented," Ammon told us. I eyed him suspiciously, wondering if he was giving us correct information. Looking at her cards, Mom folded her hand and passed. She then whacked the air in front of her in a vain attempt to clear the air, but I was still stuck on trying to understand how this seemingly drastic plan worked.

"Really? That's only like, like, no time at all. I thought this was like hundreds of years ago?!" I fanned my fly-infested pancake with my cards before tossing a single ace of hearts onto the pile.

"Yah, that's why they're only starting to feel the impact of the policy now," Mom said, clearing the table for the next round.

"But think about it. Everyone wants sons, so what does that mean for the daughters? If you only get one shot at it, what do you think happens if you get a girl?" Ammon said, planting an unthinkable seed in our heads. "I'm not saying it happens every time, but records show a definite increase in abortions and in the number of unwanted orphans, which still only accounts for fifty percent of the statistically "missing girls" in the 1980s.

"I hate men!" Bree growled.

"What do they do if they DO have more? I mean, it's kind of hard to stop that kind of thing," Mom said.

"They can only screw them over financially by levying fines and taking away benefits, that sort of thing. So yah, if a family is really rich and they want more kids, they can just absorb the cost and have more," he guessed.

"So sad that money rules the world," Mom said.

"Yah, but you'd be surprised. Somewhere it's reported that seventy-six percent of the population supports the policy. I wonder if that number will crash drastically when the negative effects start catching up. And if you don't live in the city, you can just apply for a permit to have a second child if the first is a girl."

Violently throwing her next cards onto the pile, Bree growled, "Why are they so sexist?!"

"Look who's talking, Miss 'I Hate Men!' But anyway, they can also apply if the first is handicapped in some way."

"That doesn't sound any better! That's almost like saying girls are friggin' disabled!" said Bree, quick to take offence.

"They are! Try living with the lot of you! It'd handicap anybody."

"Damn, you are such a jerk!" she said, throwing her hand across the table. "I'm not playing anymore!"

"What the hell!?" Ammon said. "Good to see *you're* in a good mood."

"Oh, you two! Stop it," Mom piped in, seeing Ammon growing more aggravated. "Now Bree, you're not quitting. You have to at least finish the round," she said, gathering up Bree's cards. "Now, did you have two fives or just the one?" Mom asked, trying to find them all.

"I'm not playing if he is," Bree said, folding her arms and glaring at Ammon.

"See what I mean?" Ammon said. For such a smart man, he somehow didn't have the sense to drop it. "Insane! And if this "man" were not here, what would you do tomorrow?"

"We're almost done," Mom went on trying to smooth over the conflict.

"Well, she forfeited the last round anyway!" Ammon said.

"I found all her cards. It's fine," she said, putting Bree's cards back in her hand. "And don't listen to him. The reason they want sons is so they can work the fields and help the family survive. More hands working the fields means more food and money," Mom explained before adding a little white lie to ease Bree's mind, "so they can buy nice things for their wives."

"But the other thing is the whole '4-2-1 Problem,'" Ammon continued.

"Hey, this isn't my card!" she said, showing a low six of hearts.

"Well, too bad. You shouldn't have thrown them all in," Ammon said, making me cringe in anticipation of the next outburst.

"And just what does 4-2-1 mean?" I asked to please him and keep the conversation going, since Bree seemed not to hear him.

"It means that if couples are only having one kid, then that one kid needs to support both his parents and as many as four grandparents when he grows up. You see how that works? So the poor seniors are being left with less support, and many have to fend for themselves entirely."

"It's in their culture to take care of each other. I'm so lucky to have four of you guys," Mom said as she laughed a bit too agreeably.

"Right now, male-to-female ratios are high everywhere. Doesn't matter if it's rural or urban. They're saying there will be thirty million more men than women in 2020, so you can imagine the social instability that will cause."

"Good, so then women can start having harems," Bree said with a vengeful laugh. *At least something pleases her,* I thought, thankful she hadn't blown up again.

"What was that last round? Who came in first on that one?" Ammon asked, jotting down the card scores and ignoring her comment.

Mom beamed as she called out, "Me!" *No wonder she was so eager to keep that round going!* I almost had to laugh.

"Okay, so speaking of girls and boys, does anyone know which bathroom is which?" I asked, while Ammon shuffled and dealt the next hand.

"Does it matter? Just go in whichever one you want," he said.

"I'd like to know, at least. For future reference."

"You've managed just fine so far," he said, not understanding my concern.

"Yah, because we always followed the crowd. Just look in your little booky-book there and tell us," I insisted.

"It hardly matters here," Mom said, reminding me that there were hardly any people in the compound.

"Well, it does to me! Especially since the showers have no doors!!!!" I protested.

"Aaalriiight, then" he said, drawing out his vowels to emphasize how much he does for us. "So here it is," he opened up his *Lonely Planet* to those translations and laid it on the table. "Here. This one is women 女人, and this is men 男人."

"Which is which?" Bree asked.

Leaning over to take a closer look at the little symbols, she burst out laughing, "Yours looks like a blockhead!!! HAH! One with legs!"

"Well, that makes sense," Mom joked along, happy that the bickering ended on a humorous note, and we played until the sky turned a beautiful, dark lilac colour with splashes of citrusy orange. We were just ordering our last round of banana pancakes when the crickets started to come out, and I was sure I heard the distant croak of a frog or two.

"Go, Mom. It's your turn," Ammon said, waiting anxiously to throw in what could only be yet another winning hand. Fanning her cards and waving them at the flies, Mom threw in two queens.

"If only these stupid flies would go away!!" she said, bothered by the numerous insects still landing on her hands and plate. "Whoa, wait, wait," she said with an outstretched hand to stop us in our places. Her eyes circled as she watched a few more little flying friends land on the table. She slowly leaned in and then suddenly slammed her open palm down. CRACK! Her brand new bracelet flew off in two pieces as if she'd planned it to hit both Bree and Ammon, who instinctively ducked. Any remaining tension broke as we all roared with laughter.

Her immediate "Oh no!! My bracelet" reaction was quickly followed by, "But doesn't that mean I get a wish or something? Isn't it good luck in China if it breaks?"

"Well, it was *your* bracelet, so I wouldn't be surprised," Ammon said. Everyone in our family and all of Mom's five brothers were convinced that she had "lucky horseshoes up her butt."

"As if you need anymore! Why don't you share some of that luck with the rest of us?" I asked.

"No really! That is what she told me! That I get a wish when it breaks," Mom insisted

"Well, then, Happy Birthday!" Bree congratulated.

Wrinkles and Dimples
19

Only one thing marred our enjoyment of the luxurious pleasures of taking a few days' rest in Dali. Bree had unintentionally brought an unwelcome little hitchhiker along from Vancouver, and we all caught a cold. As if that weren't enough, Mom's left lung became inflamed from a case of pleurisy she developed. She had also tripped on a stair on the overnight bus to Yangshuo, and her right ribcage crashed directly onto a bedrail. The next few weeks, both sides of her upper body were in excruciating pain.

Once we'd all rested and mostly recovered, I found myself hobbling awkwardly down the narrow stairwell of the bus to Lijiang on my sore feet. Like wounded gladiators shoved unceremoniously into a colosseum, we tackled the next challenge. I was not, in any way, looking forward to the inevitable walk ahead, long or short. My backpack and I were on pretty rocky terms at the time, and I'd have been happy never to see it again. "Do you know where we're staying tonight?" I asked Ammon, ever the worrywart. *Of course he doesn't.* As we expected, though, a few people waited to solicit our business, complete with pictures of the accommodations they offered. Some carried posterboard signs, while others held brochures. With nothing planned or booked, we were free to go with the flow.

Mom coughed. With each gasp and harsh expulsion she cringed in agony and tried to hold her ribs and lungs together.

"Hey, if it is getting worse," I started sympathetically, "then maybe you need to go home to get that taken care of."

"Yah. Nice try," she scowled, rolling her dark eyes.

While Ammon tackled the issue of accommodation, the bus driver tossed our luggage from the under-carriage. Bree and I grabbed the four backpacks in midair as they came flying out. I stumbled backwards with an "oomph!" as I caught mine. I sat the thing upright before reaching my arm down into one of the straps to once again hoist it onto my back. Ammon lifted and held Mom's pack for her as she slipped an arm through one strap, sneezing repeatedly. Ammon asked the little woman he'd procured how far the guest house was.

"No far, no far. Close, close," the lady started in English. "Wu. Wu." She held out five fingers to signify five minutes. My hands were too sore to carry anything, my feet were too dry and cracked to walk, I could hardly talk between chapped lips, and my back was so stiff my stomach hurt. I felt like death warmed over! And yet, there was Mom huffing along next to me, clenching her hands at her sides. I honestly don't know how she managed at all. Ammon claimed his throat was too sore to swallow. As for Bree, well, Bree probably had something wrong with her, too, but it would be nearly impossible to tell which symptoms were new.

Every street and alley we approached held hope before we'd inevitably pass it by. Our lady guide didn't even glance down any of the side streets. She was still humming along, practically running with her stubby legs and showing no sign of stopping any time soon. As we rounded every corner, I would perk up and think that this had to be the one! But we just kept walking and walking. I looked hopefully and seemingly endlessly at every building that just might be a guest house.

I contemplated slipping into the back of the line and casually dropping my pack off and leaving it in a canal, or at least dumping a couple of the books. I wondered how much trouble I'd be in if I could get up the nerve to actually do it. I could so easily imagine the floating pages drifting in the opposite direction.

"My feet are killing me. They're completely dead," I broke out instead, hoping it would somehow lighten the load. I knew I didn't have any right to complain, seeing Mom tough it out, but I couldn't dismiss the fact that I, too, was in pain. I hurt everywhere, actually, from my groggy head down to my feet, where the pressure of the pack's extra weight began splitting the already opened cracks even more.

It was not knowing how far it would be that made the walk so torturous. I began to curse the lady under my breath for lying to us. This was not – in any way, shape, or form – five minutes. We had already been walking for over fifteen minutes.

My stomach roared at me. I wasn't food deprived by any means, and yet I felt starved! A step, a limp, then growls from my midsection, followed by a slow, rebellious moan from my parched throat. *Oh shut up!* I tried to discipline my body and its constant complaints. *This isn't my fault! I didn't do this to you. Take it out on someone else, why don't you!*

Finally, we arrived at the gates of our destination. A tiny old woman wove her way through the natural beauty of the dainty courtyard to welcome us, but my heart quickened a beat or two, and I stopped dead in my tracks at the sight of her.

An unfortunate encounter only days earlier with an old Chinese woman was one I would not soon forget. We had been waiting at a bus stop, fully laden with our backpacks as people went about their daily routines. Men passed by with squawking chickens in hand, women danced by sweeping the road with bushy brooms, and little kids ran past collecting empty bottles for refunds.

One peddler stood out from the rest of the pack. When I first saw her, I bit my lower lip. Her wicker basket was blooming with what looked like homemade marshmallows melting in the sun. Her basket hung in the crook of her arm, half hidden beneath her cloaks. She brought to mind the wicked queen in the Snow White tale carrying white, poison apples as she shuffled towards us, despite my efforts to ignore her. Judging from the condition of her few remaining teeth, I guessed that the anonymous white blobs were probably a staple of her diet. We had no interest in finding out what they were, so we all shook our heads and politely said, "No, No thank you. We don't need any," before trying to wiggle away to avoid confrontation.

Though she could not understand our words, our body language was quite clear, yet she didn't simply slip back into the crowd as we expected, and before I knew it her hand, knobby, rough and crow-like, reached out for me. She grabbed me and sank her claws deep into my arm. I was caught off guard and was too surprised to cry out. My terror blocked my air supply for about ten seconds. I wanted to run, but my pack and the crowds limited my options. Had I forcefully pulled away from her, I'd likely have fallen on my back like an awkward turtle. I tried tugging to resist her, but she didn't budge. *Why me? Why is it always me?* I asked myself. The slightest conflict was enough to push me overboard at this early point of the journey. She clung there desperately, her grip becoming stronger and her nails pinching deeper into my arm. I tugged again, looking frantically for help from my family, who were close by but failed to notice my dilemma, let alone rescue me. *Whatever happened to sticking up for each other?* I thought furiously at I tried to either attract their attention or to pivot away from the old crone, but I was trapped. It felt like she and I hovered in the eye of a whirlpool as the rest of the world spun around us. I didn't know what else to do.

In desperation, I finally gave up on the idea of escape, at which point an inner strength came over me and I turned to her, still angry and terrified. Facing my trepidation directly, I experienced an adrenaline rush that seemed to reveal a completely different facet of this encounter. Suddenly, I became aware of what a rough life she must have had. Her hunched back, her weathered, wrinkled face, and her rotted, gummy snarl told me I knew nothing of her pain.

We somehow stood alone in time, and I imagined her peeling her cloak back and emerging from the shadows of her ancient roots to reveal her inner core. In her eyes, I saw a playful and innocent childhood and began to hear a story of her once shiny black hair and a cheery grin that boasted small, pearly white teeth. *What has this world done to her?* She was screaming at me with her eyes and I stood very still and listened to words only I could hear. It seemed an eternity before she was gone. Had I not had proof in the form of the bloody scratch she'd left behind, I might've thought she was a figment of my imagination.

And now here I was, having to deal with a second old lady. I cautiously stepped deeper into the garden courtyard of the guest house. I still felt a bit shaken by, and not quite able to grasp the full significance of, that first encounter. Sensing my hesitation and nudging me along, Mom advised me, "Don't let past experiences affect your view of new people."

The woman who had led us on this agonizing twenty-five minute hike reached out a hand to introduce us, "This is Granny. She will take care of you." Granny responded with a big, joyous smile. She didn't hesitate a moment before gently taking Mom's hand to lead us up the narrow, steep passage from the porch.

The wooden stairs creaked and complained beneath our feet as we climbed to the peak. It was all made of wood, and our heavy steps made dust fall from the cracks between the roof and the stairs. Numerous cats were already flirting outrageously. By nightfall, they'd be mating and scrambling in the shingles above our heads and we learned that there really is nothing that can keep you awake quite as well as a cat in heat and the obnoxious moan of the male as he begs permission.

Squeezing awkwardly into our attic space with our packs, we were able to unload them at last. There were five beds in our dorm, and a plump, unravelled backpack already claimed one of them. Luckily, the occupied bed stood apart in one corner of the room. Three beds almost touched, but that worked fine for us three girls. Ammon was in another corner, across from the anonymous traveler. He was happiest there, preferring to pretend he wasn't part of our group. Nobody believed that he had three girls tagging along anyway.

Granny was waiting for us when we came back down. The lady who'd led us here had vanished, most likely to return to the station, and we were alone with the little old Granny who spoke not a word of English. That was generally the case among the older generations. The younger a new acquaintance was, the more chance there was that we might have a few words in common. In recent years, the tourism industry had grown to the extent that we even occasionally heard some Celine Dion songs playing in city streets. People Granny's age wouldn't have been exposed to anything other than Mandarin but the language barrier didn't prevent us in any way from having a good chat with her. It took a lot more skill and effort to communicate without a common language, but it made for an exciting, mind-expanding game and, before I knew it, I was laughing helplessly. The tones, emotions, and actions devoted to our charades quite possibly explained more than simple dialogue ever could have, and immediately established a more intimate connection between us.

Granny's face was worn, to say the least, and she had thick, wrinkly dimples. She looked like an animated mole pinching its face in the sun. When it came time for us to explore the world outside her garden, she was very confident that she could direct us. She didn't know where we were headed but then, neither did we, so her directions would do as well as any. Leaning out the door, she took Mom by the hand and pointed left and right to show her the way. We watched her waving arm intently, imagining the path ahead. Mom eventually put her hand on Granny's and nodded thankfully. As a last note, Granny let us know that "eating," signified by raising and lowering her hand to her mouth in a shovelling motion, was at seven o'clock.

Our physical ailments were far less burdensome once we shed our 35lbs (15kg) packs, so off we went. Granny's seemingly random collection of motions did eventually lead us to the town centre. Twinkling canals alongside brick pathways wound their way around homes with thatched roofs. The streets were nearly empty aside from a few local shoppers scattered along the way and a little crowd that had formed in the main square, where local women dressed in blue aprons and white vested costumes linked arms to dance and spin. Onlookers joined in, raising and kicking their legs as the giant circle rotated. All the participants were smiling and laughing.

Lijiang's major tourist attractions are its large, double waterwheels and the Jade Dragon Snow Mountain located fifteen kilometres away. It formed part of the southernmost glacier in the northern hemisphere. The view of the mountain was clear from the town centre, where domestic tourists huddled with their cameras. On the bus ride to Lijiang, the driver had announced the first glimpse of the mountain as its snow caps appeared in the distance. Straining our necks to see what all of the oohs and aahs were about, we were surprised by what we considered to be an exaggerated reaction to a simple mountain. Being from Vancouver, a city surrounded by majestic mountains, we thought them lovely, but these attractions were not why we'd come to Lijiang.

It was neither the Jade Dragon nor the waterwheels we walked miles to see that impressed me. Rather, it was the enchanting beauty of the village itself. Hanging plants and vines dressed the shingled roofs and passageways. Wood planks were used to bridge the narrow waterways between shops. It was the everyday normality and the still beauty that made this town memorable. There were no signs of shopping carts, automatic doors, or escalators. My own personal normality had completely disappeared. It was all so simple and so authentic. The streets were dripping with red from bubbly paper lanterns hung one atop the other. The bold oriental lettering and designs on the lanterns added more character and spice to the stone alleyways.

A temple with many curved and then pointed roofs exuded spirituality. The snow-capped mountain's image was clearly reflected on a pond's surface. Hanging willow branches touched the still, crystal-clear water. Reflections of the many dainty, arched, wooden bridges formed the other half of complete circles. Ducks paddled carelessly as hundreds of colourful Koi, splotched and fat, surfaced with their gaping mouths begging for food. Stairs led down to brick canal ways and stone carved dragons drank from the winding waters. *It appears I had to conquer my first "villain" to reach this fairyland,* I thought, thinking back on the first old woman.

This sauntering walk led us through the quiet, deserted residential areas. We found ourselves at one of many local watering holes, each consisting of a three-tiered system of square, cement pools surrounded by a small courtyard. The upper level poured out an abundance of fresh, crystal clear water that the villagers collected for cooking and drinking. The water that flowed from there into a second pool below was slightly murky and was used to wash vegetables. The third and last pool was a pale, soapy, blue colour, and it was there that the villagers did their laundry on their hands and knees.

We noted that many of the men and women sported heavy loads. Some were hunched over, carrying large baskets of produce or other goods, while others had encased, woven baby carriers on their backs that youngsters could comfortably sit or stand in. Both types of baskets were strapped with thick fabric crisscrossed the carrier's chest diagonally for support.

Baggy topped hats with hard visors in a variety of colours, like the one we'd seen on Granny, were worn by most of the villagers. The other thing that consistently stood out was the Chinese people's apparent passion for camouflage patterns. The design decorated everything from cars to suitcases, from pants to hats, and everyone from little kids to soldiers in uniform sported it.

To absorb as much raw culture as we could, we sat around a cement table beside the wells and pulled out our deck of cards to continue our ongoing game of Daifugō. A plump, fuzzy caterpillar crawled across the table, and I poked it with my pen. I wryly commented aloud that I had better not suck my pen anymore. Of course, a few minutes later, Bree caught me with it up my nose and shrieked, "Savannah! You're going to get caterpillar disease!!" Gasping, I recoiled at the potential result of my involuntary fiddling as the others collapsed in a fit of laughter at my expense.

I counted the caterpillar exposure as my second near-death experience on this trip. I'd also thought that I was poisoned and might surely die after I touched a plant off a beaten trail in the stone forest, but I'd survived that first encounter with the non-fatal, apparently very common plant called stinging nettle, only to now potentially succumb to caterpillar disease. *One way or another, this trip was surely going to kill me.*

What started as a few locals casually doing their wash and other daily chores gradually grew into a group of men intently watching our every move as they squatted like ducks along the walls surrounding us. Others merely stopped for a quick peek as they passed by. Our card playing always attracted the Chinese men's attention.

"Oh, no. What are those guys doing?" Mom said, noticing a small group of domestic tourists, most likely from the city, dipping their hands in the uppermost well. "Don't they drink from there?" she asked Ammon.

"Yah, it is supposed to be for drinking. That's gotta make the lo-cals angry," he said. Just as we were discussing the domestic tourists' apparent ignorance of the villagers' customs, one of our squatting friends who'd been watching our game got up and flapped his arms and successfully shooed them away. Our suspicion that the locals most definitely did not appreciate this careless disregard of their drinking water was confirmed.

Our audience continued to watch our game and discuss the rules amongst themselves. The way we switched positions and how we traded cards depending on our current rankings was what always con-fused people and made it hard for onlookers to learn the game. The entire group got braver and inched closer. Every once in a while, one would come to help us and recommend a card by pointing at it, glanc-ing alternately between my hand, the rest of the cards on the table, and lastly my face to see if he was right.

"No, that one doesn't work," I smiled cheerfully at the first attempt and shook my head. He sat back down with his fist under his chin and returned to the drawing board.

The next try resulted in an encouraging, "Yah, yah. Good choice," from Ammon as he threw down the suggested two fives, but just when they thought they'd got it figured out, we'd get up and change our seats again. Perplexed, they'd sit back on their heels and again try to figure out what we were doing, and why we were doing it.

"Hey, what time is it? We better get back for Granny!" Mom said, glancing at her wrist watch. "Oh my goodness, we better get going! Can you believe we've been here for three hours?"

With a hurried adieu to the crowd, we rushed back for our seven o'clock meal.

We expected dinner to be on the table and were eagerly anticipat-ing what it might be when we got home, but all five-feet-nothing of Granny, dressed in her grey collared, button-up jacket with an apron strapped around her waist, was waiting for directions from us. We sat in the open garden as she made trip after trip to her kitchen to present different raw roots and vegetables as options. She explained the difference between spicy and non-spicy, and we managed to tell her we were evenly split. Two of us had an adventurous palette, but the other two could not tolerate a lot of heat. Mom and Bree put their hands around their own necks and stuck their tongues out to demonstrate what spicy foods did to them. Granny giggled and smiled with her beautiful, expressive eyes before running back to the kitchen yet again. Ammon didn't really enjoy hot spices but was not going to go through the trouble of explaining it as he also enjoyed the adventure of exploring local cuisines. Bobbing as she ran, her layers of skirts swinging, Granny presented us with choice after choice, a process we enjoyed despite our hunger: tomatoes or cauliflower, eggplant or lady fingers (a long, cucumber-shaped vegetable that is flower shaped when sliced into pieces widthwise) were just a couple of her suggestions. We'd point and rub our tummies to signify which ones we liked. In a surprisingly short period of time, she prepared a wide assortment of vegetable dishes accompanied, of course, by rice. Given that the toppings were fairly bursting with spices and with tasty, unfamiliar flavours, I managed to overlook the fact that rice was still just rice. After a healthy and delicious vegetarian dinner, Granny graciously rubbed a restorative honey and oat mix on my dry hands and feet before she sent me gratefully off to bed.

Don't Let the Travel Bug Bite
20

*A*s was the case in many guest houses, we were allowed one hour of free Internet service each day at Granny's. I never knew how I'd feel after that hour. Sometimes I received emails that lifted my spirits; other times, my inbox would be empty and I would get depressed. The state of my email correspondence controlled me as if it were my own personal happy meter.

I was often irritated because MSN Chat was rarely installed on the computers, and I'd have to spend half my allotted time downloading it. There was nothing I craved and looked forward to more than a few minutes of catching up and chatting with friends, but the download too often either took the whole hour or failed entirely. The time difference worked against me, too. What was noon local time was the middle of the night back home. The whole experience of trying to connect electronically using antiquated equipment was as much an exercise in frustration as anything else.

"I just want to go home!" I'd shout at whoever would listen, slamming my fists on the keyboard and wanting nothing more than to throw the whole thing out the usually non-existent window. "Why does it have to be so slow?!" I would cry when my emails were erased or when the few live conversations I managed to instigate would freeze in the middle.

After one such frustrating episode, I took a seat outside on the ground under the shade of a short tree on the patio. I slipped my dusty flip-flops off and pushed them to the side with my toes, feeling the warm stones under my dry feet and leaning forward with my elbows on my knees to feel the sun on my back. It had been chilly in the drafty, cement internet room.

The lovely silence was abruptly broken by a bearded man's comment. "I saw you on the Internet earlier. You seemed pretty upset."

He pulled out a chair at the wooden table and looking up at him I answered directly, "Yah, I want to go home. I miss my friends." Suddenly ashamed of my cracked, worn feet, I promptly crossed my legs and tucked them under my thighs.

"So, you're missing your friends, eh?" he started, using a familiar Canadian dialect. "You must be in high school. How old are you then?"

"Almost fifteen." *And no! I'm not in school at all. Do ya have to rub it in?*

"Trust me, I've been there. High school is really overrated. Kids think it's so important, but as soon as you're spit out into the big wide world, it changes. And your friends? They won't be there forever. After school, everyone goes their own way," he told me in a practical manner that effectively translated to, "My two cents worth. Take it or leave it – that's how it is."

I'd heard this lecture many times from Mom. For some reason, his nonchalant delivery made it seem that much more convincing. He wasn't saying it to talk me into staying; it made no difference to him either way. He was just a man with an opinion. Annoyed with myself for almost being swayed by his argument, I thought, *Yah, but he's a weirdo traveller, too. What's with these guys' long hair and scruffy beards anyway? He's just a bum who wants to give up his life to be here. I'm not like him.* I didn't want to believe any of them, 'cause they just didn't get how I felt.

"I mean, already you've been out how long? A few weeks?" he guessed. "How many of your friends are actually still contacting you? Are they all as connected as you'd hoped and expected them to be?" he asked, truly interested. My brows furrowed and I shrugged. I shook my head uncertainly, not really wanting to answer. I couldn't help feeling slightly angry and sorry for myself as I was forced to face the unpleasant truth that perhaps I'd been trying to overlook. *He's right. My so-called friends, even those I considered my closest friends, had only sent one or two emails, if that. Less than half of them read our family blog. It sometimes felt almost as if I'd never existed, that I had vanished and no one seemed to notice.* Though it hurt to no end, I was in the process of discovering who my true friends were. I began to realize that the people who would always be there for me were those I had usually undervalued and taken for granted, even a few I had only just met. Sandra, our helpful guide through Hong Kong, was a perfect example. Despite our brief, four-day encounter, she often sent me sweet words of support that gave me strength. "Savaaannnii, I am so proud of you." I could still hear her long, drawn out, "Sandra-ish" accent.

"The opportunity you've got here is way better," he said before I had time to respond.

"Hrmph," I grunted stubbornly.

Turning his green eyes on me, he said, a bit more forcefully this time, "You're so lucky. Seriously. I wish *my* parents had taken me travelling when I was younger!" I often got this sort of reaction to the trip from envious travelers I'd met along the way. "Trust me about this," the anonymous Canadian said firmly. "But hey, I gotta get packing for the trek tomorrow. Good luck, kid."

"Thanks," I whispered, burying my face in my palms.

The mystery man staying in our room, Ryan, was yet another scruffy backpacker, this time an American. He had to have been about twenty-five, around Ammon's age, and he'd been on the road for four months now. *Four months!!! And he seems to think we've done something impressive.*

"I cannot imagine travelling with my mom," Ryan joked, "let alone my whole family!"

"So, how long have you guys been out?" another guest with an accent I didn't recognize asked. He scooted his chair towards us to get in on the conversation.

Ammon, our leader and the one with the most experience, answered, "Almost two weeks so far." I could see the mockery his statement evoked in their raised eyebrows. Two weeks wasn't much to be proud of compared to someone who'd been "out" for four months! I felt I'd already conquered the world, but measured against his travel experience, I was just a pathetic greenhorn.

"But we're planning to go for about a year," Ammon quickly added.

"Or two," Mom jumped in. I don't know whose eyes grew wider at hearing that, mine or theirs. Two years? I nearly choked. *Since when was it two years?! We haven't even completed our second week! I'll be having a word with her later.*

The two backpackers didn't need to say anything. I knew they thought we were insane to think we'd last even two months. *If I could just pick their brains and take their bets, I'm sure they'd wager, "a couple of months, MAX," just like the rest of my traitorous family at home. No one believes we can do this.* The men slowly nodded in sync.

"Oh, that's cool! A world-travelling family," a second man with dirty blond hair and a pointy nose said. *I don't fit in here. I'm not one of them. I feel so stupid and out of place. This isn't my thing at all, so why do I suddenly feel like I'm competing for something?* The pressure continued with a list of questions we could only answer vaguely. "Have you ever travelled abroad before?" he continued. He was really beginning to get on my nerves.

"I have," Ammon explained. "I did three month trips in Europe, Southeast Asia, and Venezuela. This is the girls' first time."

"What's your time frame, then?" Ryan asked. *He's just fishin' for a good laugh.*

"Well, we know for sure that we want to be in Nepal in five months for the trekking season."

"And what comes after that? Where is the big adventure going to end?" he prompted Ammon to tell him more.

"We're headed to India from there, and then, who knows?"

"So you only know what you're doing for the first six months?" the first man butted in. I began to feel we were being interrogated about what seemed a foolish trip, even to me. *How can they take us seriously?*

"What's the route after that?"

"We haven't planned that far yet."

"Sounds cool," Ryan said, the doubt written all over his face belying his words and implying that it was easier said than done. *What do they expect from an unplanned trip? For it to simply unfold into a nice, tidy, year-long itinerary? Obviously, we look ridiculous,* I thought, angry that Ammon and Mom had put me in such an awkward situation.

I could almost hear the backpackers' thoughts. *They're going to kill each other way, way before a year is up,* or *That's what they think now,* or *Yah, right. When mosquitoes stop drinking blood!* And yet, as I watched Ammon talking, he didn't look the least bit ashamed. Suddenly feeling insignificant compared to these experienced travellers, I wanted to prove them wrong. *I can't let them be right. To think they're assuming we can't do it! They think I'm too prissy? I'll show them!* I was shocked by my impulse to defend the very trip I hated. In that moment of rage, I wanted to run upstairs, strap my backpack on, and do lots of intense push-ups, but I'd have collapsed in a heap after two of them, so I stayed put with my head held high instead.

Closing the door behind me, I cornered Mom defiantly. "TWO YEARS?! What's THAT about?"

"Oooh, I don't know," she said, backpedalling a bit.

"Two years?!" I repeated coldly.

"Let's just see what happens."

"See what happens? You can't say that. You said a year! ONE year."

"But who knows what's going to happen? There's no huge rush to go home. We already packed it all up."

"Oh, I KNEW you would do this to me." Without at least a date to count down to, this trip had become open-ended and could go on forever.

"We'll just see what happens and see where all this takes us. Maybe we won't be ready to go home in a year. Right now, though, it's just one year." I set my jaw and raised an eyebrow, daring her to continue. "Well, maybe a year and a half."

Trekkers
21

*T*he backpacks would not be trekking the Tiger Leaping Gorge with us. We stored them at Granny's place, planning to return for them later. *But if there is any justice in the world, they will magically disappear.* Just in case that happened, by some amazing stroke of good fortune, I planned to take some precautions.

"C'mon Savannah, we're leaving in a few minutes. Get downstairs," Ammon pushed.

"I'm coming, I'm coming," I said, fiddling aimlessly through our pile of bags in the corner.

"Don't forget to go pee before we leave," Mom said.

"Yah, yah, yah," I waved her away.

I heard a few stairs squeaking and cautiously peeked over my shoulder to make sure they were gone. I reached into my daypack and slid the item out. Oh it was so heavy, so massively huge. "I just can't take you with me. If only you weren't so heavy, we could stay together."

I scanned the room, holding the thick pages to my chest as I searched for the right spot. Stopping in mid-rotation, I knelt down beside a small desk and slipped the drawer open before slamming it shut again. *No! some book-hungry traveller might think it's up for grabs.* I walked over to our backpacks which were squeezed between a corner and a bed. A thief would have no use for my treasure, and I simply could not let it be accidentally snatched away. I put it on the floor under the bed, separate from the rest of our things. It had no monetary value, but I had to guard against the possibility that we might be separated before I could finish reading it. Crouching down and slipping *Gone with the Wind* under, I whispered, "Dear Rhett, I'll be back for you in only three short days," and secretly kissed him goodbye.

Glaring cynically at my backpack, I casually kicked it on my way out. "I won't be missing you, you miserable sack of dead weight."

In a few days, we'd be returning to the quiet village to restock on essentials, but right now, the two-hour drive out of Lijiang highlighted an impressive mountain range that towered over us and prompted me to imagine I was immersed in a new level of "Zelda," carrying "items" and "potions" on my back. Even here, in the nooks and crannies of a deep, rocky gorge, people miraculously managed to cultivate and farm every spare inch. Rice terraces were patched into valleys and balanced precariously over daunting cliff edges. The spotty green fields blazed brilliantly against the grey stone face of the gorge. *How do they even get up and over there?* I marvelled, as I looked across the narrow gap between towering cliff sides. A few horses were scattered about whenever our trekking trail opened into grassy fields. Men looked up from their work to wave as we passed. It all seemed so mystical.

"This'll be your second World Heritage Site," Ammon began.

"A what now?" Bree asked.

"UNESCO," he said, trying to ring a bell.

She stared blankly. "Oh, you mean the outer space thingy?!"

"No, dork! That's NASA."

"So, what is it then?" she said, rolling her eyes.

"Different natural or man-made sites around the world that the World Heritage Committee, elected by their general assembly---"

"You've already lost me," she interrupted, putting her head between her palms and squeezing as she groaned, "Oh, my head."

"A World Heritage Site is somewhere or something that UNESCO believes has historical or cultural significance to the world," he tried again, but she had already run away. "It means it's cool, okay?" he shouted after her.

Though I didn't quite understand the process Ammon was trying to explain, I did get that this place was special. Looking at all the foreigners around me with their backpacks and hiking boots was proof enough. There were not a ton of tour buses around, by any means, but it was the largest collection of foreigners we'd seen since Hong Kong. We would pass a few dozen by the end of the trek. *I'll see this World Heritage Site and I'll conquer it,* I decided, making it my mission in this still largely involuntary game to collect as many "sites" as I could.

"Legend has it that in order to escape from a hunter, a tiger jumped across the river at the narrowest point, which is still 25m (83ft) wide, and that's why they call it Tiger Leaping Gorge," Ammon said, trying something a little more creative that might appeal to Bree.

"They have tigers?!" she exclaimed.

With an exasperated sigh, he clarified, "You're not going to see a tiger, Bree."

In that moment, she grabbed me from behind, put her chin on my left shoulder, and directed me where to look. "Is that? Is that THAT guy?!" At this point we were hiking up seemingly endless switchbacks, zigzagging our way slowly and seemingly endlessly up the steep slope.

"Oh my gosh! It's purple guy," I said. He was one level above us and was still in the same peculiar outfit we'd first seen him in a few days earlier, hence the name. We never would have recognized him had he not worn his famous purple outfit. We each simultaneously took Mom by one arm, hostage-like, and whispered, "Mom! Look at him! He's so cute." We hadn't had the chance to point him out to her before.

"Yah, he is cute," she admitted, and we smiled encouragingly, our hands squeezing her tighter, "Oh, you two are so silly!" she said, yanking her arms back. "It's not happening," she stated emphatically to try to burst our bubble once and for all.

Not long after, once the trail flattened out and we'd overcome the switchbacks from hell, we again glimpsed the flowing fabric of purple guy's pants just ahead of us. He was well built and not too short, with very attractive, dark features. There was just a hint of grey hair around the edges, his eyes were warm brown, and most importantly, his nose was not too large.

"Where's Mom?" I asked stumbling over a small boulder. I followed Bree's wide-eyed gaze and saw what I hadn't noticed at first glance; purple guy and Mom had somehow started walking side by side. Purple guy had started a conversation with our Mom! "Oh my gosh, look at her go!" We both leapt behind the nearest small tree. Following as unobtrusively as possible, we snuck from bush to bush. "This is great!" I whispered to Bree, shaking my fists to contain the giddiness I felt. "And she's laughing, too!" She was blushing when we caught up with her a bit later. We had all learned to live with blushing at the drop of a hat as our own, occasionally embarrassing, family curse, but on its own, it didn't necessarily mean anything.

"He's a really friendly guy," she started, knowing we were going to force everything out of her anyway.

"Where's he from?" I asked. *Am I really asking that typical backpacker question?!*

"Iran."

"Oh, that explains his weird garb. Well, I think it's sexy!" Bree said.

"He's a yoga teacher," Mom told us.

"Yoga, eh?"

"You guys! Stop it. It's not going to happen. I'm not ready for anything like that." We knew she couldn't really mean it. He was too much of a hottie to escape her attention. She was just not interested in the idea of dating itself. Having only ever been intimate with one man in her life, it was not going to be easy for her to give herself to another. We knew this process would take some time, but patience was not our long suit. When she offered the excuse that she was still married, we rolled our eyes derisively.

"Dad is already living with somebody else. Surely, you're allowed to look!" we told her, irritated.

"Oh, he's like Costco guy," I carried on, remembering a cashier we'd picked out for Mom before leaving home. He was a slightly younger version of George Clooney, and we'd ogled him suggestively for months, making numerous special trips to do groceries and purposely choosing his till. We never got much past asking if he liked baseball, though, and were a long way from arranging a date.

"Oh, I dunno. It is a close call," Bree said, snagging a leaf from a tree hanging over the narrow trail. "I think this purple guy might even be cuter---"

"No! How can you say that about Costco guy? Ok, fine. Then I get him," I said.

"Hey. That's not what I said. You can't have him," Bree complained, selfishly.

"They're both too old for either of you," Mom mumbled as she shook her head, bemused, as we continued to bicker in her wake.

As we passed other hikers, everyone was making friends and sharing stories. I was so happy to be around familiar words and accents. I had been craving any English that was not spoken by my family, because that was as unsatisfying as listening to my own voice. I quickly learned that as much as I wanted the backpackers to be my messengers from the other side, they weren't. They were not there to tell me the latest gossip about my friends, which movies had come out, or which fat girl slipped on a banana peel. They were only interested in one thing – travel.

"Where are you from?" "How long have you been out?" "Where have you been?" "Where are you going next?"

The conversations never seemed to change. Despite this, I soon learned that travellers were really there for each other. During one of our hikes, Bree developed a nasty blister. Forced out of her stiff, new hiking boot, she started working on getting a callus under her foot, something she somehow didn't seem to mind. Luckily for her, though, she didn't have to trip and skip over rocks and twigs for long before a young trekker came by. She must have been in her late twenties; her hair was a thick matt of curls tied up above her visor.

"Hey, I've got an extra pair of flip-flops I don't need. If you want, you can have them," she said, noticing that Bree's bare foot made an odd match with her clunky boot.

"Oh wow! Thank you. You are too sweet!! I totally owe you one," Bree said.

"Oh, don't worry about it. It's my pleasure." It seemed there was an unwritten travel rule about passing on help in the future, even if it's the smallest thing. It could be anything from information to a used book, or even an old pair of flip-flops. Offering help was an unwritten code between travellers.

Just when I was getting used to having company and people to talk to, the 22 km (13.6mi) stretch of trail slowly spread everyone out. Some continued longer than others before calling it a day, and hikers stayed in different guest houses along the way. Before I knew it, we were alone again.

The trail got narrower and narrower the higher we climbed. It was rocky and bare, with little vegetation. Despite the gorge getting deeper and deeper, the white painted peaks never seemed to get any closer. I suddenly felt as miniscule as the grains of rice which I was surprisingly learning to like. I felt pretty darned tiny from a top-of-the-world perspective.

"The Yangzi River," Ammon announced. "That right there is the longest river in China. It's like the Amazon of Asia," he told us, leaning over to peer down at the narrow gorge. "And it's one of, and possibly THE, deepest gorges in the world – 3,800 metres, which is about, what? 12,000 feet? Maybe a bit more." I moved in behind him to lean forward to see the river, cautiously putting my weight on my front foot. There were no rails or fences of any kind. If you tripped, you were a goner.

"Whoa!" I gasped when a few rocks fell loose, disturbing the dust as they tumbled down the sheer, sharp cliffs. Just when I thought the trail couldn't get any narrower, our passage was constricted even more. We were occasionally forced to shimmy along with our backs pressed hard against the rock face. My legs started quivering visibly only halfway through the first day, and I had slipped a few times, tripping forward as my legs gave out for a microsecond. I was suddenly grateful that Rhett was safe at home rather than weighing my daypack down. As soon as we found a guest house, I would collapse anyway, with no energy reserves left to entertain my new-found "crush."

"I swear, I'm going to go flying off this cliff," I told no one in particular. "And how long until we get to stop?" I asked, when I noticed that once again, my complaints had no effect. To be fair, even I could see that we could not stop until we reached a place to stay, hopefully as soon as the path was wide enough to accommodate such a facility. We hadn't passed by any houses or potential accommodations in a few hours.

Until then, our only comfort was the sight of a few scattered companions who enjoyed nibbling the tufts of dry grass growing in the cracks of rock, and even the goats generally kept to themselves, either above or below the path. The apparent ineptness of blocky hooves didn't thwart their mobility in any way. They climbed fearlessly to the edges to reach the last bits of untouched grass and twigs. I couldn't decide whether they were too brave or too stupid to realize or care that gravity kills, but watching them kept my mind off the walk ahead.

It also wasn't uncommon to see horses or mules along the wider sections of the trail. Although we had plenty of water at that point, I was comforted by the sight of the occasional waterfall glistening and splashing over different parts of the path. I readily conceded that the trail's vistas were breathtaking, but I hurt everywhere, and my forehead was sunburned and itchy beyond belief from the sweat of our exertions. All I wanted was to get this trek behind me, but I also knew that as soon as it was only a memory, I'd be wishing I was sitting on some ledge next to a daring goat, straining to hear the current of the river far below.

Luckily, it was a flat walk, compared to the one-kilometre stretch of murderously steep switchbacks. I occasionally experienced an intense adrenaline rush when I found myself at the rear end of a wild horse on my left and a sheer, final drop on my right. Their rough tails flipping the flies from their rumps close enough to hit me in the face also set my heart racing. We sometimes inched by them so tightly that I could smell the dusty, grainy odour of their dry hair. Bree didn't seem bothered in the least, casually patting their bums as we passed. I dared not, preferring to creep past completely unnoticed whenever possible. I could picture one of us getting kicked off like a video game target. "YES! I got the tall lanky one – rack up five-hundred points for me," I imagined hearing after one of them reared up and kicked someone over the edge. "I count two-hundred over here for that little one. Look at her fly!" Their proximity and their muscular legs and hard hooves taunted me. Barely taking a breath, I crept past them, one after the other.

Get Lost!
22

*A*mmon caught our attention as his stork-like legs slowly stepped backwards and he twisted and turned the map he held in his hands.

"What's the problem?" Bree asked when we finally caught up. He scowled, investigating the crinkled folds and lines, glancing off to the right in the direction of the gorge and then at the road ahead. He hadn't needed the map prior. We had simply followed the high road and the solo path that squeezed between 5,000m (16,404ft) high cliffs on either side along with the rest of the tourists.

The dinky road we'd trekked had somehow and somewhere opened up into an actual street covered with tarmac. A few villages had been built up on plateaus and we passed human life more regularly. We were far from the sight of any backpackers, so in that sense we were alone, and we went back to waving our arms and hands around to be understood. The challenge now was to find our way amidst forks and T-junctions that lacked road signs of any type.

Our immediate goal was to find a ferry that would bring us to where we'd catch a three-hour bus back to Lijiang. Finishing up our banana pancakes that morning, we listened as our waitress helpfully offered advice. She had leaned over our table when she'd seen the map spread out.

"No, no. Much fastest old ferry. Better, better," she explained with her few words, and as she was a friendly local, we believed her. The other advantage was the minimal dent the fare of the Old Ferry would make in Ammon's wallet compared to the First Ferry.

But not long after breakfast, Ammon was standing perplexed in the middle of the road, obviously struggling to make a decision.

"Well?" we prompted him, asking to be brought up to date despite the fact that none of us had had any prior interest in, or responsibility for, the map.

"I dunno. I'm not sure, but I think we missed our turn," he told us without looking up from the map. The thought that we might have walked even one step further than we absolutely had to made me groan. *All that energy wasted!*

Bree jumped over and started putting her fingers all over the map, bringing it down to her eye level and examining it. "Let me see here, hmmm…."

"Get off it!" he said, not wanting to be bothered explaining it all to her. She was not by any means a map person, but her curiosity understandably got the best of her. When somebody says something like, "I can't figure it out," or "I can't twist this lid off, it's stuck," we are sometimes tempted to respond with, "Give it to me, then." The instinct to try even when you are pretty sure you won't be able to help is strong. You want to make *sure* that you can't. Curiosity combined with the urge to help seems to be an inherent, instinctual part of human nature.

"I'm serious! I don't know where we are in reference to the road that she told us we needed to take." The lines on the map were faded, the towns unnamed. "Geez. It's gotta be just over there." He pointed down at a dirt track winding off in the direction of the gorge. The paved main road we were standing on headed further inland, away from the water. "This map makes no sense. I think we missed it." He muttered to himself for a while before giving his opinion. "That's got to be where it is. It probably connects back to the road we missed."

"So it's *not* the road we missed?" Bree asked, thinking she'd missed something.

"Yah, yah, it is. It's that one," he said, finally making a decision. After all, somebody had to do it, or we'd be standing there until our year was up, given our family's mutual tendency to procrastinate. I was just glad to hear that we didn't have to backtrack and could access the right road just below us instead.

Bree then mischievously tugged the earphone out of my ear, and I skidded and scrambled down the steep gravel hill screaming behind her, "Hey!! Where do you think you're going with that!" We stirred up clouds of dust as the four of us slid down towards what we hoped was the right road.

Catching up to a skipping, jumping Bree, I grabbed the second earpiece dangling from her right ear and promptly stuck it back in mine. She was in charge of the MP3 controls. The MP3 player which was actually mine to begin with had conveniently wound up in her pocket after hers had mysteriously broken.

"This has got to be it. It's got to be the right one," Ammon assured himself.

Bree and I continued on our way, linked arm in arm and loudly screeching along to a Whitney Houston tune.

"Okay, next song is yours," Bree generously offered, continuing with another of the games we often played. Listening to randomly chosen songs, we had to consider every word and relate them to our lives. It was easy to do this now, lots easier than it had been at home. Many more songs seemed to resonate with me now. I related strongly to tales of missing loved ones and broken hearts, pain and weakness, sweat and tears. In fact, I realized as we walked that I had rarely before been all that moved by song lyrics. Music had just been the source of a pleasant beat to me, and I had somehow managed to largely miss the point of every song I ever listened to. But now, the lyrics took me through layer after layer of emotion, some of which I didn't always want to feel.

Quickly switching off the song, Bree said, "No, no! You can't have this one. We aren't allowed to listen to *this* one."

"What? Bree, you were listening to it just the other day," I protested.

"Yah, but I decided we can't until we've been gone for a hundred days." It was 3 Doors Down's, "Here Without You." Despite only hearing the first few beats before she snapped it off, the lyrics played in my mind, "A hundred days have made me older, since the last time that I saw your pretty face."

I thought of Terri. I had been counting the days in my journal. We were at day twenty. The hike I was facing seemed at least that long, but it was only three days, a thought that made me shudder. As we continued to sing away, the trail grew fainter and fainter until it eventually faded to nothing.

"Uumm, Ammon?" Mom quietly began.

"What!" he barked, displaying a bit of the tension he was feeling.

"This is taking kind of long. Wasn't it supposed to be a short cut?" She said, not daring to mention the more obvious reality that the path had virtually vanished. Our neat quartet had spread out slightly, like confused hounds that had lost the scent. Ammon slowly stopped and turned around. Bree and I slowly peeled our earphones out and stopped singing.

"This stupid map is impossible to read! I don't know where we are anymore," Ammon was furious with it and with himself.

"Well, we know the river is down that way," Mom said, pointing to the right down the hill. The landscape we were walking through was initially dry and relatively flat, but it had become increasingly steep. Before we knew it, we were on a rough mountain side.

"Bree, run down there and check. See if you can see a boat or a ferry port or something," Ammon said, waving her off in the same direction Mom had pointed.

"Are you serious?" she asked.

"Well, we've gotta know if we're on the right track or not. Maybe we just *think* we're going the wrong way. You never know with these things. I mean, this *is* the less popular trail. That's why it's called the OLD Ferry. Just see if there's a ferry," he told her.

"What would you guys do without me?" she asked, placing her daypack on the ground and taking the second earpiece from me. She plugged herself into some "pumped" music, as she called it, and ventured off to complete her assignment. Her athletic figure disappeared slowly behind some dry, lifeless bushes down the hill.

This detour had already cost us four hours and the rest of our water. Well, that wasn't entirely true. The only thing worse than having no water was having only two sips left at the bottom. I considered taking it for myself and claiming it was already empty, but I didn't dare. I didn't think I could live with the guilt, so I just told myself the bottle was already empty.

"I have no idea anymore." Ammon continued spinning in circles with his map held out in front of him. "This is obviously just an old goat trail!!" he finally admitted.

"Well, where the heck are the goats that made the darned trail in the first place??" I demanded. "They *would* have the nerve to disappear! Cowards! Getting us into this mess with their trompy old hooves!" The trail clearly led nowhere. *Even the goats probably never made it*, I thought, subconsciously scouting for any tell-tale remains of goat skulls and bones as my impulsive condemnation haunted me.

"It's not me, it's the map," Ammon kept insisting.

"You know, that's really comforting. I feel *lots* better now," I said.

"You're not helping, so shut up," he retaliated, and I did. About ten minutes passed.

"Where is she? Why is she taking so long? Can you see her, Ammon?" Mom nagged, as if his single foot of extra height somehow gave him super vision.

"She'll be fine," Ammon said.

"Well, what if she slipped and fell off or something," she continued to fret.

"If she's stupid enough to walk off the bloody---" he began.

"Oh Ammon, stop it!"

"I'm just saying, don't worry about her."

Bree and I had learned how to make a strange but very loud and accurate screech using our bottom lips from a Venezuelan guy we'd once hosted. Only we two could do this, so I whistled for her using our secret signal. Nothing. Again, and no response. Again, again, again. Popping out from behind a nearby bush, she whistled back piercingly loud right next to me and said "WHAT?" as in, "Ow, my ears! What the heck is all the racket about?" Her face was beet red, but she was hardly puffing at all.

"See? Stop fretting," Ammon said as if he had been in control the whole time. "Well?" he continued.

"And?" I added with a squeak that was a little less cool than intended. I inched over beside her and squeezed her by the arm, clenching my teeth so as not to show her I had been worried.

"There is nothing down there. It's just this humungous cliff that drops into the river. That's not the way to go," she said again confidently. "What time is it at home anyway? I'm sensing Full House might be on right now!"

This was horrible news. Knowing what was ahead of us, I lifted the water bottle to eye level and shook it, acknowledging for the second time that it was virtually empty.

"Is that all there is?" Mom looked round at us, trying to remember who'd had it last.

"Yah, only a tiny bit," I confessed, holding it up again for her to see. We shared the last drips of warm water to wet our lips. It was a lot less pleasurable than I had imagined. I found myself unable to feel it slip down my throat.

There was absolutely nothing around us. There weren't any little huts, let alone a village or a place to buy water. Even the goats didn't show their faces, and the gorge was a million and a half miles down a sheer cliff, so that was a dead end if I ever saw one. There was nothing for it but to start out again. We were headed inland, which meant upland, which meant straight back to the road we'd originally abandoned, if we could find it. We might not even recognize it, since we had left that road over four hours ago, and it probably would not look the same wherever we intersected with it. But then, it didn't matter so much if it was *the* road. Any road would do, for that matter, as long as it led to water.

We were in this together, and we had our music game to keep our minds off the heat burning our flesh. I never liked hiking or pushing myself to those kinds of limits, and luckily, I'd never had to. I was more like Mom, who hated exercise, and very unlike Bree, who got high from the exertion of spending hours on end doing gymnastics and working out. She removed one of her earpieces and held it out to me so we could again share tunes. I was still looking up at the obstacle ahead.

"C'mon, Savannah. C'mon! We can do this! Imagine you're part of a secret CIA mission." For the first time, I felt I could relate to her and Rocky Balboa's obsession with sweating to the "Eye of the Tiger" song that she listened to as she did sit ups and push ups in her room. My singular contribution to her fitness regime was to sit on her bed and shake my head in general disapproval.

"Rising up to the challenge of our rivals." The lyrics inspired me, and the beat pounded in my chest as I became one with the music. Cresting the summit, I envisioned myself triumphing at the top, raising my hands above my head to celebrate my victory. I was almost there! Two more steps, one more, and then, and then---

My arms dropped before I got a chance to do my "Rocky on the steps of the courthouse" impression when I saw yet another hill. I felt like crying. *Now I remember why I never cared for work-out music. It makes you feel like crap!* I became a good deal less enthusiastic from that point on.

Not knowing how or when our blind route would end was torturous. My mind began to drift and imagine the worst, because over analyzing is what the developed mind does (at least mine does). The sun would get hotter and hotter before it inevitably, and too soon, started sinking. We would be left in total darkness, with no shelter and no light. We'd get turned around and lose our way completely. Who knew what animals would come out at night to nip at us as we lay terrified though the cold night, in a fetal position in the prickly dirt.

I had never hiked, nor had I experienced 35°C (95°F) degree weather, and now I was being challenged by both. There was no escape from the harsh sun. Nothing was tall enough to provide us with shade or shelter, and despite my 30SPF sun block, my skin was burning. The rasping wind worked together with the sun to suck all the moisture from my body and gave me chills, despite my sweaty skin. I felt so defenceless. The swooping breeze felt like a bodiless vulture circling overhead and slowly sucking the life out of me. I could not touch its ghoulish presence and was unable to bat it away. We were exposed to whatever harsh conditions this strange land cared to mete out.

After what seemed an eternity, a big fat pipe gushing water miraculously appeared in the middle of the plateau at the top of the next hill. *Oh, no. That is mean! Now I'm hallucinating? What next?!* But as we drew closer, I began to hear splashing from the cement platform it stood on, and that wasn't all! A shallow valley with a few cottages was tucked away below the water source. It was a fair bit down the hill, still quite some distance away, but it lifted our spirits immeasurably.

Not knowing the source of the water and unsure whether it was safe, we all kept our distance – well, almost all of us. Bree dashed into it before anyone could stop her. There was no holding her back, and she was soon sopping wet from head to toe. Filling up the water bottle she still carried, she offered it to us. "Anybody want some? Yum, yum!! This water is amazing!" It certainly looked like nothing less.

"No, Bree, you go ahead," Ammon told her, knowing she'd already had half a stomach full anyway, but not wanting the rest of us to risk contracting Giardia. "You can be our official guinea pig," he added. Newly refreshed, she was now joyously doing cartwheels and other gymnastic tricks.

"So now we'll know, if you die, we shouldn't have drunk it," Ammon smirked. *She better die,* I thought, *'cause not drinking it is going to kill me anyway.* I was jealously grumbling under my breath. I wasn't brave enough to drink it, but I sure was going to get my hands wet. When I felt its icy chill, it was even harder to hold back. It was like caressing temptation itself. I was furiously envious of Bree and her lack of fear. *Maybe dying would be worth it just to take a few sips.* Instead, I stepped in and felt the ice cascade over me, thoroughly soaking the minimal clothing I wore.

"It's a good thing we got an early start," Mom said, aware that there was still a long road ahead. And somehow, the rest of the day became a steady, draining series of "just a bit furthers." First it was the water spout, but we didn't indulge because we saw the village, but before we could get to the village, we saw a tiny sign to the ferry and trudged on, and somehow we STILL had no dang water!

Winding down in the direction the sign indicated, we finally reached the river. "Whoa, where the heck is it," Bree said, leaning a hand on a rocky wall as we approached the dusty trail beside the river bank. We couldn't see any dock, shelter, or ticket booth.

"Just keep going," Ammon said, sure he was on the right track this time.

"I'm not sure I have all that much faith in this guy anymore," I whispered to Bree just before I tripped and fell into her back. Bits of rocks blended with the cracked dirt. The trail became so narrow I had to hold onto the rock face of the canyon towering over us while the river rushed past at my feet.

"What kind of mission did that woman send us on?!" Mom exclaimed. Around yet another bend, a couple of men were standing around, but we saw nothing else aside from a tiny wooden raft secured to the shore with some woven rope.

"See!" Ammon announced triumphantly as they approached us.

"Really?!" I couldn't believe this was happening.

"Ok, let's go," Ammon urged us after an effective round of communication charades with the fellows. "Well, here's the good news," he began once we were all cautiously standing on the raft, "after all that trouble, the lady was right about at least one thing. It only cost ten yuan, so we saved twenty-five cents."

"That's all!!??"

"That's twenty-five cents EACH," he said, to clarify that we'd saved the princely sum of one dollar at the expense of an extra six hours of walking, not to mention our discomfort or my fear of expiring along the way.

"Yip-frikkin-pee," I said, with the most uninterested, unenthusiastic face I could muster. *I could've sold a lemonade for more than that!!!!* I wanted to strangle him in that moment. Had I been able to find the strength to lift my arms, I might have done just that, but then I realized how exhausted Mom must've felt when she didn't even correct my language.

Despite recent events, I couldn't turn against them. We were all suffering. *Except Ammon*, I thought. *He loves torturing us! Why would we ever think there would be a shortcut that was cheaper too? There had to be a catch! Shortcut and discount just don't go together!!*

I let my fingers trickle in the cold water and soaked the back of my neck as we crossed. The ferry ride only lasted a minute, and Ammon was still talking as we stepped off. A dust cloud formed around our ankles immediately. Ammon tilted his head back and stared at the monstrous cliff we now faced. "The bad news, like, the really bad news, is ..." No further words were needed, but he continued anyway, "I have no idea what's at the top or where we are."

Fortunately there were horses for hire. *Or maybe they were donkeys. No, they weren't even donkeys; they were mules.* Two of them, to be exact, so they had to make two trips to get us all to the top. I was now glad we didn't have water, or Ammon would surely have made us hoof it up that steep mountainside to save the three dollars it cost to rent the mules. Seeing how exhausted and dehydrated we were, though, he had the grace to cough up the price of a ride, despite Mom's nagging reminders that we'd now spent far more than the dollar we'd almost killed ourselves to save in the first place!

Ammon and I waited at the bottom, and it took almost half-an-hour for the mules to make the return trip, much longer than I had expected, but the mules eventually came back and we were saddled up. We are both afraid of heights, Ammon more than I, but I think our level of fear was the same during that fifteen-minute walk. It was literally a narrow switchback forming a "Wild Mouse" rollercoaster-type path just wide enough for the mules' dainty ankles. Every sharp turn made me close my eyes and pray sincerely to the heavens. One missed step and we were done for. I positioned myself very loosely in my seat so I could jump off the second the mule slipped on one of the many loose rocks along the path.

"Oooh, I don't like this. This is terrible," Ammon grumbled from behind me. His audible discomfort brought a short, but deeply satisfying smirk to my face. Thankfully, there was a dusty little village at the top.

"Xie, xie," I said, thanking the mules before I rushed ahead, knowing Mom would have a drink waiting for us. We were headed to a restaurant of sorts where Mom and Bree were already seated. A donkey tied to a wooden pole in a clearing was hee-hawing. The sound was cloudy and dull like the colours around me, and the place smelled of dusty hay. We were led through a bushy passage and under a flimsy doorway to a table where we were greeted immediately with an odd question.

"Do you want to join the staring contest?" Mom and Bree inquired.

"What?" I replied, totally confused and sure I'd missed something.

"Look at them," Mom said unable to repress her giggles.

"Them? Who is ..." I hadn't yet noticed a long table against the opposite fence where a dozen men stared awkwardly at us, and I do mean stared: jaw-hanging, eyeball-bulging stares!

"They haven't moved since we came in," Bree told us as we slowly crept in and took our seats.

"True!" Mom insisted, finding their behaviour quite odd.

"Not once," Bree emphasized. They looked as comatose as they come, and they had odd, frozen expressions on their faces except for when they drooled.

"I bet these guys have lived up on this plateau their whole lives," Mom said.

"Are you sure they don't speak English?" I double checked.

"Nah. Definitely not," Bree said confidently.

As confirmation, Mom added, "They hardly understood when we asked for Coke." *They had probably responded with "Oh, you want Joke,"* I thought, reminded of the way the locals had pronounced Janada.

"I feel like I'm in the movie *The Hills Have Eyes,*" Mom said. She was really getting a kick out of it.

"Oh, oh! Look. He moved," I said, referring to the one with his finger up his nose. "At least we know they're alive."

"Wait a sec. Wait just one second," Ammon said, noticing the Coke in front of her, "I thought you were going to quit drinking that crap."

"No, I stopped drinking Dr. Pepper," she said, gripping it in her hand with all the strength she could muster.

"Oh, Mom. Stop lying to yourself! You were quitting pop and you know it," I said.

"NO! I stopped drinking Dr. Pepper."

"That's because they don't HAVE it here," I insisted, reaching out for it.

"Well, it's hot and I really needed a treat after that nightmare of a hike," she confessed as she reluctantly handed it to me.

"What I want is water," Ammon said.

"Good luck explaining that to this bunch."

"These guys are a bunch of scary scaries, let's just keep walking," Bree suggested. We reluctantly agreed, even though it was getting late in the day and we were already supposed to be on a bus heading back to Granny's, and most importantly, to my Rhett! But this day simply refused to end. We walked and walked and walked some more through thick layers of flies hovering in the air. The sight of a giant pig head skewered on a stick in the back of a wagon seriously turned my stomach.

"Well, it's getting late," Ammon was always good at stating the obvious, but he explained the ramifications of his statement once he'd lifted his head from his guide book. "We're not going to make it back tonight, but I think there's a little village that'll have a guest house somewhere not too far up this road."

"Somewhere, shmumwhere! I wish I had a virgin strawberry margarita. Oh yah, and Chippendales, too! They can just pick me up in their air-conditioned limo any time now," I stipulated.

"Yah, that would be nice," Mom agreed with a smile.

"With their big muscles," Bree added, drooling a bit.

"Oh my gosh," Ammon groaned.

"Oh, and they'll bring chocolate dipped strawberries---"

"With whipped cream!"

"And their smooooth, soooooffttt, seexy, muuuuuscles---" Bree teased.

"Oh please, please! Somebody get me out of here," he pleaded, sounding as desperate as us for a change.

"That's my line!" I retorted, enjoying his pain.

"C'mon Ammon, you can't tell me you wouldn't want a big slab of rare steak right now!" Bree said, naming another of our most desired and missed foods.

"Not the kind *you're* talking about!" he shivered, despite the heat. "Nope. Can't say that I do."

"You're such a liar! You just act all tough," I said. "Oh, or sushi! That would be amazing!" Our list of wants continued to grow and become more tangible as we slipped deeper into our fantasies. An hour went by and we were still babbling on about our Chippendales adventure when a woman caught up to us on the road.

"Where are you going?" she asked, riding alongside on her bicycle, her basket full of fresh vegetables.

"Star Hotel," Ammon responded as he kept pace with her.

"Oh? That's my hotel. It's just up there. I'll show you."

Oh thank you, thank you, thank you! You're an angel from heaven. I thought, delirious at the prospect that it was almost over. I could have kissed her, hairy wart and all, when she later came out of the house with a tray of cold drinks.

"Look how fast your priorities are changing already!!" was Ammon's instructive response to how quickly my anxious hand went for the Sprite. I would never have thought that a slushy sprite could taste so good, 13km (8mi) hike or no. The snowy slush slipped down my throat as if I'd never before tasted the sweet syrup. Even the million-and-a-half fat black flies stealing a sip or two from the tin can's rusty lip couldn't diminish my appreciation. There was something completely magical about it. Water would have been the smarter choice, but nothing else seemed to matter.

We all had our journals out on the table, which was almost more fly than table, while we waited for our meal. It was impossible not to salivate as we smelled the aroma of wine sauce and other homemade dishes coming from the kitchen. I was continuously shocked by the delicious flavours placed before me, but then I had such a huge appetite those days that I never seemed to get enough. I woke up craving breakfast. After breakfast I started wondering what was for lunch and dinner, and then after dinner, I fell asleep dreaming about breakfast.

My stomach was growling and I just couldn't bear the thought of writing in my journal. Already I was falling behind, avoiding it and missing days at a time. Looking for an excuse not to write myself, I leaned over to see what Ammon was writing and couldn't believe my eyes. "Despite what you may read in later posts from the girls, **we were not lost,** only temporarily delayed as a result of a map malfunction---"

"Is that for the blog?? You are such a cheat!" I objected.

"What?! Pft! Map malfunction? Ya, right!" Mom laughed.

"It was!" Ammon said defensively, smacking his hand down on the table and scattering dozens of flies.

Flashback
23

*T*he room was dark and dank. "Man, I can hardly see in here. Bring that flashlight over here, will you?" I called to Bree who was shuffling around, looking for the toilet paper.

"Give me a sec. Okay, what do you need?" She pointed the light in my direction.

"I just need to find something in my bag." She shone the light down and when I grabbed for the strings on my pack, an eight-legged demon skittered across my hand. I screamed and flung my arms up in the air, nearly knocking the flashlight out of her hand.

"What?!" she shrieked.

"A HUGE spider!" I choked with disgust. Leaping into the safety of the centre of the room, we yelled for Mom as we huddled together, pointing the light in every direction to avoid a sneak attack.

"What *are* you two doing?" Luckily, Mom came armed with her own flashlight.

"A spider!" we yelped, pointing at my bag.

"Oh, good grief. It could be anywhere by now. What do you expect me to do about it?" Mom asked, looking under the bed and around my bag in an effort to be helpful.

"Kill it!" we begged her. A faint shadow scuttled across the floor and we shrieked again, jumping up and down with our arms around each other. Mom didn't even flinch.

"Oh please. Not MY bed!" Bree whimpered as it made its way over the uneven floor boards.

"You mean *that* tiny thing?!" Mom said with her hands on her hips.

"Just, just get it!" we pleaded.

Ammon hated spiders as much as we did, but he was in the other room. Nonetheless I knew that he'd be checking under his pillow and sleeping with one eye open, too.

"There it is! There, there!"

"Savannah, that's a gecko," Mom said, unimpressed.

"Then don't kill it!! He can stay," I said immediately. "But where did the spider go?!"

"There he is. He's on the move!" Bree shrieked and pointed. He was so big his eyes glowed when we shone the light on him, and I just knew his legs would be hairy and bristly. The very sight of him sent shivers up my back.

The sudden sound of Mom's phone ringing startled us into silence. The phone was only there for emergencies, mainly concerning Skylar. Mom, as if she'd been drilling regularly for this moment, abandoned her spider-killing duties to find her cell phone. She trembled as she held it to her ear. I'd never seen Mom so pale, despite her tan, but we soon heard a sigh of relief. *It must be Sky. Thank the Lord it was not an officer of some sort calling to tell us he was gone or missing in action.*

The rest of us sat close by. Even Ammon had mysteriously appeared at my elbow. Sky was safe and unharmed, stunned by recent events, but still alive. He just needed to hear a familiar voice. Mom's initial fright faded, and she spoke calmly and soothingly. A lot had been happening in his part of the world, too much of it traumatic. He didn't want to talk or think about what he saw and the friends he'd lost; he only wanted to listen to our voices. He even expressed concern about *our* safety.

"Don't you worry about us," Mom said firmly. "We are fine! Just take care of yourself, and don't get distracted."

Distracted – Hhmmm. When I looked back, the spider was gone. I glanced back at Mom lying in bed on the phone, one hand crossed over her belly while she subconsciously picked at her eyebrow with the pinkie finger of the other hand as she had always done, and the memory prompted a startling reminder of the past. I began to tremble.

"My heart is pounding," I'd whispered to Bree three years earlier, peeking through the strips of light between the closet doors.

"Mine too," she said, pressing my hand to her chest. "Here, just come in closer. Get behind the clothes." We huddled together, safely out of sight in the shadows.

"I just---"

"I know," she cut me off. "It makes no sense. We should tell Mom."

"It just makes no sense!" I repeated, reliving what I'd heard. Dad had been on the phone. He told me he'd been talking to a friend, but he couldn't seem to give me straight answers to the most basic questions. After I'd made a few more aimless visits to his room, he had kicked me out and locked the door. His actions set off unfamiliar alarms. I had gone to Bree, who was sitting on her bed drawing at the time, and told her I felt weird about something and just wanted her to come check it out. I didn't know exactly why I followed through on my suspicions. I didn't even really know what I suspected.

Of course, because the door was locked, she couldn't fully understand what I was talking about, but she was always up for a mission and she absolutely loves anything remotely related to spying. The closed door in front of her presented a challenge, one she didn't intend to pass up. We rested our heads near the seam of the door against the pin-sized keyhole, but we could hear nothing but the low hum of his voice. I ran to the bathroom and picked a single toilet paper roll out of the garbage and jammed it under the door. Lying flat on my stomach on the carpeted floor, I was surprised by how well it transferred the sound. I could now hear him clearly.

"You like the way the massage chair jiggles you around?" His words ripped through me like a knife.

"Wait, wait. Can you just---? I think I heard someone," he began.

I grabbed my "tool" and ran in the nick of time. Bree dashed past me in a flash and we both jumped into Ammon's closet at the far end of the house, where Bree and I tried to make sense of it all.

"But what if it's nothing?" I said, trying to convince myself as much as anyone.

"What if it *isn't* nothing?!" Her words filled me with doubt. *But still, it's not enough proof.*

"We have to find out more," we agreed.

We crept back, sneaking around every corner to get to the kitchen which was just down the hall from where Dad lay on the king-sized bed, talking passionately to some unknown person on the phone. Bree took the lead, crawling on hands and knees over the marble flooring. I poked my head over the ledge of the counter to make sure the coast was clear and signalled the "all-clear" to Bree.

She stealthily lifted the receiver and slowly let go of the button. In what seemed like no more than ten seconds, we heard a door opening down the hall, but we already had all the proof we needed. We shared a look that said Go! Go! Go! and took off.

"Well? What did you hear?!" I demanded the moment we were safely back in the closet.

"Shhh!" she scowled at me, returning to her post. She sat on her knees near the door, listening and watching. A good five minutes later, she scooted backwards to lean against the hard inner wall for support.

"Bree! What did you hear?" I asked her again, this time more forcefully.

"A woman's voice," she confessed.

"A woman? Like, what kind of woman?" I asked carefully.

"It was, like," she didn't want to say it, but the words slipped like melted ice from her lips, "a sexy voice." Her head hung low and she buried her face in her hands. We struggled to breathe normally again, our hearts racing. *Are we dreaming? This is a bad dream, right?*

"Could Dad really be?" I choked, scared to say the words out loud in case voicing the fear would make it real. "Cheating?" The next words came even more awkwardly off my tongue. "On Mom?" I never imagined I would be saying such a thing in relation to my own family. *EVER!* We huddled together in that closet for over an hour as we tried to figure out what to do next.

When we told Mom later that day, she didn't cry. She didn't shout. She didn't act angry or shocked, nor even sad. She did not defend, did not accuse. But she didn't deny it, either. Her composure in the light of our revelation confused Bree and me. *News to us HAS to be news to everyone else, right???* We tried to convince her that it was a bigger deal than she thought. *She obviously does not fully understand what we're telling her.*

If we'd known then that she already knew what had been going on for the past twenty years, we might have handled it differently, but this is how she handled it. She never turned her back on Dad or tried to make him look like the bad guy. She kept their relationship issues private. We were what people would consider the "perfect" family. Our parents rarely appeared to be unhappy, and there were no signs of conflict, like avoiding or snapping at each other, or sleeping on the couch. I never thought we had those kinds of problems. *They not only fooled the outside world but us, as well.*

Only weeks after our discovery, we received a call from Dad while we were visiting our cousins. Our Aunt Diana had been warned about the coming phone call's content and was prepared to comfort and support us. Bree and I were each led into a room and given the telephone so Dad could try to explain that he had moved out. Bree emerged from the room a blubbering, slimy mess. I walked in next, feeling intimidated and confused, but also determined that, whatever I heard, I would not react in the same fashion.

"When you get home, I'm not going to be there, and neither is any of my stuff," he'd said. "But it doesn't mean I don't still love you. I'm still going to come see you guys, and I'll never stop loving you." I walked out as composed as I'd walked in, my features unchanged. It had not yet fully sunk in.

It still didn't hit me when I walked in the house to find half our stuff gone. There was no TV, no desk, and no couch. It didn't affect me much until Mom came home from work and was shocked by the missing items. I realized then that they hadn't discussed any of this. She'd had no idea what was coming. It hit me when I saw her cry.

"He just walked out. It was going so well, I thought he was doing so much better," Mom had said, tears welling up as she confided all to Aunt Pam over the phone. That really hit home. Then my tears came in a flood of rage that he could hurt her and us like that. I suddenly felt abandoned and, like the house, my soul was empty and hollow. He had been renting an apartment with money he'd been stashing away for months before he was finally able to work up the guts to leave, and we felt used and deceived by someone we loved and trusted.

Then, lo and behold, he turned around and came back. Oh yes! He was "just going through a mid-life crisis." I don't know how or when it turned around; it might have been months or weeks or even just days, but everything went back to normal again. Gradually, the TV reappeared and furniture filled the empty floor space. It all returned, along with my guilty father, like nothing had ever happened. But that was just the beginning. His third wave of moving in and out generated a much stronger reaction than the first, and he left with Mom's final words ringing in his ears – "I am NOT taking you back!"

And she didn't. She'd turned a corner in their relationship. She would no longer plead with him to come back. Why should she try to keep him someplace where he obviously wasn't happy? You cannot offer more than you are to try to please someone. She'd given her love and support freely through all of their years together and pulled him up when he was down. She finally accepted that it was not her fault, that she had done everything humanly possible to keep their marriage together. If that wasn't enough to make him happy, then there truly was nothing more she could do.

Our lives as a complete family seemed to fold in and collapse upon us like a castle built of cards destroyed with the flick of a finger.

It was unreal to see where that discovery and all the ensuing drama had led us. There was Mom, lying on a cramped little bed in the mountains of China because of Dad. That knowledge accounted for some of my resentment towards him. I also often blamed him for losing Harrison and the life I'd had before the trip. I watched Mom a while longer as she talked to Sky on the phone. I had seen her hundreds of times working on the phone back home just like that. Everything was so different here, though, that I hadn't thought of the oh-so-familiar scene in weeks.

The setting was cold, dark, and slightly decrepit, and yet she seemed happy, lying contently on the old bed and chatting with Sky while the curtains billowed loosely in the wind. I saw something different in her. For one thing, she didn't have that aura of underlying worry and grief I'd so often seen before. She was strong, full of energy, and most importantly, healthy. She had changed somehow, but I couldn't yet pinpoint how.

I imagined the phone call she'd had with Aunt Pam, particularly the question that smacked her in the face and revealed a whole new range of possibilities to her. "What do YOU want to do? Don't do what you think you HAVE to do," Pam had said. The realization that she wanted and needed to travel hit her over the head like a sledge hammer.

NO! She did not HAVE to run the business alone. She did not HAVE to be a slave to anyone anymore. And she did not HAVE to do anything she didn't want to. What better circumstances could a person ask for? This was her time to go for what she'd always wanted: what she deserved and what she'd already paid for, ten times over. I imagined she'd have been in the exact same position as she was now, sitting in bed picking at her right eyebrow while talking on the phone with Aunt Pam.

For just a moment, I saw her as a woman instead of as just my mom, a woman making choices that worked for her, for a change. She is living her dream and loving every minute of it, after all those years of worrying how everyone else felt, solving everyone else's problems, and being the rock everyone else leaned on. And who had been there for her? Certainly not Dad, I thought cynically – or me either, for that matter.

She had finally and triumphantly escaped her previous life of untruth and deceit. I felt mine had been torn away from me, and yet it was the only way hers could be restored, re-established, and re-energized. I could now see that she appreciated every single moment of this freedom, something that was easy for me, who'd never had any real responsibilities or suffered any significant hardships, to overlook.

"To Hell with it," I imagined her heart screaming, and I was proud of her for standing up for what she needed after all this time. And then the emotional reality of our situation finally hit me. *After everything she's done for me, maybe it isn't too much to ask that I might sacrifice a year of my life for her!*

Bree's Birthday Fun
24

"*H*ey! What is this? You're trying to get rid of it already, are you?" Ammon accused when we got back to Granny's. He slid Rhett out from under the bed where I'd safely left him.

A sigh of relief that the book was still there escaped me before I simply replied, "No," in a non-defensive manner that I hoped would not reveal too much of my new perspective on reading. I wanted to leave them guessing for a while.

"What!! What is she doing now?" Mom asked curiously.

"This was conveniently kicked under the bed," Ammon said, holding up my copy of *Gone with the Wind*.

"Savannah! C'mon," she said, loosening my pack and putting it back where it belonged. *Little do they know.* After they'd left, I snuck over to get him out and said, "Don't you listen to them. I would never!"

Making my way down the attic stairs, I slipped in next to Ammon at the table. He acknowledged my arrival by asking, "What is she doing?" with an eyebrow raised in Granny's direction. Hunched over in her little vegetable garden, she was slowly sneaking up on flies; every so often, she'd whack one! When she finally noticed that she had an audience, she looked up, smiled, and waved the big yellow swatter at us before returning to her task.

Seeing the mob of fat, black flies surrounding our table, I felt sorry for the poor woman. *She doesn't have a prayer of keeping up with them!*

There was such a lovely, quiet atmosphere at Granny's that I began to regret having to leave so soon. She was a gentle, sweet, and humorous soul I would not soon forget.

The next morning, we were all sitting on the beds, packing our bags.

"I can't believe my whole birthday has to be spent on trains and buses!" Bree exclaimed.

"Yep, eight hours on the bus followed by a thirteen-hour train ride. I can't think of a better way to spend a birthday!" Ammon said, ever the brat.

"We aren't going to do anything fun?" she double checked.

"You won't even get a cake," he told her, and that was a fact.

"This is my eighteenth birthday!! That's a big deal! Well it *would* have been a big deal," Bree said, slumping in her corner. "What does Savannah get to do on *her* birthday?" she demanded, diverting the conversation to where I was bending over to grab a boot from the pile I'd emptied onto the floor after the last trek.

"I don't know yet. That's like, what? A month from now? How am I supposed to know?" Ammon questioned.

"Well, you *are* our fearless leader," I pointed out, bringing the boot up to my nose and taking a brief sniff. I recoiled with a forceful "Phew!"

"We could be anywhere by then. Probably on a bus, too, for all I know," he said after a moment.

"Hrmph," I brushed him off, before stringing my boots to my pack by their laces.

"No wonder you're always complaining about the weight! You should wear your heavy things so you don't have to carry so much on your back," Ammon advised. I glanced down at the clunky boots he was wearing. Maybe he had a point. My lack of experience made it hard to get this stuff right.

"But it's way too hot to wear them!" I said, not mentioning the fact that, because they were not yet broken in, they were still stiff and uncomfortable.

"Whatever you decide to wear, Savannah, tomorrow we're going to Leshan to see the biggest sitting Buddha in the world," Mom piped in.

"Hey! Wait a second; tomorrow it'll be my birthday at home," Bree interrupted gleefully. "That means I get *two* birthdays – Sweet!!"

Turning around in his seat, Ammon wished Bree a happy birthday for the fourth time before noon. *Poor Bree,* I thought. Maybe Ammon was rubbing it in to be his usual tease or he could just be letting her know it was not the end of the world, though I thought the latter seemed a rather ineffective strategy.

I twiddled a little lucky charm that Granny had given each of us in my hand, inspecting every tiny feature of the doll made from a purple cloth sack of rice to relieve the restlessness resulting from having already spent three hours on the bus. The constant chewing, slurping, gurgling, and hacking noises coming from the other passengers really began to weigh on my nerves. I could see the man across the aisle noisily chomping on an apple and spitting out the peel from the corner of my eye. The man next to him was hacking loudly. The noises ripped through me until I reached the limits of my tolerance. All kinds of garbage was also building in the walkway that had initially been spotless. I could not wrap my mind around the fact that there were open windows everywhere. It would take even less effort for people to drop their apple cores or banana peels out the window for the birds to enjoy, but everything went onto the floor.

Two common snacks were always displayed close to the tills of Chinese supermarkets, much as M&Ms were used to tempt customers back home. The most popular impulse-buy items were spiced boiled eggs and chickens' feet both sealed in airtight packages. I was actually surprised that Bree never tried them, since her favourite part of chicken is the fatty skin off the legs. For her, chickens' feet should've been like buying the centre of an Oreo cookie.

Several people were gnawing contentedly on the clammy, dead claws. I'm also pretty sure I saw a man picking his teeth with a bird's toenail after he'd chewed off the "meat," which was more like a thick layer of skin. I began to feel more than a little stir crazy. My head tilted involuntarily and my eye twitched compulsively. The sound of every piece of egg shell hitting the ground was magnified, as was the next dead-chicken-foot wrapper, the next peanut husk, the next thick loogie. Rather than scream to vent my increasing frustration, I opened my book and let Rhett whisk me far away from the hardships of another full day of travel.

In little local restaurants, we had more than once seen customers throwing chicken bones on the floor instead of stacking them on their plates, almost as if they were waiting for an imaginary dog to come by to clean them up (strangely enough, we'd seen very few dogs, wild or domestic, in China). The only even slightly negative reaction we saw was when one poor waitress who ran the family's restaurant grimaced at a man who'd dumped his leftovers on the floor. I could only imagine what kind of reaction I would get if I started throwing half-eaten burgers onto the floor of a McDonalds in Vancouver, but that's just how it's done in China. The bus got more and more suffocatingly filthy before it reached its final destination eight hours later, where someone would again painstakingly restore it to its impeccable state.

Another contradictory thing about China was how amazingly clean the cities were in comparison to the buses, trains, and toilets, all of which were uniformly atrociously filthy. We commonly saw people sweeping the streets with big branchy brooms. They'd trail behind the locals, gathering up their eggshells and apple cores so the garbage never had a chance to pile up. We never had to dispose of our water bottles either, because there was always a kid or an old grandma around who collected them to get the tiny refund. The people eyeballing our water bottles could be considered beggars, but we never had a problem with them coming up and asking for them; we certainly did not want to go to the trouble of saving and turning them in for the bit of change the effort would net us, though sometimes, I'd wonder what Ammon would've done if he'd known where to return them. Half the time, I would simply hold the bottle above my head and it would disappear within seconds, like magic.

On a few occasions, the locals fought over our recyclables. The beggars often asked for bottles so subtly that Mom made a big mistake early in our travels. A little old man was waiting patiently and unobtrusively for our bottle to empty. Because he was so considerate, Mom didn't even realize he wanted it and just handed it to the first kid who came by. The old man chased after him, shouting at the kid to claim his rightful prize, and Mom felt terrible. The kids, though, were not always so considerate, and one would occasionally try to snatch a bottle before we had even taken our last sip.

Author's Note: If you are the type who does not care for the crude nature of toilet scenes, please skip ahead to the next author's note.

But truthfully, the garbage in the aisle of the bus was pretty minor compared to the bathroom stops. Every day was truly a toilet nightmare, one that somehow kept getting progressively worse. I was so proud of myself when I'd finally conquered the squatty, and then I surprised myself again when I'd learned to use a toilet that had no doors, but the facilities' standards just kept being lowered as quickly as I met them. The three-sided, cement barrier in the stalls got lower and lower until there were no walls at all, and the public toilets became just one big room with ten holes lined up in a row – that's all there was. That was IT!

"What am I supposed to do with this!?" I'd asked horrified after running out of the chamber. *They can't be this cruel! Show me the real bathroom, please!* I couldn't simply stand there watching the half-dozen bare bums hanging out. The split second I had already seen was enough to turn my stomach, not to mention the foul smell of the room that clung to the shrivelling hairs in my nostrils. Cringing, I stood with my back against the outer wall as if something might miraculously change. I had hoped to wait out the rest of the people inside and try to get the room to myself, but a load of women from the next bus came in and nixed that option. I banged my head against the concrete wall. *It is what it is, and I have to face it, alone. I simply MUST go.* There was no kind of support or help to deal with this problem except my own willpower. I know it sounds like a petty thing, but it took all the strength I had to walk myself back into that bomb shelter of a toilet in front of all those people and do what I had to do.

I would like to say I closed my eyes, at least, but the risk of falling right into one of the holes ruled that out! I chose my hole and went as fast as my poor body could empty my bladder. I wanted out. I wanted to block from my consciousness the sight of a girl changing her bloody pad, the sounds of the grunting girl poohing next to me, and all the attendant smells, but the best I could do was to take one quick, desperate wipe and pull my pants up as I ran out.

We stopped again a few hours later. I looked around, not sure what we were waiting for. I didn't hear a tire pop or any engine problems. We had simply pulled over to the side of the big highway, but there were no buildings or shops to be seen. We were basically in the middle of nowhere.

"What are we stopping for?" Bree asked Ammon, who was seated with Mom just behind us.

"I don't know, but I gotta pee," Ammon said, excusing himself. I saw the gooey muck ooze under his heavy boots as he walked down the filthy aisle, and that was the best reason I'd seen yet to wear mine instead of carrying them. After about fifty people had done a few turns up and down the walkway between the seats, the initial "crunch, crunch" under their feet turned into more of a "slosh, slosh." It was like walking through a partially disintegrated compost box.

I was well and truly horrified when I opened the window and heard Ammon say, "Hey, if you want to go, you better go now. This is your potty break."

"What!?!? No!"

I didn't know how much longer I could hold it. I knew my only options were to muster up some courage quickly or face an exploded bladder, so I took my sorry little white bum out there to the field.

Mom had given the previous bathroom break a positive spin, pointing out that at least it was only girls using the washrooms. Now,

I regretted my cavalier, dismissive, "So what's that worth, big deal" response to her statement. I truly didn't believe it could get any worse, but it did. It always did! The best we could manage out in the field was girls to the left, boys to the right, but I think it actually turned out to be more like squatters left, standers right, because there were some men very near me.

"You better just do it now before you're the only one out there and everyone on the bus is waiting and staring at *you*!" Mom said, wisely.

Ohohoh! "I need toilet paper," I asked Bree, the official toilet paper stasher.

"I don't have any more."

"Stop kidding me. Just hand me some. Anything," I said, desperately reaching my hand out to her.

"Use a bush," she said as she squatted. I knew she was serious when I saw the clump of grass in her hand. I also knew that I couldn't waste any more time on this discussion. We were never sure how long the bus driver would wait or whether they might drive off without us.

I don't think I had ever used the public bathroom at any of my schools because of my paranoia about peeing in front of other people, and here I was, standing in an open field with piles of strange men and women squatting and doing their business. The other women didn't seem to mind at all. They pulled their pants right down and went with no hesitation, despite the men. *They've been doing this since they were babies. They just go anywhere: in the streets, on train station platforms, anywhere and everywhere!* I thought, trying to force the earlier images of such things from my mind. For me, it was like having to overcome one of the biggest obstacles of my life. *If I can do this, I believe that I will truly be able to do anything. I will be invincible.* I paced, circling like dogs do to find the right spot. I felt totally awkward and found myself once again not knowing where to start. I felt completely exposed and did the fastest squat in history to date. I dipped down in a patch where the ground was slightly lower and the grass perhaps an inch or two higher and "hid" awkwardly.

That kind of "girls left, boys right – go!" stop was a regular feature of many of our long distance bus rides. Privacy is a luxury I had always taken for granted. It was on the buses that I learned its significance and what it meant to me. Overcoming that part of the trip was one of the hardest adjustments I had to make, but I stretched more personal limits than I'd ever have thought possible in the process.

"Shouldn't we get some more food or something?" Mom had asked, ready to go hunting around before boarding the train.

"Nah, we'll be fine! They always have people running back and forth selling snacks. You'll stop regularly and there're always little shops on the platforms," Ammon explained.

Once on the train, we watched the passengers go by with cup after cup of steaming tea or hot soups. Bree traced a trail of drips from someone's mug back to a hot water tank at the end of the carriage, and instant noodles became one of our main travel essentials from then on. Of course, we could not read the labels on the packages, so we had to go by the simple pictures. We usually had a choice of a big green chicken, big blue cow, big red pig, or yellow vegetables.

I preferred train travel for a number of reasons, but mainly because of the freedom it offered. On trains, you could use the toilet as the need arose, and getting up to stretch your legs was a big bonus. There was a lot more flexibility in what and when you could eat, and last but not least, they usually had small tables against the windows where we could pass the time playing cards. That said, much like the buses, the trains were quickly covered in trash amidst clouds of smoke, and the bathrooms left just as much to be desired. Our first trip to the train's bathroom was a real eye opener.

"How? How is it? How?" I stuttered.

"Even physically possible---" Bree helped me.

"To get---"

"So---"

"Is it really everywhere?" I finally stammered out the rest of the sentence as I clenched my teeth and shut my eyes in defense.

"I'd rather use nature than that!" Mom had decided. I saw her point, but amazingly, I was willing to put up with the disgusting odours and so on in return for some privacy. There was a door with hinges and a lock (not that they always worked), and the fact that it smelled like dirty diapers and had diarrhea splattered everywhere faded in comparison. There was even filth in places that made me think, *Gee! Like, that is really quite a feat! Honestly, how could you even get it up there?* Whenever I entered, I had to dodge pieces of toilet paper dangling from the roof. I can't even begin to describe the filth, and every toilet was like that, in every carriage on every train.

I finally had to accept the fact that this was the best I was going to get. To put it into perspective, I'd had to use a public toilet on very rare occasions back home. I once found myself so discomfited at finding a floaty in my chosen stall in Wal-Mart that I had to quickly find another open cubicle. That event actually stood out vividly in my mind up until we began travelling in China! Now, traumas like that were quickly being replaced by much more disturbing scenes, and even the option of flushing was something that was offered less and less often.

Going on a train always seemed a rush. I could hear the roar of the train as I looked straight through the hole in the floor to the blur of gravel and railroad ties below. For a beginner like me, squatty toilets on wheels always posed a problem. The train rocked back and forth as I tried to balance on my tippy toes, threatening to toss me off balance at the most inopportune times. I would pray I didn't have to reflexively grab hold of the handles that were literally covered with brown smears. At the same time, I had to try not to get thrown face first into a wall, which commonly had the same smears and other unspeakable things stuck to it. I had to be cautious, too, not to fall backwards onto the wet floor. That's where Bree came in handy. I rarely went without bringing her to help hold me upright or guard the broken door.

But enough about potties. You get the picture, and it was not a pretty one, to say the least.

Author's Note: This is where squeamish readers can re-join the story.

I did manage to look up from my book every so often. The glistening rice fields and the unnaturally bright green grass created such stunning scenery that I almost couldn't believe it wasn't photo shopped, but with my head buried in the pages of my book, I often completely lost track of time. My irregular cries, gasps, and exclamations of "OH! My heart!" or "Oh Rhett!!" became more and more frequent.

"She's enjoying it now," Ammon said, picking up on my complete absorption with the classic.

"Sssshhhhh," I scowled at him without looking up from the words on the page, "I'm at a good part."

"It must be good if you're blushing like that," he teased. I just shrugged him off. I thrived on the stories and adventures I was reading about. I really could escape my troubles just by opening up those pages and jumping in next to Scarlet in her buggy or onto the back of Rhett's stallion. I could feel the quality of the 1860s mahogany desk beneath my hands and the laces and fabrics between my fingers.

I was so in love with Rhett! I could almost taste the whisky on his breath and smell the swirls of thick smoke clouding his parlour as he puffed on a strong cigar. Oh, wait! It wasn't Rhett smoking. It was the man next to me, and the man next to him, and the man next to him!! The entire cabin was grey with smoke. Every single man on that train was either lighting, smoking, or throwing away a cigarette, and at least eighty percent of the passengers were men (I also couldn't help but notice that we were the only Caucasians on the train again).

My cough prompted Bree to lodge one of the few complaints we'd heard from her since the trip started. "I know!! I've probably lost five years of my life already from all this smoke!" Bree was very protective of her health, given her athletic focus. She never drank alcohol or smoked, and she definitely never used drugs of any sort. She didn't even drink coffee, and it had been almost impossible to convince her that it was safe to drink green tea.

But she was right about the smoking, and I felt the same. The smog and pollution in the bigger cities combined with the nearly constant public smoking really irritated our lungs. When I'd asked Ammon why none of the women smoked, he explained that female smokers would indulge only in the privacy of their own homes. *I hope the excessive smoking calms down a bit in Mongolia.*

I pulled myself up onto an elbow to check the other passengers. Everyone was still sound asleep. It amazed me how tiring travel days could be. Ammon and Mom, both in a fetal position, looked as though they hadn't moved all night. Bree was flat on her back on the bunk opposite me with her earphones still on and her shirt crumpled up to expose a bare belly. Her outstretched arm and leg hung over the rail while the other arm was bent above her head. I couldn't believe she was already eighteen. It seemed like just yesterday we were giggling little girls, taking baths together, putting socks in our shirts to pretend we had boobs, and dreaming of one day reaching the "mature" age of thirteen.

"Happy birthday," I whispered as I pulled her sleeping bag over her feet.

A Sacred Mountain and the Stairway of Hell
25

*A*s there was no other option at four in the morning when we got off the train in Emei, we had taken a taxi and broken Travel Rule #2. The exhaust was beginning to cloud up and stick to the virtually dripping moisture in the damp air. Our last bag was pulled from the trunk and, without a word from the taxi driver, we heard the airtight seal of his door close. The tires squealed off down the wet brick road, trailing a puff of smoke.

We arrived in the foggy predawn at the front door of a hotel with a tall glass entrance that was shut tight. All was quiet and we dared not talk above a whisper. Pipes were dripping from balconies and electrical wires were strung along and between buildings all up and down the misty alley. I pretended it was the early 1700s and imagined a man in a tailored coat sneaking past us to enjoy a secret rendezvous as his carriage waited in the night.

We knocked and rang. A small light, barely enough to cast a shadow, glowed from deep within a hallway. A round, robed man with messy hair and eyes that squinted even more than usual appeared behind the screen door. He inspected the four of us carefully for a moment before moving aside to let us in. He couldn't have been aware of the pink robe he was wearing.

"I hope that's his wife's," Mom said out of the side of her mouth as we followed the tails of flowing pink up the spiralling staircase. She normally would have said it aloud, but tonight she didn't want to gamble on his not knowing any English. He didn't seem to be in a particularly humorous mood. Turning to leave, he handed us a clunky, old fashioned key on a heavy metal chain.

"I guess we'll take care of payment later," Mom said as she closed the stiff door behind us. Too tired to deal with any business, he presumably went straight back to bed. I pictured him hanging up the pink robe next to his own before slipping in beside his wife, completely unaware of the first impression he had just made.

The following day's schedule took us to the foothills of the sacred Emei Shan. Walking sticks in hand and daypacks on our backs, we were awed by the sheer legion of stairs before us.

"Two days? That's not too bad," I said, underestimating the brutality of what it would take to reach "sanctity." "It's not like we're going to be hiking or anything. It'll just be like taking the stairs to the top of a tall building!" *Finally, my fear of elevators and the practice I'd had climbing long flights of stairs to avoid them would pay off!*

"Yep, and the views are supposed to be amazing, so it'll be well worth it," Mom told us eagerly.

"I just want to see the monkeys," I said, and took off enthusiastically just before a light drizzle began to dampen the leaves of the bamboo forest surrounding us. It took less than an hour for my morale to plummet as the stairs went from easy-peasy to downright miserable and uninspiring.

"When is this going to end? And where are my monkeys?" I whined, shaking a droplet from the end of my nose.

"Isn't this place supposed to be crawling with them?" Bree asked.

"With all these "Beware of the monkeys" signs, you'd sure think so," I said, glaring at Ammon. We'd seen a number of pictures of rabid-looking monkeys beside plastic bags that had a big X over them. They weren't really "beware of monkeys" signs; they were meant to warn tourists not to carry plastic bags.

"We need to go to a store," Mom said.

"Why?" I asked, annoyed that she probably wanted a pop.

"To get some plastic bags. The monkeys obviously want them!" she giggled as we passed yet another warning sign.

"Are you sure this is the right season for monkeys?" I asked Ammon.

"Yah, Ammon. Maybe they're hibernating or something," Bree said accusingly, trying to outsmart him.

"Who cares about the monkeys? This is one of the ultimate sacred places in China," Ammon replied.

"I bet it's a Unicorn Site, too," Bree said. She was the only one who still had lots of air left in her lungs.

"UNESCO, you mean? Yes, actually. It is," he said, only slightly annoyed.

"Unicorn sounds better," Bree laughed to herself.

"It became a UNESCO World Heritage Site in 1996," Ammon continued, "but people have been making pilgrimages to this place for two thousand years. So it's got major history! This place goes as far back as the time of Christ," he finished, putting it into perspective for us.

"So, while He was over there in the desert walking on water, these guys were over here hiking up this mountain?" Bree sounded impressed.

"Yah, I guess that's basically what I'm saying," he confirmed.

My head fell back in awe as I passed under another decorative gateway. Red pillars reached down from the arched and pointed roofs, and a black wooden sign displaying golden Chinese lettering hung in the center. It looked incredibly mystical.

"The slopes of Emei Shan have been inhabited for ten thousand years. It's one of the four sacred mountains in China, but this one is a thousand metres higher than the other three," Ammon continued.

"Oh gee! Aren't we the lucky ones! How far is it to the top?" I asked.

"A little over three thousand metres," was his immediate answer.

"Oh, man," I said, "how high is that in feet?" Though I was not that familiar with the metric system, I could already tell that this "walk" was going to be a bigger challenge than I'd anticipated.

Ammon did a quick mental conversion and replied, "About, ten thousand feet or so."

"Holy crap!" I exclaimed, regretting my initial enthusiasm.

"Seriously, Ammon, how do you remember all this?" Bree demanded. A bit impressed with himself, too, he just laughed and carried on.

Stopping for a moment to catch my breath, I looked back to gauge our progress. Below us, the roofs of the gateways, each with their gallant arches, were layered one upon the other and looked like Viking ships sailing between the branches. The appearance of the pillars had changed from pure red to a deep, smoky rouge. Seen through the mist, they were a bit eerie and yet stunningly beautiful in their own way.

"This is awesome!" Ammon said.

"There's hardly anybody here, either. It's so peaceful," Mom observed.

"No one except them," Bree said, as we jumped out of the path of two men jogging past carrying a fat man in what looked like an old war stretcher with a modern twist. It featured a built-in seat made of sticks of bamboo painted blue, green, and red. They had come up behind us through the grey fog, never faltering or slowing their pace in the least.

"My gosh! How do they do that?! They are so strong!!! They aren't even shaking; they're hardly even sweating," Mom noticed.

"Couldn't we do that?! Why do we have to walk it? There is nothing to see or do except, ugh!" I said, demonstrating slow, heavy movements up one more stair and then another, dragging my arms like the monkeys I wasn't seeing. My feet felt damp and soggy, and droplets fell from the tips of my baby curls that were beginning to spring up all over the place from the moisture in the air.

"It costs a hundred bucks to do that. Plus, we wouldn't experience the same sense of accomplishment when we got to the top," Ammon explained, but I knew he was only thinking about his wallet again, or should I say, his money belt.

"We could all sit on top of each other and we'd still be lighter than him, so now it's only twenty-five bucks each," I said.

"It's not about the money," Mom said.

"That's such a lie," Bree laughed.

"That guy's beating me to enlightenment," I said, and realized even as I said it just how cheesy I sounded.

The man sitting so comfortably (at least as comfortably as one could expect while bouncing between two men at a steep angle) didn't have to tackle the stairs, and that seemed very appealing at this moment. But as two more porters passed by carrying another sallow city man nestled behind a huge potbelly, I began to reconsider. I just couldn't picture myself sitting in that chair.

At the top of the next bend, we came to another million-and-a-half stairs extending endlessly on into the fog and then narrowing away into nothing amidst the overhanging trees. There were no signs or directions, nothing but a giant stairway to "heaven." The stairs that wound through the lush natural vegetation were mostly made of concrete, but sometimes they were just dirt. A single green handrail appeared and disappeared, apparently without design. The trees glistened from the morning showers, and I had to admit it was enchanting. *Two steps, one more. Two steps, one more.*

A lion statue called out to me as I neared. I felt its wet nose hard against my inner palm and then bent my head forward against its nose, holding onto his menacing fangs with both hands. I closed my eyes and its teeth became prison bars, the stone figure a barricade blocking my ability to move forward. I lifted my head and rested my chin on the statue's snout. The drips beneath its chin soaked through my left pant leg.

"Ugghh," I groaned and pushed off from the lion statue, patting his drenched side as I passed.

The others were about a dozen stairs above me and still climbing. Mom was standing to wait for me and catch her breath at the same time. *Two steps, one more. Two steps, one more.*

"For someone who hates hiking so much, you sure don't show it!" I gasped between words.

"I don't hate hiking. I love it. I just hate exercise for the sake of exercise," Mom explained as she pushed on. "This is a long walk with beautiful scenery. It just kills me to be stuck in one spot on a treadmill. Yuck!" I'd often wondered how she stayed so slim through the years. I'm almost certain she'd never had a gym membership in her entire life, but then again, she'd been a gymnast like Bree back in her day.

Ammon was always far ahead of us, his longs legs allowing him to cover in one step what took us two or three. But at each bend in the stairway, he would stop and wait, ready to tell us more about what we were seeing.

"Did you know, Emei Shan literally means 'Delicate Eyebrow Mountain'? Its name comes from two peaks that face each other and look like the delicate eyebrows of a classic Chinese beauty."

"Yah, yah, yah," I said, dying for oxygen. We'd been walking for seven solid hours, and the last thing I wanted to hear more about was this damn mountain. The few other tourists we'd seen on the trail were all domestic, and they somehow climbed those stairs dressed in suits and heels.

The natives of the holy mountain were very fit and active from carrying, not only the city folk, but also loads and loads of bricks. If they were not actually carrying things up and down, then they were trudging alongside their mules as they carried them. At one stretch, we seemed to pass by many of these quadrupeds. There was only one way up the mountain and parts of it were very awkward, steep, and/or slippery, which made me wonder how on earth those donkeys/horses/mules, or whatever the heck they were, got up here in the first place.

The steps were short and wide in some sections, steep and narrow in others, but in either case, they were never the perfect height or width to allow me to develop a steady stride. We were finding it hard enough just to walk the stairs, and they were making their poor animals carry very heavy loads. It just felt unnatural in every way.

At one point, there was no guard rail or even a fence to hang onto, so I was focusing on the ground, watching my mucky boots plod along up the mud-covered stairs. Just ahead of me, I saw the skinny hindquarters of a small, quivering horse bearing two wicker baskets bulging with red bricks. He looked totally squashed, and my heart hurt for him and the few others ahead. *They're struggling so hard to finish their day's work to please their masters.* I cringed as I saw that he was ready to collapse under the weight of his load, his dainty ankles trembling as he searched for each narrow, jagged step. It took all his strength to hold himself up. Rooting three legs to the earth, he'd struggle to find the next step with his fourth, scraping his hoof on the uneven stair.

"C'mon, let's get around this guy. He's not going to make it," Mom said frankly as she picked up the pace. We hurriedly made our way past, expecting the worst.

"You really think he won't?!" I asked.

"I really don't know, but I do know that you can work a horse to death! If you push them hard enough, they'll drop dead from exhaustion before they'll give up," Mom explained. That's what I was seeing right before my eyes. He wasn't going to stop. It was taking longer and longer for him to take each step. He foamed at the neck and beneath the straps of the baskets. My heart tensed. I didn't think he could go another step, let alone the hundreds more to come, and I was watching when his legs buckled as his knees completely gave out, and he went tumbling down end over end.

We gasped as flecks of mud flew from the creases in his hooves as he fell down dozens of stairs in a full backwards somersault. Shouts from local men seemed timeless as his feet stretched high in the air and exposed his soft belly. He finally came to a halt by crashing into a tree.

The alarmed owner quickly ran down to unload the bricks. The horse looked like he was fading fast. We waited and worried and watched to see what would happen next, glad to be taking a breather ourselves. A little more than stunned, the poor horse eventually began to move. I was both amazed and concerned when he rolled over and hoisted himself back onto all fours, somehow righting himself even though he still had at least half the original load on his back.

The lighting hadn't changed all day through the fog, but I knew it had to be getting late.

"A whole dang day and no monkeys!" I exclaimed, finally catching up to Ammon at the edge of a clearing.

"Well, I just saw one on the roof of that monastery," Ammon said.

"What!!" I exclaimed. Rushing further into the clearing, I looked side to side and shouted, "Where? Where?"

"What? What?" Bree asked as she bounced around, not sure what she was looking for.

"It's gone now. See? If you weren't slacking all the time, you'd have seen it," Ammon said. I glared at him and he laughed.

"Hey, look! It's the horse," Mom shouted and pointed as the tired animal actually crested the summit where our monastery was located. I was more than pleased that he'd made it; it meant I would be able to sleep that night.

"I hope they don't make him work tomorrow!" Bree said.

"He deserves a vacation!" I agreed.

"Are you kidding me? If he's lucky, he'll *get* to work," Ammon started, "Otherwise he's just considered damaged goods, and they'd probably just retire him and then eat him."

"That's terrible!" Mom said.

"Why!? If he's no use to them, why keep him?" he said. *Is that really the mentality here?* I didn't want to think about that and went back to wondering what role the horse would play in my dreams that night.

Now that we'd reached our goal for that day, Ammon led us into the little wooden monastery which we knew had rooms to rent. He poked his head in, and his "Hello" and the *ding* of the doorbell echoed in the chamber-like entry. I crept in after him, inhaling the essence of this damp monastery nestled into the clearing halfway up the sacred mountain. We had visited several monasteries before, but this one made me feel like I had to tiptoe.

The floor boards creaking beneath our feet were followed by a sudden, "Ni hau." What was usually offered as a light-hearted greeting sounded low and unusually haunting this time. The small head of a young woman whose slick, black hair was pulled back in a severe ponytail poked over the wooden counter.

"We are four people," Ammon said, holding up four fingers.

She cocked her head like a little bird to see us, and then shook her head and almost shouted, "No! No!"

Hearing sighs of disbelief behind him, Ammon pushed on. "We need a dorm, please."

She repeated herself, looking for all the world like a gasping goldfish trying to intimidate us with a big mouth. "Noooo! Nooo!" We were not daunted by a Chinese woman who only reached as high as Ammon's belly button, and she seemed to realize the futility of disagreeing with his statement, because she then took out a paper that listed options for rooms.

"These aren't what we want. I know you have more than just doubles." There was nowhere else to go at this time of night, but I knew Ammon would choose sleeping on the ground and eating mud before he would pay the price of a double room. After putting up a bit of a fight, she caved in and offered a four-bed room, but Ammon still wasn't satisfied. Going on the basis of the list of room options posted on the wall ahead of us and his gut instincts, he pushed a little harder to get us a dorm. The "nooooes" kept coming, though, each time with more force, and her mouth soon resembled that of a whale more than a goldfish. Not knowing what else to do, Ammon finally broke down and echoed her persistent "noes" with "yeses" that mimicked her tone perfectly.

With a sour look on her face, she finally gave in, twisted around, grabbed a key off the wall, and signalled for us to follow her. It was as if Ammon had stumbled upon a secret code that somehow granted us entry.

"Geez, mareez!" Bree said, unable to make sense of most things that happened at the best of times. Keeping her distance, she silently lipped "nooooo, noooo," with fish lips and the same wide eyes Ammon had used to impersonate the woman.

On the other side of a paper wall, monks sat cross-legged in a candle-lit room permeated with incense. Its smell was everywhere. As we walked past, I peeked in the doorway for a better view of the individual mounds of red robes that were lined up in such neat rows that they looked like a game of checkers.

We were escorted silently to a seven-bed dorm in a back corner of the monastery. Judging from the severe slope of the room and the bottomless view from the window, the room must have been literally dangling off the side of a cliff. The creaking floor boards did nothing to allay our fears that we might tumble over in the night. There was no place to buy food, so it was lucky we had brought our own bowls of instant noodles and incredibly sweet cookies.

The bathroom was nothing to be proud of, as we suspected. We only knew from the increasing intensity of the smell that we were on the right track as we took a long, creepy walk through the dark to get to it. Given that the monastery had no plumbing system, it was yet another hole in the ground with walls about knee-high. There were slopes inside the hole for the excrement to slide down and off the cliff, at least in theory. It didn't work as well as they'd planned; very little actually slid down and off the cliff, and so much had piled up that it came up over the top of the hole. *Charming!*

It was much cooler at this altitude, so Bree and I huddled under some blankets around our tiny kettle on the floor to keep warm. We then stole blankets from the five empty dorm beds and slept in the same twin bed so our body heat would help us stay warm through the night. The room flickered with candlelight and smelled of burning wax throughout the icy night.

When I finally got my monkeys, I was reminded why we should always be careful what we ask for. Hordes of them swung in the trees outside our window in the dark, bouncing and running all over the roof and banging loudly enough to keep us up the whole night, or what little there was of it. Chanting monks woke us at four in the morning.

Their devotions echoed throughout the monastery. We listened as they repeated "Nanoo nanoo nee maa haaa" over and over again, and it was one of the most enchanting and wonderful sounds I'd ever heard. My reaction surprised me, as I would never before have understood its simple, calming beauty. I might even have derided it. I would never have listened to the sound of chanting monks sending off their prayers long enough to see it in a different light and appreciate its unique splendour. With no other option, I found myself falling sway to its undeniable grandeur. Twenty-odd voices blended into one melodious hum that came from deep within. The vibrations of their rhythmic chants penetrated my chest and soothed my mind as swirls of incense washed over me, and I felt wondrously weightless and free.

It was raining when we started off the second day, and after only an hour I collapsed. Bree shouted, "Timber!" as I dropped my walking stick and hit the ground. I didn't care that it was muddy and cold – I just wanted to rest.

A woman from one of the few "shops" we'd passed by began to laugh. It was clear she was immune to stairs, having walked up and down them every single day, probably her whole life long, to get to work.

"C'mon, Savannah. You can make it," Mom encouraged.

"Just go away. I need a minute. Please. No more stairs." I begged. *I'm really not here. I'm down on the flat lands where it's dry and wonderful. No stairs. I'm back in the guesthouse.* I hoped if I lay there long enough picturing the places I wanted to be (which was almost anywhere in the world, as long as stairs weren't involved), that it might just happen.

I opened my eyes and saw the bottom of Ammon's mud-caked boots instead. "Don't start quitting already. You've got a full day ahead of you!" Ammon said, stepping on my bum for good measure before walking on.

There is always a certain amount of peer pressure involved in being part of a group. The family was willing to wait periodically, but only for so long, and I owed it to them not to hold them up. I was totally outnumbered, and I could not just sit down and give up.

I thought I might rather die than lift my leg another two inches for another stair, but there was no help for it as far as I could see. I was trapped and began to feel stressed and coerced like that poor horse from yesterday.

Another man being carried went by. They almost stepped right on me, but even then, I could not bring myself to move. It was like being left behind in the mud and forgotten. I'd finally been thrown from my cushy, teen-princess throne and put in my place, and I didn't like the feeling one little bit. Before I could break down completely, though, Bree poked me with her walking stick until I reached out and grasped it and held on tight as she pulled me to my feet. She sympathetically let me hook the crook of my walking stick to her backpack and helped drag me up. I was carrying only my small, day-trip backpack, but even that weight made the stairs feel higher and more unreachable.

Then I heard a hoot and a howl, and the bushes began to quake in the distance. The mountainside was bright green and glistening, covered with clumps of ferns and tree-strangling vines. We were completely surrounded by bamboo jungle, and as we leaned over the rail, we could see the tops of trees shaking off to the right. Like the famous scene from *Jurassic Park*, the trembling patches of dense foliage got closer and closer, and the hoots and calls grew sharper.

When the commotion reached us, we were finally treated to close-up interactions with the monkeys we'd been waiting to see – monkeys on the roof in the night didn't count. From that point on, they were our ever-present companions, fighting and playing and swinging from branch to branch all around us.

Much like the Chinese, they were intrigued by this new group of bizarre, hairless white "monkeys." They'd peer down their long, narrow noses to inspect us from the stairs. They plunked themselves down on the handrails or blocked the stairs completely, as if they had worked out the art of collecting road taxes. They scratched each other's backs, breastfed their babies, and groomed each other's dense, rain-streaked fur. We often gave in to their irresistible charms and fed them whatever food we were carrying, encouraging their begging behaviour. They walked up to us on their hind legs and took our offerings in their small, rubbery hands. Even fully grown, they were only about knee high. The baby monkeys had loose, naked skin on their faces that was replaced by red masks as they matured.

They reminded me of the raccoons in Vancouver that played havoc with our trash cans and occasionally got trapped in our house. Interacting with the monkeys gave me a sense of the achievement and satisfaction Ammon had referred to, and the energy to carry on.

Along the way, we caught up to a group of domestic tourists chasing the monkeys around with their cameras. It was drizzling lightly, and a few tourists wore plastic bags on their heads to keep dry. One daring monkey leapt out from where he'd been lurking in the shadows of the underbrush onto a woman's back and balanced his feet on her shoulders. As she ducked her head and spun in circles shrieking, he tried to pry the plastic bag from her head. A man who was apparently the woman's boyfriend tried to pull the crazed monkey off her as she began to cry, terrified and hysterical, and kept holding onto her head and the plastic. The monkey continued to yank at it and crawl all over her, completely dominating the situation. *Just give him the bag!* I wanted to shout, but I knew they wouldn't understand me.

"What do you expect if you wear a bag on your head!?" Mom laughed. "I guess they didn't see the signs."

"He's not getting any after that performance!" Ammon joked, watching the boyfriend get slapped across the face by the hairy troublemaker.

"You couldn't even save me from a stupid MONKEY!!!" Bree imitated what she expected the woman might well be saying that night.

But the show was soon over, and Bree and I dragged ourselves ever higher, again asking why on earth we were doing this. Mom pushed us through fog thick enough to chew. Despite knowing there would be no view, her determination forced us to climb for the last hour to get to the summit. When we finally reached the finish line, I could hardly see my own outstretched hand, let alone the big golden temple that was supposed to be on top.

I could barely see Mom beside me but I realized, despite my fury, that it would have been even worse had we paid a hundred dollars to be carried up. Then it slowly dawned on me that, even if it had been a clear day, this was about far more than just the view. It wasn't reaching the top that made it so precious. It was experiencing it, breathing it, even cursing it a little (okay, okay, so maybe a lot) along the way. That journey helped me climb not only the physical stairs but the symbolic ones in my life. It was about setting a goal and accomplishing it, no matter what. I learned the boundaries of my own strengths and weaknesses, and then how to move beyond them.

Somewhere beside me, Bree's half-crazed laughing reminded me that we were a team, and that a team effort had got us there. When I'd dropped my walking stick and fell to the ground, with the locals snickering and cold, wet mud on my face, they were the ones who got me back on my feet. Being in a situation where failing or giving up is not an option, you reach limits you didn't think you could and begin to believe that anything is possible. Trips like that increased my confidence in my abilities and in myself.

Postcard
26

Ya, these are Terra Cotta Warriors! They don't seem that great but the history behind them is amazing. They are 2,000 years old and it took thousands ▢▢▢▢▢▢ of people **POST CARD** 40 years to complete. It was pretty sweet to be there, especially on my birthday ☺. It's great out here, I wish you could've been here with us but maybe India is a better plan. This was too short of notice. I'm in Xi'an right now eating breakfast about to leave to Datong then straight to Beijing. YAY! This should be great. We're going to see the Great Wall, circus, shop and other stuff. I'm excited! This place is crazy because they sell baby bunnies and puppies on the side. It's so tempting. The rabbits only $3.00 and the dogs $16.00. People are crazy. It's fun to smile and wave like always, since I like crazy. People to people. Not only because you feel like a star but because you make the people so happy. Also people literally come up to you and say "You are so beautiful! Can I take a picture with you?" Of course you just say yes, what else can you say? Haha I'm going to feel so unimportant when I get home ☺. Aaw, Terri, they were selling cantelope slices on the stick (they were so big we didn't think it was possible to be a cantelope!) and it reminded me of you and Yegen froz. Oh, and I was on a boat for three days! My first one ever too! I slept and I felt like I was on a TV show once (I'm such a geek) hehe.

秦兵马俑一号坑内景
Panoramic view of vault I

Keep reading the blog! Love you Soooo much

Savannah Grace xoxo (K)(L)

Terri

West Vancouver, B.C.
Canada

June 15ᵗʰ, 2005

**Ya, these are Terra Cotta Warriors! They don't seem that great but the history behind them is amazing. They are 2,000 years old and it took thousands of people 40 years to complete. It was pretty sweet to be there, especially on my birthday ☺. It's great out here. I wish you could've been here with us but maybe India is a better plan. This was too short of notice!! I'm in Xi'an right now eating breakfast about to leave to Datong then straight to Beijing. Yay! This should be great. We're going to see the Great Wall, circus, shop and other stuff. I'm excited! This place is crazy because they sell baby bunnies and puppies on the side of the road. I was so tempted. The rabbits only $3.00 and the dogs $16.00. People, like always, stare like crazy. It's fun to smile and wave to people. Not only because you feel like a star but because you make the people so happy. Also people literally come up to you and say, "You are so beautiful! Can I take a picture with you?" Of course you say yes. What else can you say? Haha I'm going to feel so unimportant when I get home ☺. Aaw, Terri, they were selling cantaloupe slices on the stick (they were so big we didn't think it was possible to be cantelope!) and it reminded me of you and Yogen Fruz. Oh and I was on a boat for three days! My first one ever to sleep on. I felt like I was on titanic (I'm such a geek) hehe. Keep reading the blog! Love you sooooo much.

Savannah Grace xoxo (K)(L)**

Sitting at a round, concrete picnic table, I endlessly twirled my pen in my hand. Terri's blank postcard was waiting for me to write something – anything.

I started with the easiest part, the date: June 17th, 2005, and then wrote the opening lines.

"Hey Babycakes!! Oh how I miss thee. Do you know how long it took us to get here from Xi'an, the place I sent the last card from?! Eighteen hours!! Eighteen bleep-jeeping hours on a train!"

"Did you tell her about the Terra Cotta Warriors?" Mom reminded me, still excited about ticking something off her bucket list. "That they're discovering new things every day. I can't wait to come back when they've finished digging the whole farm and the replicas of the livestock!!!"

"I put that in the last card Mom, and no, I---"

"Or how every soldier is completely unique? How every single man was given different armour and features," she stated more than asked.

"Mom! No! I didn't tell her any of that. I didn't have enough room!" The heat was giving me a headache, and she wasn't helping. Yes, of course there was a lot I wanted to share with Terri. I had wanted to tell her that they were discovered by an unsuspecting farmer digging a well. That in itself was incredible, but again, I didn't have room on the card.

"The picture on the front is of the Cloud Ridge Caves, that's where I am right now. On our walk here, you wouldn't believe it, I saw a camel! And I'm not talking a statue one like a real live one just sitting there on the side of the road…. (it's got a double hump and apparently their humps are just essentially big boobs) speaking of boobs… mine, Mom claims, are getting bigger!! I've got boobs!! Wish you could be here to see them!"

Oh geez, what if some pervert mailman reads this…how embarrassing! Maybe if I change the b into a k? Then I'd get humps made of books? I've got books? Man, that makes no sense at all!

Quickly moving on to cover my idiocy, I jotted down what I'd learned from Ammon.

"The Cloud Ridge Caves are more than 1,300 years---"

Before I could finish the thought, Mom was piping in again. "I thought it was fifteen hundred years old? Ammon said fifteen hundred. Right Ammon?"

"Yah, it says it was the sixth century, so about fifteen hundred years old."

"Mom! Are you reading over my shoulder?! Stop it. I hate that!"

"Just making sure you get it right."

"Well, stop it."

I put my pen down and flipped the card over defensively. *There's no way I could ever fit everything I wanted to say on it anyway.* I started chewing the pen as I held up the picture on the front of the postcard. It was a giant, solid-rock Buddha carved into a cliff face, but the picture didn't do it justice. I lowered the card and looked ahead at the real Buddha. It was humongous! The few people passing by looked like tiny ants in comparison. *I'm actually here.* Looking out at the camels on the lawn and the cliff wall crawling with religious carvings, I saw how far we'd come. Picking my pen from between my teeth I neatly changed the three into a five and continued.

"1,500 years old and are still mostly in good shape. Some even still have paint! The caves are manmade and there are 51,000 Buddha statues carved into the walls inside the cliffs. Some of the Buddhas are huge like the one on the front of this card. I'm looking at it right now, actually. Lots of tiny ones are quite eroded because they were more exposed to the elements. It is very hot out and I got a bit of a burn ☺.

The food out here is way better than I thought, when it's not peanut butter sandwiches and instant noodles. We play a lot of cards because we wait around lots for trains and buses and things. We saw panda bears in a sanctuary place and also went on a trek into the mountains on horseback."

I rested my head in my hand as I thought about what to put in next. *She'll never understand through these measly words and one photo. There's just so much to say!*

I'd seen snow falling in June and ridden up 4,000m (13,123ft) on horseback, even higher than when I went skydiving when I was thirteen years old! But I knew saying that would never give her the feeling in your lungs as you gasp for air that seems not to be there, or how our Chinese cowboy guides went into the woods to cut down trees to build our tents and fashioned beds out of evergreen boughs, or how we'd used horse saddles for pillows, or how cute and incredibly lazy panda bears are as they lie on their backs eating bamboo all day. I wanted to tell her how the local ladies in our dorm room on our Yangtze River boat cruise had brought a plastic bag FULL of duck tongues to snack on, and to see her face when I told her I had eaten one myself. Or even that the Yangzi River is the third longest in the world, after the Nile and the Amazon! I wanted to tell her about the crazy Belgian guy who carried his fishing pole with him everywhere he went and how his wife only shook her head, because he'd never once caught a single fish on their seven-month backpacking trip, but he still insisted he was a fisherman and would one day catch a great big fish.

But with so little space, how could she ever understand? I felt like I'd lived an eternity without her, and that there was so much we'd missed from each other's lives. I was already fifteen, and she wasn't even there for my birthday! I just wished she could be here. I wanted to tell her my every thought and wish and dream. I wanted her to feel the same things I'd felt and see what I'd seen, but she wouldn't. No stretch of imagination could give her that.

I flipped the postcard back over. There could never be enough room on that tiny card to tell her all I wanted to say. *How can I write this in a way she can understand in the space I have left?* I picked my pen up one last time and simply ended it.

"It's pretty crazy out here. I miss you so very much. Love you. Your best friend, Savannah."

I kissed the flat card and wished she could just smell a hint of the land around me. Letting go, I slipped it down the wooden mail box and heard it fall onto the unseen pile within.

Stepping Back
27

I was staring out at the Great Wall of China at last. It slithered like a centipede across the hilly horizon, and I found myself trying to imagine all that had gone on over the years along its path. In a way that was similar to how I wished Terri could grasp what I had experienced, I became frustrated at how much *I* couldn't possibly grasp. Although I was there in body and spirit, my brain could not access the millions of tales I knew were trapped beneath my feet.

I grabbed my pen and notepad, the two things I always carried lately, and jotted down a few words, doing my best to describe what I was observing. I could see all the way out and over the mountaintops that looked like snow moguls, but with an ever-present trail of bricks dipping up and down, until the very furthest stretch appeared to be no bigger than a piece of Lego.

I had heard of The Wall from teachers and textbooks, of course, but hearing about it was far removed from the experience of standing on it. *How could I not take it seriously now?* Trying to comprehend the dates always gave me butterflies, now even more than ever. It had always been easier for me to avoid history and pretend it was just fiction, but seeing it in the flesh made it real in a way that I simply could not just brush aside.

We had taken a short walk through the forest to see a quieter part of the Great Wall. Although we had chosen to go off the main tourist track, there were still a few vendors waiting when we arrived.

We first climbed a passage to the top of the ancient stairs of one of the many watch towers. Of course, Ammon had his lessons ready as if he'd prepared lecture materials the night before. "This is the longest manmade structure ever built, from Shanhaiguan in the east to Lop Nur in the west. It's about 6,400km (3,977mi) with all the little side walls and everything included. During the Qin Dynasty which was from 221 BC to 206 BC, under the rule of Qin Shihuang-something-or-other, the warring feudal states finally unified. Shortly after that, they started building it," Ammon continued. "Well, there were actually some walls made before that to defend specific pieces of land, but then they started to connect them and make it this huge project."

"How many men would it take to build something like this?" Mom asked in amazement. From a distance, it looked very smooth and seemed to flow over the land like a ribbon, but walking along it was nothing short of strenuous.

"Well, let's just say that a million men died doing it, whatever that tells you," Ammon answered.

"Holy-karolly! I can't even begin to imagine a million people – I can't even imagine twenty thousand. That's, like, a thousand times twenty!!!" Bree said.

"It's good to see you haven't forgotten your math," he teased.

"Couldn't they have used those men as soldiers instead? Wouldn't that have worked as well or better than making 'em build for years? What were they trying to keep out, anyway?" I asked.

"A bunch of the nomadic forces kickin' around from Mongolia and stuff. To protect the Chinese Empire."

"Maybe it was more about keeping them in than it was about keeping them out," Mom thought aloud, probably relating it to China's strict rules for using the Internet.

The sun lay low in the sky by then and was a bit blurry behind the layers of greenish/grey fog, but I was overheating anyway.

"See these?" Ammon continued as we explored the inside of one of hundreds of watchtowers dotting the hillside. "Archers would sit in here and shoot invaders." There were narrow holes on three sides of the small tower as well as along the wall itself. The wind gusting through the small passages made them a good place to rest and cool down.

"And this part. See how it's shaped? How it goes into a V, with the narrow part on the inside? That's so there's less space for enemy arrows to get in, but it still gives the defending archer good sightlines and range."

"Wow! That is so cool!" Bree said, jumping into formation with one elbow pulled back, ready to shoot. Something which would normally have bored her silly was transformed into a real live history lesson.

The extent of our Mandarin consisted of all of four phrases: 'thank you', 'hello', and sometimes, on lucky days when we were able to reproduce the right tone, we could say 'ice water' and 'not spicy'. Plus, we could count to ten, something I always practiced in the markets along with the required hand signals.

The Wall was much more eroded and torn up than any of us had expected. A tiny woman who looked as decrepit as it did, one of the few peddlers tagging along, took me by the hand and insisted on helping me down, instead of the other way around. I was rehearsing some words and trying to learn a couple more with her. As I was trying to pronounce the word for stairs, I was also wondering if the men who built them had been giants. They were much too tall for the people of today, and I imagined great big warriors, armed with giant bows and arrows and wearing pointed helmets, leaping up and down them, defending their territory.

"Didn't they do more harm to their empire by making everyone suffer to build this?" I asked, moving ahead to talk to Ammon.

"Yah, but I don't think they really cared. Empires are just about royalty and keeping the uppity-ups happy."

"I hate that the big, head-honcho guy gets all the credit and probably just sat on his butt all day eating and getting fat! And he probably had a whole big harem and screwed everybody, too. Errgg! That makes me so angry," Bree said.

"But you know it wasn't all just one guy. I mean, this thing took centuries to build. It was built over the course of a bunch of dynasties. And it probably even went through stages of no production at all," Ammon continued, partially ignoring her outrage.

"Die nasty? What kind of accent are you trying to have? I bet lots of people had nasty deaths!" Bree said, getting angrier.

"I knew I should have explained that one," Ammon said, shaking his head. "It's not 'die nasty', it's *dynasty*. That's like a period of time that was ruled by emperors from the same family. Most of the parts still around were built in the Ming Dynasty which ended in 1644," he added to show off just how much he knew.

"Okay, this is getting annoying. Do you have the answers for EVERYTHING, or are you just pulling this completely out of your arse, Ammon?!" I commented. Laughing, he threw his head back and smirked at me instead of responding.

"You're so vain," I told him, unimpressed by his cocky manner. He just moved on, taking the last sip of water. The moment his bottle disappeared, a peddler magically appeared with a bag full of ice and bottles of water.

"EE KUAI, EE KUAI," the hawker insistently called out the price he was asking, the equivalent of fifteen cents. Ammon swung his daypack off his back and pulled out a second bottle of water. The hopeful seller's shoulders slumped with disappointment, and he immediately retreated to wherever he'd come from.

"By the way, I'm still bummed about my go-kart!" Bree said.

"They would never have let you do it anyway, so your dream was shot before it started," Ammon said realistically. Bree had always dreamed of driving a go-kart on the Great Wall of China, but her fantasy was immediately crushed the moment we saw The Wall. Unlike the wide, smooth, city wall we'd seen in Dali, the town where we'd spent Mom's birthday, the Great Wall was a bit on the narrow side for any go-kart, even if it hadn't had extremely steep, broken brick stairs. If anyone out there has similar crazy ideas, I'm here to tell you it's not going to happen! I'd imagined that The Wall would be a smooth masterpiece of cobblestone paths gliding along like a silk snake, complete with accessible ramps, so this was another reality check for me. I grew up in a glossy world where everything was pristine and exact, one where almost nothing was more than two hundred years old.

"I heard they buried people in the walls!! Alive!!" Bree announced to change the subject.

"Oh, c'mon, Bree! Stop with your horror stories," I said.

"Hang on a minute. This time she's actually kinda right," Ammon began.

"Sweet!" she said, once she'd recovered from her initial surprise at being right for a change.

"They *say* that archaeologists unearthed the bodies of a bunch of workers who were buried inside the walls. I sorta doubt they were alive at the time, 'cause they needed them to work, but who knows?"

"They dug up The Wall?!" Bree asked, "Isn't that, like, bad??"

"Not really. You see how worn this wall is?" Ammon said, as he made his way down another steep stairway littered with rubble. "And this is the part that's preserved and taken care of. I mean, this thing is looong. Most of it stretches over mountains and remote grasslands and desert. It's been exposed to rain, snow, wind, and such for thousands of years. Some parts are collapsing and lots of parts were buried in sand before anyone discovered them. But if it makes you feel any better, a lot of the workers were criminals," Ammon stated, more to present the other side's argument than because he truly felt that made it any better morally.

"That does make me feel a bit better!" Bree said seriously.

"Criminals. Pft! For what crime, I wonder?" I asked. "Stealing a rice cake? They were probably just looking at someone funny and got arrested."

"Well, now I feel bad again," she said, looking back and forth between me and Ammon.

"Speaking of rice, did you know that they used rice to build The Wall?" Ammon went on. "In the last phase, they used a sticky, rice-pudding-like compound mixed with slaked lime." He opened his book for a split second to check his facts and then continued, "It was the main ingredient for their mortar. And it's super-strength stuff that even weeds can't grow through. You know how tiny sprouts can somehow grow up through the concrete? Well, this rice stuff they used is better. It's stronger and a lot denser!"

"Holy crap!!!! I thought that was just a joke!" I said.

"How much rice would that take, though?" Mom asked.

"That's such a waste of food! They make them use all their food while they're starving. Oh, that's so mean," Bree said.

"Well, that's the thing. The farmers and commoners would've been pretty upset. First the ruler takes their men, then he takes all of the harvest in the south to make The Wall and to feed the men working on it," Ammon said. "During some periods, boys of all ages were forced to join. It got to the point where the women were afraid to have sons. With the men all gone to The Wall, it was nearly impossible to keep the fields and manage the rest of the required household chores. Those who lost their husbands or sons were left without the support or manpower they needed to manage their farms. Many died as a direct result of that, too."

"Yikes! That is just horrible! In a sense, even the women were slaves to The Wall," Mom said.

"Of course they were. It's a ripple effect. How could they not be affected?" Ammon said. The whole story just kept getting worse and worse, and I began to doubt just how "great" the Great Wall was.

"Isn't it stupid that people worship things that people suffered to make? You know? Do you ever think like that??" Bree asked.

"Yah, I do. And isn't it insane that millions of people will go along with one crazy person's idea?" Ammon added. *How is it that the manpower of millions of people cannot right a wrong? How can they be controlled like helpless sheep that way? Surely the forces of a million people would be enough to stand against one man and his army. But how would they get the army in the first place? Shouldn't they be the first to realize and try to protect the weak? How does it get to that point?* I could not wrap my head around that kind of power dynamic. *Or is it justifiable because it was under the name of protection? Maybe they really felt they were protecting their families.*

"It is an incredible structure. It's so impressive to think that mankind can create such a monument, even without cranes and stuff, but it's pretty awful to think about the sacrifice it took to do it," Mom said, looking slightly depressed by the notion.

"But how did it protect anybody? I mean, if it took hundreds of years, wouldn't the enemies have been a little quicker than that? Or did they just stand around and watch while it was being built?" I asked.

"I think that they started with the assumption that it was going to protect them, but it obviously turned into some kind of obsession," Mom suggested. I couldn't fathom it. All the land around me exuded history, and my head ached from the strain of trying to picture all those men working so hard and giving their lives to build it over the centuries. I tried to imagine the personal sorrows that went into The Wall. Thousands of years ago, people left their marks on the same stones and rubble I was walking on. I couldn't help thinking that only a few could claim any credit for the masterpiece, but that the credit should go to those who sacrificed their blood, sweat, and tears for a project that led to so many early deaths.

Was it built to protect their homeland and to please their emperor, or did they try to please him to save their heads? The rulers didn't care about the people. They certainly wouldn't have sent a million horses with a million letters to tell people when their family members died. They just wouldn't have done it. I bet many of the families assumed their loved ones would die on the wall and weren't coming back, but there is always some hope left if there's no proof of death, or at least a written letter. They probably sat for days at their doors waiting, then weeks looking up at the sound of every horse, and years just wondering if he would suddenly come walking through the front door.

I began to suffocate under the strain of trying to grasp the sheer enormity of the lives lost and the pain and suffering of the families who were left wondering forever. I laid my palm flat against the worn bricks, imagining I was touching the hands of those who created it. I wished I could uncover the thousands of lost stories. I tried to imagine somebody digging up *my* story in two thousand years and wondered whether even *I* would remember it that long from now?

In five hours, we'd conquered only ten of The Wall's 6,400km (3,977mi), and it really helped put things into perspective. When we'd seen enough, we chose to take the zipline across the river where we could catch a small boat and then find a bus to take us to Beijing. The way the zipline's platform was suspended somewhat precariously off the wall gave Ammon even more incentive than just the budget to suggest that we should walk the rest of the way. Despite his fear of heights, we successfully combined our female powers and overruled our leader.

A year ago, I never would've guessed I'd be doing this. It's crazy what the future can hold. I turned and watched the wall disappear into the smog behind me. The river below was sparkly and perfect. For a minute in time, I was alone up there, literally hanging between earth and sky in the zipline's harness. It was the furthest I'd been from my family in weeks, and I was enjoying hearing nothing but the soft, zipper-like sound of metal scraping cable above my head. The deep fog obscured where we'd been, but I knew what was behind me. My destination was also hidden, but I somehow knew that there was a foothold waiting for me there. Some would call it faith, and I guess, in a way, that was how Mom felt about the whole trip. She knew there was going to be something waiting for her on "the other side," and that everything would work out. She didn't need to see to believe. *One hundred percent. That's how strongly Mom must feel. She just doesn't doubt for an instant.* I couldn't see the platform until just before my feet touched the hard surface, and I had a feeling I wouldn't be seeing the end of this journey until I tripped over the finish line.

A Series of Beijing Events
28

*W*e arrived at a dinky bus station in Beijing late at night, and even at that time, it was incredibly hot and muggy. The following days were no less smothering. Each time we went out to explore the city and surrounding sites, the sun seemed to get hotter and the shade less plentiful. At times I truly believed the skin on my back must be bubbling up like a thin slice of bacon on a hot frying pan. Temperatures reaching as high as 38°C (100°F) sizzled upwards from the pavement, roasting our bare legs.

The humidity and the ever-present layer of smog over the city only added to our suffering. From the moment we'd arrived in Xi'an, the major city we'd visited the week before, a thick cloud of pollution descended upon us, and we hadn't seen blue sky since. The ground-level cloud of cigarette smoke added to the deadly combination. We had been coughing constantly to try to clear our chests, especially Mom.

Air quality was not the only downside of visiting the big cities. Super-sized, baseball-capped American tourists wearing uniformly unattractive white socks with sandals tromped about with big cameras strung around their necks, many of which rested on surprisingly large beer bellies. They literally swarmed everywhere, their guides' megaphones blaring as they flocked around the gates surrounding the Terra Cotta Warriors and formed long lines at sites such as the Temple of Heaven and the Forbidden City.

The Forbidden City was a palace used by emperors and their house-holds for five hundred years. No one other than servants and lovers could ever enter, hence the name "Forbidden." The whole complex had shiny, orange-roofed buildings and many big, open courtyards. I marvelled at the number of tourists, me included, wreaking havoc there as I imagined the old emperors rolling in their graves.

Despite my reluctance to be either a tourist or a backpacker, it was apparent, even to a novice like me, that there was a huge differ-ence between the two. Tourists came fully prepared with all the nec-essary comforts of home. They were able to afford the extra weight of things like hair dryers, facial creams, high heels, and a clean pair of underwear for each day of their trip, maybe even more, and their travel is usually just for a limited time.

Backpackers, on the other hand, embrace discomfort. The ideal backpacker would fit everything needed for the entire journey in a pair of cargo pants – toothbrush and a change of underwear in one pocket, passport and money in the other. That would define the ulti-mate backpacker, AKA, a hardcore traveler.

I noticed another key difference. Tourists tend to drop in for a nice, leisurely vacation. They hit the main sites and are on their way, uninterested in other tourists, whereas backpackers, despite constant-ly seeming to play a game of one-upmanship about things like who packed the lightest or who travelled the longest or the furthest, are always watching each other's backs and sharing information and sto-ries. That part of it felt reassuring, but after nearly two months on the road skipping from village to village in rural China, the obese size of "my people" pouring in on tour bus after tour bus was embarrassing.

I found that the local city folk were noticeably larger, too. It had never been more obvious to me how much village and city lifestyles influence people. The farmers and villagers worked very hard and ate a healthy diet of rice and vegetables, yet they looked rather weathered and worn. They were very friendly people who always took the time to explain directions and seemed happy to help us. City folk were more fast-food oriented and physically inactive, and they looked very soft and stylish. They always seemed to be in a hurry and much too busy for us, evidently having something more important to do, with their ever-present brief cases and cell phones, and somewhere more important to be. It was really like living in two different worlds, and we found both experiences fascinating.

There were also a lot more beggars in the city areas where tourists flocked. We had seen very few, if any, in the five weeks before we reached Xi'an, but from then on, we saw more and more. Obnoxious kids chased us down far more aggressively than anywhere else, as did lots and lots and lots of cripples. They were scattered everywhere, many rolling themselves around on skateboards or crawling on their hands as they dragged lifeless limbs behind them.

Before travelling, I could remember every single beggar I had ever seen – all three of them. I recalled each face and how one held up a sign that read, "Hungry. Out of work. No food. Help." When I was only ten or so, a bearded man had actually asked me for some spare change in Seattle. This was one of the most traumatic things to have happened to me up to that point in my life, but China was a whole new ballpark. It made the poor man sitting on cardboard begging with his dog and his upturned baseball cap pale to insignificance in comparison.

When I first saw limbless beggars, I tensed up and shied away from them as if they might be leprous. Their knobby limbs looked to me like they were disintegrating right off their bodies. The pungent smell of greasy sausage cooking in the streets made me nauseous, as I imagined I was smelling their rotting limbs and fatty tissues sizzling on the concrete. I knew I could not continue to jump like a spooked mouse every time a one-armed woman approached me or run out of my flip-flops if a man with two stumped knees wheeled over to grab my ankle. This inescapable reality was another challenge I had to overcome. I learned to acknowledge the brutality of these all-too-common scenes and develop thicker skin and a new mindset. *How can I fear someone who is so helpless?* Even when my legs ached to the bone, I grew ever more appreciative of what I had and was truly grateful for even things as basic as my ability to stand up and walk.

Along with the beggars, we saw the occasional drunk staggering down the street at nine in the morning. On one occasion, Ammon declared, "Now there's a sight for ya!" A man who was happily on his way to a serious hangover was swaying down an alleyway carrying an empty beer bottle in each hand. This was not such an unusual sight, but this guy was wearing nothing more than just his hiked-up socks, dress shoes, and tightey-whiteys. One side of his hair lay flat against his head, while the other half stuck out like a mad scientist's. He did not seem to be aware of his state. In fact, he looked quite pleased with himself.

"I mean, he's wearing no clothes, but he still found time to put his best shoes and socks on," Ammon smiled. Mom suggested that he might never have completely undressed.

I loved a lot of the street food, particularly because I seemed to be constantly hungry. The streets were overrun with venders shouting "EE KUAI, EE KAUI!" (fifteen cents) and waving their items in the air. There was a wide variety of fruit, freshly cooked meat, and various dumplings to choose from. Although food prices were easy to gauge by watching how much the locals paid, bargaining was still very much part of their culture. After visiting so many markets on our journey, the constant haggling and pantomiming became almost second nature. Sometimes bargaining took little effort, while other times it involved a long "discussion" over a hot cup of tea. However, despite Ammon's insistence that "it's part of the culture," I still found myself feeling guilty when we haggled prices down from one hundred ninety to ninety yuan, or from thirty-five to four yuan.

"Hallo. Come you look," a middle-aged woman shouted from her little shop in the middle of the market's excitement. Ammon slowed down slightly, something which happened rarely, if ever, when we shopped. It was always he who pushed and pulled us along. We loved to window shop, even though we were never allowed to actually buy anything, firstly because of the weight and lack of space, but more importantly, because of our strict budget.

He glanced in the shop window and wiggled his chin before whispering, "Well, I was kinda thinking about getting one of these silk shirts." He initially kept his distance so as not to show interest and thereby immediately lose the upper hand in the negotiating game.

"You come. You looking. Is nice," she said, waving an arm at the dozens of shirts hanging above her head. Ammon kicked the dirt and swayed his head side to side. As part of his strategy, he was stalling just long enough to give her time to make the first desperate move.

"Dis. Three hundred fivety. Is nice?"

"Three hundred and fifty?!!" Mom repeated, as usual. This time I couldn't tell if she was supporting Ammon's bargaining position or if she was truly shocked, *again*, but I was not surprised to feel her warm breath on my neck and hear her ask, "How much is that anyway?" It was fifty-two dollars and fifty cents.

"Three hundred twenty," the woman said immediately as she stepped out of her shop, sensing us warming to the product. I knew Ammon would never pay that much for a shirt and really doubted he would be able to negotiate the price down to one he *would* be willing to pay. In fact, I hadn't yet seen him buy anything that wasn't absolutely essential, like water, food, bus tickets, accommodations, or toilet paper (and not much of that!). He was a real cheapskate, unlike we three girls who would splurge on pop, hair conditioner, and chips.

He stood still and maintained his sceptical look for a bit, as if to say, "Hah! Never in a million years!" "But what is the discount price?" he finally asked cheerfully.

"Three hundred. Is good price."

"I am a poor man. I can't afford that kind of price. You'll have to do better than that for me," he said in a friendly, joking manner.

"Okay, you come. You look. Feel. Is very good silk. Real silk," she said as she ran back inside to get a sample for him.

"Ammon, that's a really nice shirt," Mom said, when the lady was no longer within earshot.

"Yah, they are actually pretty nice," he admitted, shortly adding a strategic and honest, "but what am I going to do with it, even if I could get it for a good price?" Just then, she reappeared with a very attractive, black silk shirt with a subtle but sexy Chinese dragon stitched on the front. He obviously liked it, because he lifted a brow in the woman's direction and started low. "How about thirty?"

She waved her hand out in front of her to signal, "No, no!" and defensively clutched the shirt. We girls could tell this was the start of a long process with that kind of price difference, so we left them to it.

When we came back forty-five minutes later, he was sitting just inside the doorway on a tiny wooden stool, his knees practically hitting his ears, sipping tea. We entered curiously, wondering how the bargaining session was going and whether they had come to any kind of agreement.

"Is good man," she told us when we entered. "Is good bargain man!" she said, almost proudly. She immediately began telling us how so many tourists came by her shop and bought things without even trying to bargain. "My friend there, with bracelet shop, she say fifteen. American, he buy fifteen! No bargain. No even try," she said, shaking her head like it was craziness. "We laugh at this people. We don't give respect. Next time we say twenty, France, he pay twenty."

I was surprised and relieved to hear that. I had been slightly worried about how our bargaining appeared to the locals, despite Ammon's reassurances. A few times when I had negotiated a ridiculously low price, I had felt somewhat guilty that I may have ripped them off. But she confirmed that bargaining was a respected part of the culture, and that they wouldn't drop their prices any lower than they could afford to go. At the same time, I hated that Ammon was right again!

In the cities, more people spoke a bit of English, so we were able to get some firsthand information about their culture, lifestyles, and perceptions of things. She appeared very proud of her culture and was not impressed by the tourists' evident lack of awareness.

While the three of us took this opportunity to refill our stock of feminine needs, like trying to find tampons or deodorant and any type of skin lotion that didn't contain bleaching agents. Due to light skin being highly valued in China, virtually all skin-care products contained some sort of bleaching compound. Ammon had managed to get a lot of information from her. While they had enjoyed tea, he learned that she lived above the store with her parents. Since her husband's house was too small for them to live together, it made sense for her to care for her elders there. In this culture, children often took care of their parents when they reached the age of retirement, and many of the shops are family run and have living quarters upstairs. I felt a bit sorry for her, and wondered if she had any siblings, and whether she and her parents got along.

When she saw that we were ready to take Ammon away, she got off her small stool and grabbed the same silk dragon shirt we'd seen before.

"Here. You take. One hundred," she said, smiling graciously. Ammon raised his brows and then let out a surprised laugh.

"You are a good lady," he said, nodding to her as he took it.

"And you, very stubborn man," she said with a wink.

On second thought, she doesn't look unhappy. She seemed to be quite light-hearted and energetic, and not the slightest bit unfriendly. I couldn't see how that was possible. I could not quite comprehend how someone with so little could still appear to be as happy as she. At home, I'd somehow come to believe that only homeless people lived in apartments. The only nice apartments I remembered were five-bedroom penthouses, so now, I couldn't even come up with what I considered a suitable word to describe her circumstances, living in a two-bedroom flat above a shop with her aging parents. *But still, poverty and happiness don't go together...do they!?*

Every day that we got closer to Tiananmen Square and Mao, I felt myself becoming more and more anxious. I couldn't believe I was really getting excited about this. Ammon had gone over the basic historical facts with us earlier and managed to really intrigue me. It was like reading a textbook out loud and then jumping straight into it. The information was still fresh in my mind, and I was as thrilled as if we were going back in time to see cavemen. I never imagined how fascinating a boring square and a foreign leader could be.

I was surprised to hear how recently the 1989 protests and the massacre had taken place. I didn't think things like this still went on. Heck, Bree was born just before it all happened! The story of the "unknown rebel" who singularly made history by standing up to a whole column of tanks impressed me the most. With nothing more than an outstretched hand, he stopped the military tanks that were ready to crush him like a tiny bug. I couldn't believe I'd never heard of him and was eager to see the famous photo one day.

"That guy became a powerful icon of the last century," Ammon told us as we emerged from the crowded streets into the third-largest square in the world.

"What made him do it!? What did he say about it?!?" Bree sounded equally impressed, but I was busy watching the pods of soldiers kicking one leg straight into the air as they marched in unison. There was no doubt the square was huge. It was 440,000 m² (4,736,120ft²), almost as large as eighty football fields. A very large museum of history, Tiananmen Gate, an old railway station, and the Great Hall of the People made up the square's perimeter.

"Well, that's the thing. No one ever found him." *Wow! A real live mystery! Imagine if we found him and could talk to him in person? That would be amazing!* The fact that I found myself unintentionally inspecting each young male on the off chance that I'd be able to pick out a face I'd never even seen before gives you some idea of the effect the story had on me.

When I spotted a particularly large poster of Mao Zedong, I remembered what we had come for. We quickly found the long line snaking outside his mausoleum, and we stood and waited in it with hundreds of others. The old dictator could often be seen on posters, and because his face was displayed on all Chinese bills and coins, I felt like I already knew him.

"So, what can you tell us about this dead dude?" Bree said.

"First, he's not just a 'dead dude'," Ammon said almost defensively. "This is major history. He's been dead for thirty years, since September 9, 1976, and he's fully preserved and looks as if he'd died yesterday. So you're literally going to see his body. You won't just be looking at a coffin."

"Oh, gross!" Bree said, realizing the implication of that bit of information.

"Crazy! Who would want to do that?" I asked.

"I think he, like Ho Chi Minh – the guy who won the Vietnam War, actually wanted to be cremated. They both specifically said they didn't want to be put on display, but the people missed them so much that they did it anyway. Lenin was preserved because he was "The Man" in Russia, and Mao made China what it is today. They're the great communist leaders, and now I'll be able to say I've seen all three!"

"Good for you. You go ahead and collect your dead body sightings. Next you're going to expect *me* to have an embalmment count," I said, refusing to become caught up in anything so ghoulish.

"I've never heard of any of them," Bree said, and I nodded in agreement.

"You will, especially since we're going to Russia soon," Mom said, shuffling along in line.

"People seem to really love him," I whispered an hour later, acknowledging the number of people laying flowers for him just inside the building.

"He was, among other things, a scholar, a poet, and the founder of Communist China. Oh, and he killed seventy million people," Ammon threw in casually but very quietly before entering the chamber where he lay. I choked at that. My eyes bulged and Ammon, moving forward with the line, warned me with one of his looks that I should stay silent.

"Seventy million!?" I mouthed silently. I was still reeling over that figure when we entered the room where the great emperor lies for eternity. There is no speaking, taking photos, or stopping allowed; you just trundle along in single file on the red carpet encircling his crystal coffin and glance at him as you pass. I stared curiously at his sallow skin and imagined him standing in Tiananmen Square just outside the doors in the sunlight. *I guess this must be what evil looks like.* There was no remorse in his expression as he laid with his arms crossed nobly over his belly. I wondered whether his spirit lingered there in the room, full of guilt. *Would the spirits of all those people be chasing him, holding him down or standing guard at the gates of heaven to refuse him entry? Or would they be able to forgive in heaven? Why would I even assume he'd get as far as the pearly gates?*

"He looked a bit like Snow White!" Bree said when we were back out in the daylight. "Do you think if a princess came and kissed---"

"Bree, how impossibly irrelevant can you be?"

"Very!" she said stubbornly, ignoring Ammon's jibe.

"Plus, the bigger question is, why would anyone want to go down in history with that haircut?!?" he said, abruptly changing his tune and smiling at her.

"But seventy million?! That's unbelievable," I said.

"Yep! Hitler is said to be accountable for only seventeen million, and Stalin killed twenty-three million with his genocide and everything else," he continued. "That makes Mao the single, greatest mass murderer in human history. And just to make things really interesting, you know our most wanted criminal, Bin Laden? If what they say is true, he killed only a few thousand in the Twin Towers, and we're talking millions here. It's truly unfathomable."

"This just boggles my mind," I said.

"They worship this guy even after he lived an evil life and murdered millions of their people?!" Bree asked, understandably clueless for once. "How did he even manage to kill so many?!"

"He was responsible for the mass famines, which resulted from how he implemented the Great Leap Forward. But I don't think he necessarily did it intentionally like Stalin, who purposely cut off the food supply to starve the Ukrainians. Never mind, I'll tell you more about Stalin later." We were grateful Ammon left it at that and didn't go into whatever the Great Leap Forward meant. We'd been overloaded enough for one day.

"How could you ever forgive, let alone worship, a person who killed that many, even if it was an accident? I mean, he was responsible for the number one death toll in history?!" I was appalled.

"I can't believe this many people are bringing flowers. They must have incredible censorship going on here," Mom whispered, observing the long line-up and the dozens of vendors selling flowers as we looked for a spot to play cards. "There's no way they could possibly know. They have to be in the dark."

"That would seem plausible, wouldn't it? If we can't even open our blog site, it would make sense for them to block any negative information on their leaders or government," Ammon said practically. "But that's how they keep people suppressed. Like you said before, how come millions couldn't stop the insanity of one man who wanted to build a wall halfway across the country? Mainly, it's 'cause they weren't connected, but from now on, people will be united through the Internet. It all starts with one person's actions setting an example, like the 'unknown rebel' of Tiananmen Square. He's the kind of leader you need to start a movement. The whole world saw the picture, but I bet if you asked the locals here, most wouldn't know about it. Which makes me think, maybe he doesn't even realize his worldwide fame and that's why he never came out. Maybe he never even knew the effect he'd had. Either that, or they killed him."

Venturing out the following day, it was hard to resist popping in for quick looky-looks as we passed shop after shop. Every few feet, the three of us would skitter off into one of them, leaving Ammon on the curb tapping his foot impatiently. We'd obediently return and then set off with him again, but five minutes later, we'd run off like disobedient ducklings yet again. We had five kilometres to go, but Ammon finally snapped when we entered yet another bra shop.

"I'm done with this! I'm not going to miss the Temple of Heaven for bloody lingerie shopping." Throwing us a simple map of Beijing that was reproduced on the back of a business card and marked only with our hostel and the temple, he hissed, "And stop sharing clothes! I can't tell who's who from behind anymore. You three are driving me nuts!!" And with that, he stomped off in a huff. The three of us looked at each other rather perplexed, but then we couldn't help laughing.

"But we have to shop so we don't have to trade clothes anymore!!" Bree shouted after him, but he was already gone. I'd like to say he merged into the crowd and disappeared, but it was more like watching the dark ringlet of his short ponytail bobbing above the ocean of people until finally the distance between us became too great to see it anymore. The constant stress resulting from being outnumbered undoubtedly made this a long trip for him. Understandably, I don't think his personal checklist included sampling every shop in Beijing.

"I guess we have been acting a bit like Donald Duck's nephews, Huey, Dewey, and Louie," Mom said, feeling for him.

We could understand Ammon not wanting to spend all his time shopping, but the issue of sharing clothing was something else entirely. We each had our colours, Mom generally in red, Bree in black, and me in pink, and even I got confused when Mom wore Bree's black shirt or Bree sported Mom's red one. The three of us were around the same height and we all had long brown hair. On the other hand, we found sharing quite liberating, as it tripled our meagre, five-item wardrobes. Unfortunately for Ammon, this was a habit we wouldn't soon be quitting. We shrugged off his concerns, possibly underestimating the needs and frustrations of a man who is attached, sometimes uncomfortably, to three related females.

As we made our way uncertainly towards the Taoist Temple of Heaven, we wove through narrow side streets boasting shops of all kinds. It felt like there was a garage sale on every corner where you could find absolutely anything, all of it unbelievably cheap. By the time we arrived at the temple, we had run short of money, and we were grateful Ammon wasn't there to witness it. Without our leader to keep us in line and enforce the rules, we'd clearly lost all self-control. We tried the few ATMs we found along the way, but none wanted to give Mom any money. We were really not looking forward to asking Ammon for dinner money with our tails between our legs, but the more immediate problem was that, without him there to bail us out, we couldn't even afford the price of full admission tickets. We had to rely on Mom's amazing ability to "always get what she wants," and she came through again, somehow wangling discounted student tickets for each of us.

Stepping into the gardens surrounding the Temple of Heaven, Mom filled in for our tour guide, "So, this temple was built in the fifteenth century."

"And Taoism is the one with the yin and yang symbol, right?" I said, remembering what Ammon had taught us at previous Taoist temples.

"It represents balance: black and white, heaven and earth," she agreed.

"That's so romantic!" I said.

"So how long did it take to build this?" Bree asked.

"I'm not sure," Mom admitted.

"I know who would know," I chipped in helpfully.

"Where is Ammon anyway? We're never going to find him in here!" Bree said, suddenly inspecting the area. We twirled and spun as we walked down pebbled pathways in the beautiful garden complex, taking in the beauty of all the gorgeous flowers while keeping an eye out for the trusty leader who'd abandoned us. The Temple of Heaven gardens were too much like a maze for us to have any hope of finding Ammon, though, so we left before too long.

Though we'd paid the cheaper student rates, we had only enough left to buy a small bottle of water for our long walk back to the hostel. We set off in its general direction, this time with Mom leading. After inspecting the small map carefully, she decided to take what looked like a shortcut, a plan that gave me a distinctly uneasy feeling. Nonetheless, someone had to take charge, so off we went. As we might have predicted, before too long, we didn't recognize any signs from the tiny map that only named major roads.

"Hmmm ... This must be the right way, but I'm just going to ask someone to make sure." Mom walked over to a man on the curb who was idly watching traffic go by. She began speaking in English and pointing in the direction we were walking. He nodded in agreement. "Okay, so he says it's down this way. We're on the right track." When we'd gone a bit further and still not seen any familiar street names, she tried again and stopped a young couple, this time showing them the hostel's business card map. They looked at each other uncertainly before they, too, nodded. "Well? Is it that way?" Mom pressed them for more and pointed again down the same route we'd been taking, and they again responded with one more simple bob. "Okay then, we must still be heading in the right direction," she assured us, and we kept walking. The streets were getting busier and louder with a lot of honking and shopkeepers shouting. My head was buzzing and I wasn't at all confident about the directions we'd been given.

"Oh, I don't remember any of this," I said, having hoped that we'd start to recognize things again after walking thirty minutes. "This isn't getting us anywhere. Ask another person."

"I can always backtrack. I know how to backtrack. I just want to try this shortcut for a while longer before we give up on it." This time when she asked someone, she pointed in the direction we'd just come from and got more nods. "OOH, okay, so we went the wrong way. Maybe we walked a bit too far."

"Mom, I think they just don't understand anything!" Bree insisted.

A couple of the people we'd asked without pointing had simply shrugged and walked off. As a test, we purposely pointed in what we knew was completely the wrong direction the next time, and that person also nodded.

"It's probably your terrible pronunciation," I complained, feeling too hot and tired to be gentler about it.

"But I'm showing them the map! They should be able to understand that," she said, as she reached out to another couple and started pointing at the map all over again and asking for a specific street.

"Oh my goodness! We are actually getting lost," I grumbled.

We stopped to ask a couple of young military men. "Is it this way?" Mom asked pointing to the right. They nodded. "Or is it this way?" she ignored their nods and pointed to the left. Another nod. "So it's in this direction, this way?!" Mom repeated, her arm motioning to the right. They nodded, then gave a confused shrug. "Okay, thanks anyway. Xie, xie."

They must be thinking, "Just agree with them, and they'll leave us alone," I thought as I watched Mom struggling and sweating. After walking a few more discouraging steps, she gave up. "Yah, they don't understand. We'll just have to backtrack then, if we still can." Our shortcut had turned into a very long exercise in frustration. Two hours later, we finally arrived at the hostel with blazing red cheeks, our hair all frizzed and fly-away, and our clothes dark with sweat from going way over our daily average of 10km (6.2mi).

I wondered if Ammon even knew about Travel Rule # 4 – Never point any particular way when you're asking for directions, and if he did, why he never told us about it. Maybe he didn't want to give away all of his leadership secrets and didn't expect we'd ever need to use them.

When we finally walked into the lobby, Ammon was sitting there and looked up from his book with a cheeky grin. He was just sitting there, seemingly unworried and wearing a smile that said, "SEE? You need me."

I knew it was true. As annoying, anal and downright mean as Ammon could sometimes be, we wanted a smooth, successful journey, and he was our ticket to that, in addition to being a dearly loved family member. I realized that, beneath his smirk, he couldn't hide a subtle sigh when we arrived safely. Nothing but worry would cause him to sit and wait in the lobby like a watchdog. I'd seen how expertly he could control his emotions when he'd dealt with his cancer, but for the first time, I saw past his beard and furrowed brows and into his heart. Of course he was going to razz us that it took a few extra hours roasting in the sun to get back without his guidance, but it was all a cover-up. He had abandoned us in a big, strange city, and he felt responsible. At that moment, I understood how much he cared for all of us, and I directed an equally cheeky grin right back at him, pleased that I'd discovered his secret. *I think I can live with that.*

New Territory
29

"**W**hat?! What do you mean, 'we have to separate'?" I gasped when Ammon brought back "the good, the bad, and the ugly" news from the insanely chaotic ticket stand.

"I thought you checked it all out yesterday?" Mom said.

"I did! I got our four tickets. But now they're saying there isn't enough room on one bus. It's kind of hard when they're all jabbering at me in broken English, you know? We're just gonna have to meet up at the end. The buses are supposed to go in tandem, though, so we shouldn't be too far apart."

"I'm going with Mom," I said eagerly. As a hopeless Momma's girl, I naturally felt safest with her. The many honking, roaring noises of the bus station made me nervous, especially with this new plan added to my standard sense of unease. Ignoring the few scattered, metal benches, we sat on our big backpacks in a circle, as if around a comforting campfire, and pulled out the cards. I still felt the weight on my shoulders from carrying the heavy pack all the way there. Smiling at them beneath us, I wondered why we didn't use them as portable seating more often. The daypack that secured my journal and Rhett was strapped around my foot as a safety precaution.

Before long, we'd drawn the usual crowd of onlookers who wanted to join in on our card game. We'd surrendered our first deck of cards a couple of weeks earlier to the cowboy guides from our horse trek in the mountains around Songpan, but the new deck was already looking worn. As Mom dealt the next round onto Bree's upturned daypack, Ammon started talking to whoever was listening.

"You know how people say the ideal amount of exercise is ten thousand steps a day? They did a study showing that between the daily lifestyle of work, walking around the house, buying groceries, and the usual stuff people do, the average American takes somewhere between a thousand and five thousand steps. Well, we've been averaging 10km (6.3mi) a day," he continued proudly as he picked up his newly dealt hand. "That's fourteen thousand one hundred steps for me," he stopped a moment to let that sink in as he sorted through another winning hand, "and I take about two steps to every three you guys take," he ended, acknowledging for once that our standard mode of travel was more demanding for us short people.

"Yah, we walk everywhere," Mom nodded in agreement as she tossed her next card.

"We never STOP walking!" Bree complained.

And I, for one, felt the effects of all that walking as I nudged my backpack forward a bit to get close enough to throw down my best cards. *It might be nice to be trapped on a bus for a while. Then there's no way Ammon can drag us around and make us walk all day. Still, we'll be sweating either way.*

Ammon smirked as he laid down a pair of twos to score yet another win.

Between finding embassies to secure the various visas we needed, getting our hepatitis A booster shots, sightseeing, and "shopping" in the markets of Beijing, we'd walked 91.25 km (56.7mi) that week, according to the pedometer that hung on Ammon's belt. That far exceeded our daily average, and inspired me to think about how proud my gym teacher would be if I could report having walked that far! But that thought immediately resurrected the constant question lingering in the back of my mind; *what am I going to do about school?* I still couldn't let those worries go, and continuously beat myself up about it. *How can Bree be so unbothered by it?* She had barely finished Grade 11 before we'd left and had conveniently convinced herself that she'd graduated. She appeared not to have a worry in the world.

Just because I'm not in a school doesn't mean I'm finished. It means I'm skipping, which means I'm going to have a mile-high stack of studying to do when I get home. Which means when I'm finally there, I won't have a moment of fun because I'll be locked in my room for the next five years. How will I ever face my friends? The fear that each day I was away added yet another assignment to the pile never slipped my mind, but I was losing my battle to reduce that waiting pile. Being so preoccupied with future worries was definitely interfering with my ability to enjoy the present.

Mom's approach from the beginning was, "You can't do anything about it now, so don't bother fretting about it. Enjoy this while you can, and think about the rest later. There's no sense in stressing yourself out. Learn what you can about where you are. It's not as if you're not getting an education. It's just a different kind of learning." As my complaints about my heavy backpack grew louder, so did Mom's insistence that I should lose the weight. "Oh, just chuck it! You're obviously not going to do it, so stop carrying all that deadweight around."

Over the course of using and sorting the things in my backpack, the schoolwork had eventually slid to the very bottom. *Mom's right; I'm never going to finish this stuff within the year. Who am I trying to kid?* Internet availability and China's censorship made it way too difficult to do research, plus we never stayed in one place longer than a few days so I never had time to really get into it.

I was well aware of how much difference five pounds could make in my life. By the time we reached Beijing, the hard reality of my situation sank in, and despite my worries, I'd finally thrown both courses in the garbage. I could still visualize the pile of paper sitting in the trash in Beijing, and of course, I began to wonder if I'd done the right thing as soon as I'd let them fall.

Later, my choice was confirmed as I sat crammed on the bus floor. Apparently being separated wasn't the worst possible dilemma we had to deal with on the thirteen-hour bus ride to Mongolia. Women, children, and boxes of two-day-old chicks already occupied the beds we'd hoped to use. As it turned out, the bus trip originated a few towns back, and its aisles were crammed with boxes and burlap sacks tied firmly to the bedposts. Mom and I only managed to secure a bit of floor space in the front where people had to climb over us to get on and off. The sudden arrangement change was bad enough BEFORE an extra man and woman were assigned to "bunk" with us, too. The pretty Asian lady with thick black hair tied neatly in a French braid began shouting at the driver as soon as she couldn't get a bunk. Clearly, she was also under the mistaken impression that she'd paid for a bed. After she vehemently let the driver know how she felt about him and his organization, she plopped herself down next to me against a bedpost, arms crossed in an almost audible "hrmph!"

Surviving the night took priority over anything else. With no light except for the sudden bursts of lightning streaking across the sky, I couldn't have done much homework anyway. I imagined myself struggling with my nose literally pinched between pages and enduring all kinds of paper cuts. My elbows would've whacked the girl next to me, making her even angrier. My writing likely would not have been legible even if I'd managed to do enough work to send to my teacher.

"Sorry teacher, my dog *did* my homework," would be more believable than trying to explain what was actually going on.

Mom was curled up on her side on the floor with her back to me. "This is torture! I need to sleep on my back," she complained more than once. "I never should have done both ears at the same time!" A couple of days earlier we girls had abandoned Ammon to go in search of a beauty parlour. We'd taken turns sitting in blue, plastic chairs while three young ladies sputtered in Chinese as they prepared to take a piercing gun to our ears. We probably shouldn't have been surprised when they slid open a dirty drawer full of loose earrings and placed one randomly into the gun.

"Aren't you going to sterilize it!?" Mom asked incredulously. The ladies shared a perplexed look before moving closer to Bree, who was sitting restlessly in the chair as her tan faded before my eyes.

"Wait, wait!" Mom shouted, holding her palms out to stop them, "Clean? Sterilize? Alcohol?" They finally understood the obligatory game of charades and soaked the earrings in a bottle cap of vodka.

"I guess that's what you get for two bucks, eh?" I shrugged. We'd paraded into the hostel to show our brand new piercings, unashamed by our pink and swollen ears, to Ammon, who just shook his head and rolled his eyes.

"See what happens when I let you guys loose in the streets!? I'm not surprised that you two would do something stupid, but I didn't think Mom would too!" Bree now sported four new holes in her ears, Mom had the cartilages in both ears pierced, and I had the cartilage in my second ear pierced; Bree'd done the first one for me at home with ice and a needle years ago. So Mom wasn't particularly enjoying the bumpy ride as she was forced to lie on at least one sore ear. (For the edification of any who might not know the finer points of such beauty routines, the healing process of a cartilage piercing is a good deal more painful than those done in the fleshy part of the ear lobe.)

A man who had been sitting in the bus stairwell made his way over to the space we three girls were sharing and slowly, with each bump, slid closer and closer until he was leaning all of his weight on my knees. *Go away. I hate you!* I thought as I subtly tried to kick him off. My whole body was squished, and my legs were completely numb. I had to turn slightly when I adjusted my position to relieve their tingling, thus creating a small space that he used to try to insert himself between me and the other young woman. In an effort to prevent the unknown, stocky man from getting any closer, the girl and I instinctively squeezed together. We shared not a word in common. I didn't know if she was Chinese or Mongolian, her age, or even her name, but I freely welcomed her closeness.

As I dozed in and out of consciousness, my chest burned and my limbs ached with the need to get a moment's rest. I felt like my innards were turning grey, like a slab of meat exposed to the sun, and wished a hundred times over that this infernal ride would end. My head was swimming and my throat strained to keep the hot lava deep in my belly from forcing its way up. Naturally, the man was just as tired as I, and he continued to lean and push, despite my new female companion occasionally snapping strident complaints at him.

She and I clung to each other in that crowded prison the whole night long, my head on her shoulder and my breath on her neck. For that single night, I had a companion, and our shared ordeal made us a team. I felt as if I'd completely lost touch with the world, and I really missed having a friend. It made me think of Terri, and I didn't have the energy to wipe away the tears that trickled down the side of my cheek and into my ear.

I learned the next morning that the pesky man was the second driver, not just some anonymous pervert, and I couldn't help but worry when he took over at the wheel. I kept imagining his heavy eyelids nodding off and his head drooping over the steering wheel as he drove the overloaded bus at typically high speeds.

When we finally arrived, my unnamed companion slipped away without a word and I got busy finding an appropriate place to relieve my nausea. Hanging on to a chain-link fence, I could produce nothing more constructive than a few violent dry heaves. I could feel Mom's presence near me. Her face first displayed real concern, but she pantomimed the silly morning sickness joke once I'd assured her that I was alright. Ribbing me about being pregnant was by now a running family gag, though I did not find it all that funny. Given my growing boobs, the increasing frequency of the nausea that no one else experienced, and the fact that I'd missed my period, even I sometimes wondered. But unless I was the next Virgin Mary or had missed a major lesson in sex education, I knew I could not be with child. The symptoms I shared with many pregnant women were relatively easy to explain: missing my period was a clear sign of built-up stress and the drastic change in my environment; my boobs were just growing (finally!) from the natural development phase I was going through; hunger was often associated with growth spurts; and intermittent nausea can be explained by any first-time traveler.

I waved Mom's inquisitive look off. *But I do feel awful!* I thought, as a little water dripped from my mouth. My backpack balanced me as I leaned forward to heave again, but it was no use. There was nothing in my stomach.

The place we were dumped was nothing but a dull, square cement building. There appeared to be no food or lodging, only dust and more dust and some stern-looking officials with machine guns. I remembered my fervor to partner up with Mom for the journey and began questioning whether I actually felt safer with her when we arrived at our destination before Ammon and Bree. I realized how completely lost we were, and knew that Ammon would at least have known where we were. It felt strange to feel that way. Up to that point, I'd pretty much always believed my mother could right all wrongs.

I'd seen my siblings at a couple of the stops during the night, but when we arrived at five-thirty in the morning, they were nowhere to be found. The last time we'd crossed paths they were ahead of us, so it didn't make sense for them not to be here. *What if we aren't in the right place? What if they crashed? What if we never find them again? Where will we go? Where will we sleep?*

After a nerve-wracking, two-hour wait, they finally came trudging in. I can't express the relief I felt, but there was no time to celebrate. After briefly explaining the time it had taken the driver of the other bus to fix a flat tire, Ammon raced off with us in tow to figure out the next leg of the trip, as we had still not actually reached the border.

It didn't matter that we hadn't slept all night; it didn't matter that I was sick; it wouldn't have mattered if I were suffering epileptic seizures – we had to keep going. I thought back to the countless times I'd stayed home "sick" from elementary school. Then, I was mostly faking to give myself time to catch up on a project to avoid losing marks for being late, which Mom knew all too well, but here there was no way to cheat or fake it. We couldn't just stop at the halfway point, as I'd learned when climbing the hellish stairs at Emei Shan.

Bree and Ammon had lucked out and gotten beds the night before, so they weren't nearly as exhausted as Mom and me. It was particularly painful to hear that there were even spare, unused beds on their bus. They had also met a really friendly Mongolian woman, Khongorzul, who was traveling with her daughter, so their experience of the trip was drastically different than ours. Bree promptly introduced us. "This is Khongorzul, the lady we met on the bus. She's great! She gave us cookies and she speaks English!" Khongorzul appeared to be an affluent, educated woman with an oval-shaped face and a tall, slender body, though I suppose five-feet-six wouldn't normally be considered tall. The twelve-year-old daughter had the same charismatic, intelligent air as her mother.

Strict personnel denied our request to walk the few kilometres to the next border post, to my great relief, and luckily, Khongorzul agreed to share the cost of hiring transportation to cross the border. She raced off with us to find a driver, insisting that he had to be Mongolian. Period. No discussion. There was no way to deter her from this fixation. "Chinese, they are crazy drivers. Not safe!" she kept saying as we ran alongside her, weaving in and out between the waiting jeeps in order to determine their heritage. All the while, she continued to tell us what heathens the Chinese are. The only reason she was in China at all, she vehemently added, was because she, coincidentally, was applying for a Canadian visa at the closest consulate, which happened to be in Beijing. Had there been any other way, I'm sure she'd have traveled twice that distance to avoid stepping foot in China. To her dismay, she had been refused a visa and, worst of all, this denial would prevent her from applying again.

After talking to a few Chinese drivers, she proclaimed, "I don't like those guys. I don't trust them. Don't go with them or they'll rip you off. They are dishonest." Ammon agreed, though his dislike was directed at taxis in general. In his mind, cab drivers belong to a race of their own.

Ammon had warned us of the hatred the Mongols felt for the Chinese, but I was surprised that it was so blatant. He had shown us on the map how Mongolia was sandwiched between China in the south and Russia in the north when he explained some of their historic enmity.

"Mongolia was originally a province of China. During the collapse of the Qing dynasty in 1911, just before World War 1, they declared their independence, but it took until 1945 to gain international recognition. Because they were helped by Russia, their greatest ally, they converted to the Cyrillic alphabet, were the second country to adopt communism, and Russia became a principal trade partner."

After a few minutes of checking jeep after jeep, Khongorzul finally found a driver she approved of. "He is from my country. He's a very good man." Our well-chosen driver then bustled around to make space for the eleven passengers and the luggage he intended to transport across the border. He plucked his cardboard box of fresh fruit out from inside the jeep and opened the hood to somehow fit the fruit into the engine compartment.

"Now, we can go," Khongorzul translated as he signalled us in through the side door. The tiny five-seater, war-torn Russian jeep was already occupied by five sweaty strangers. Three members of our group took up the space where the fruit had been. Once the rest of us had squeezed in, we headed down the bumpy road towards immigration, with arms and heads protruding from every window.

Ammon and Bree were bursting with excitement, a feeling I did not share. I can't say that I was particularly thrilled about going to Mongolia. They had germinated a plan to spend some time there even before the big family-trip concept came up. When Ammon returned from his latest trip to Southeast Asia, he'd planted the seed in Bree's head, showing her where Mongolia was on the world map that covered an entire wall in our house. It wasn't long before they started "putting it in the air" that they'd like to spend an entire month volunteering on a Mongolian horse ranch together. As I looked back on those conversations, I figured it was probably their plans that got Mom subconsciously dreaming of travel and moving it to the forefront of her brain. I remember Bree insisting to Ammon, in her inimitable, know-it-all way, "I'm coming on your next trip. Just you watch!" I also remember feeling very grateful at the time that I would be at home and wouldn't have to live without a shower in the middle of nowhere for weeks on end, and that I wouldn't have to leave the comfort of home – ever. Little did I know. I laughed cynically at the memory. Inevitably, Mongolia had somehow become a major destination for our trip. *Who dreams of visiting the wilds of Outer Mongolia, for goodness sake? It's probably Bree's fault that we're here!*

There being no direct flights to Mongolia from North America, we started in China, the closest place to it. The whole idea just scared me silly. The stories I'd heard of Mongolia were even worse than what I'd heard about China, and they'd come from travelers who'd been there. I knew the worst part was going to be the food.

But here we were, and part of me could not believe that I was waiting in line in a little immigration building in the desert to get into a country I already hated. I was so tired I could hardly fill out the simplest form – surname, date of birth, nationality, visa validity, expiration date. I squinted in an effort to focus properly, but it all seemed like way too much to ask of me. *Why do they even care?* I wondered as I scribbled in what would have to pass for answers.

Bree was literally dancing by my side as we made our way to the train station once we finally officially got into the country. *I didn't wish for this,* I thought, trying to understand how I ended up in this remote country on the other side of the world. *Doesn't fate know any better? I hadn't wanted to travel in the first place, but I most certainly wanted nothing to do with this part of the plan.* Noticing the steam coming out my ears, Ammon barked, "What's your bloody problem!?"

"Look where those idiots stamped my passport!!" I said, waving it at him angrily and glaring in a way that normally would have provoked a tongue lashing, but this time he responded by laughing.

"Hah! I told you you'd start to get into it!" He ignored my dismay and was pleased, instead, by my concern about my passport's appearance. In his mind, it was a sure indication that a seasoned traveler was blossoming within me.

"I am not! It was just so pretty and they ruined it! Why would they want to ruin their own visa?"

"Who cares what it looks like? That's two fewer stamps I needed to fill my passport!" Ammon said, walking faster and leaving me smoldering in the dust behind him. At that point, I only had a grand total of four visas in my passport and about twice that in stamps, but it was starting to feel full. Though I'd never tell Ammon, I'd secretly memorized the shape, text, colour, and placement of every one of them.

The six of us finally made it through the heat and the dust to the deserted train station, only to spend an exhausting six hours waiting for an overnight train that was supposed to leave at seven o'clock in the evening. Aside from picking up a few necessities for the trip from a tiny shop, mainly water and cookies, we spent hours playing a few dozen more rounds of our ongoing card game, with Ammon and I taking turns being in first place.

When we finally heard the train rumble into its sandy port, we hurriedly swung our packs on our backs and ran outside. Assigned to the very last car on the train, we were unable to board from the concrete platform which wasn't long enough to accommodate the train's length. From ground level, the metal step and the handlebars were a long reach, but team work made it possible. With whistles urgently blowing for the last call and my blood rushing in my veins, Bree pushed my backpack from behind as I grasped Ammon's extended hand and clambered in. Instantaneously turning around, I reached for Bree's outstretched hand and tugged her in with only seconds to spare.

It seemed that the moment we crossed the invisible boundary line and left China's gorgeous green rice fields behind, the land before us was transformed into a lifeless desert. We found the stark demarcation completely bizarre. "It's almost as if the earth knew it wasn't China anymore," Mom said, looking out the window.

"Whoever made the toilets knew, too," Ammon said. "I wouldn't call them award winners, exactly, but they're definitely an improvement. The doors actually lock, and they're not nearly as filthy."

The little men wearing straw cone hats had vanished. There wasn't a soul in sight for miles. Every time I glanced up from *Gone with the Wind,* I expected to see the lush green fields and terraces we were always treated to on our train rides. Unsure whether I missed the fertile vegetation more than I was now captivated by these wastelands dotted with camels, I was surprised to catch myself smiling, even laughing, as I reminisced about my experiences in my very first foreign country.

I couldn't believe all the things we'd done in the seven weeks we'd spent there. It seemed that months had passed since I was nearly squashed running across ten lanes of traffic among the City of Chengdu's ten million people, yet I could still feel the buzz of the big cities in my ears. If I had ever, by any stretch of the imagination, independently chosen to visit China, I would've visited only the most advertised and "safest" places. But it was the beautiful landscape and sweet authenticity of the local people in the small villages and in their markets that provided our richest experiences. The remote nooks and crannies that at first seemed to be the most intimidating actually turned out to be the most amazing.

It seemed like forever since we'd landed in Hong Kong. Perhaps the impact was due to being thrown into it all so suddenly and a bit harshly. I'd certainly gotten to know the squatties. I'd literally faced the toilets, at one point thrusting my head into one, sick as a dog. I'd also seen a bum washing his bum in a puddle at the edge of a busy highway. The biggest eye-opener, though, was watching a young mother clutch her baby to her breast while lying on a curb, scooping soggy rice from a trash can into her mouth. *That picture will probably stick with me for a while,* I thought. Luckily there was always so much going on that I rarely had time to dwell on any one image.

Lowering my heavy book to look out the train window, I was struck mostly by the scarcity of towns and people. Aside from a few lost wanderers on foot or atop child-sized horses, we were alone in the desert. Predictably, I began to worry. *What if we broke down? How would we survive? How much water is on this train? There isn't a speck of shade anywhere. How long would our food supply last if we got stranded here? How long would it be before we'd have to start cutting throats to get a share of noodles?* Following close behind the anxiety, though, I began to feel some excitement welling up inside me. I could see that it was a perfect place for the horseback riding I'd been promised. We occasionally saw herds of what we thought must be wild horses, given the absence of any farms, barns, or even fences.

Every so often, an isolated, circular white tent would appear like a buoy bobbing in the vastness of the sea. These small, round homes usually sat alone in open fields. Sometimes there were pairs or even groups of them. I was shocked when Ammon explained that those white tents were the most common form of housing outside of the capital city.

"You're kidding! They LIVE there?!" I ogled a few through the glass.

"Yes, and 'there' is called a ger," he told us.

"Grrrr!" Bree growled, devising her own, more creative, version of the word.

"And about a third of the entire population of this country lives that way."

"How do they get food, or water, or clothes, or anything?!" I asked.

"Well, that's part of what you'll learn while we're here," Ammon told me. "Something you should know is that twenty percent of the people live on less than a dollar and twenty-five cents day."

"Whoa!" Bree couldn't quite comprehend how they could do that. Neither could I, of course, but I thought about different parts of their lives as I peered out through a minor sandstorm to where a flock of goats were tended by young boys who looked to be about nine or ten years old. *Do they even go to school? Where do they get their food from? How do they live out here?! How do they find people to date?* And then a final, anxious thought. *Where will I ever find a date?! I'm gonna be a worn-out, if well-traveled, spinster before I ever have a man in my life!*

The thing that impressed me the most, though, was seeing the train randomly stop to unload passengers who'd then just walk off into the never-ending distance

I must've passed out as soon as the fiery sun sank into the hazy horizon because, before I knew it, I heard everyone waking around me. People passed me to line up for the bathroom and freshen up for the new day just before we got to Ulaanbaatar, Mongolia's capital. We exchanged warm hugs with Khongorzul and her daughter as we said our farewells.

"You will have a great time. You will love my people. If you are again in U.B. and need my help in any way, this is my number." And with that, she was gone.

Arriving again without reservations or plans, I was pleased to see a girl on the platform promoting a guest house. The benefit of going with her was the free ride to the hostel – just what I needed after two straight days of travelling. The first thing I noticed during the ride was that the steering wheel was on the right-hand side of the car. Though I'd seen this in Hong Kong, it was the fact that they did not drive on the left side of the road like they did in Hong Kong that really threw me. I eventually noticed that roughly half of the steering wheels were positioned on the left, but regardless of its location, everyone luckily drove on the same side of the road.

The luxury SUV we rode in from the station did not extend to the cheaply priced hostel's quality. The dorm we were presented with was dark and dank, and hosted ten cramped bunk beds that would accommodate twenty guests. I was ready to turn around and walk right back out when we saw it, but not Ammon.

"You know what? I like it," he said, surprisingly.

"You WHAT?!" I asked, watching him swing his pack off to claim a bed.

"I like it," he repeated before turning on his heels to leave. "Now drop your bags. We're going out. We've got to go figure out what we're doing next."

"Oh my heck!" I exclaimed, but we all left our bags on top or underneath our chosen bed. I felt tons lighter when I finally got to drop that load. When you are attached to something that heavy for so long, it slowly becomes a part of you, and dropping it feels a bit like when you get off a horse and suddenly feel much shorter.

We got caught in a heavy downpour that filled potholes and formed muddy rivers in the streets of Ulaanbaatar as we searched for a place offering the cheapest tours. A quiet bell dinged four times, once for each of us, when we passed through a little wooden door and climbed the stairs to Narran's Guest House. The business was run from a small apartment, so Bree and I waited in the stairwell while Mom and Ammon booked a twelve-day tour that would begin the following morning. We were both sopping wet and began wringing the rainwater out of our long, braided hair.

The door through which Mom and Ammon had disappeared was closed, but the open door opposite looked like a kitchen. Bree and I were just chatting when I began to notice her leaning awkwardly to get a better look inside the open door.

"Stop it!" I finally said as I looked over my shoulder to see what was so interesting. "What on earth?"

"Shhh, shhh! He might hear you."

"You've gotta be kidding me," I said, rolling my eyes when I saw the topless guy rummaging through the refrigerator to get a bite to eat. His skin was as smooth and perfect as a baby's. He looked no older than twelve, but I figured he was probably in his mid-twenties.

"Don't you think he's cute?!" she asked, not taking her eyes off the slender guy's lean, mocha-coloured figure. "His aviators are so sexy, like he's from *Top Gun*," she whispered, leaning over me to get a better look.

Pushing her away and speaking in a normal voice, I asked, "Who wears sunglasses indoors?"

"But they are SO sexy!!!" she insisted.

"Ugh," I groaned, annoyed. I stood up and slammed the door shut.

Her eyes nearly popped out of her head. "Oh my gosh, Savannah! He was getting up. You just slammed the door in his face." I turned warily when I heard the door slowly creaking open. He stuck his head cautiously through the crack and peered at us.

He pulled his sunglasses up and with a charming smile asked, "Are you two fighting?" Bree was too weak in the knees to answer, so he carried on. "My name's Baagii," he said, pleasant as could be.

"Rhymes with doggy?" I asked.

"Yes, exactly!" he laughed, taking no offence.

"So, what are you doing here?" Bree asked, striking up a conversation.

"I work here," he said with a cheeky smile. "I help with the tours." *That's just great! That's all the encouragement Bree needs!* From the instant she heard he was an employee, she couldn't shut up about him. She talked about him at the hostel, in the big covered market when we bought food, and even at the bank when Mom became a millionaire. Okay, only a togrog millionaire, but the thick stack of new currency made Mom giddy nonetheless, but all Bree could do was say, "Baagii's worth a million togrog," and giggle childishly at her own cliché.

She paced like an idiot the following morning, hoping against hope that he would be there. The vehicles arrived late, something we'd rarely experienced in China. One Russian van pulled over at the roundabout where we waited, followed closely by a jeep similar to the one we'd driven across the border in. I held my breath as the grey van's side door slid open and Baagii emerged from the shadows, his aviator glasses catching the sunlight first.

"Oh, here we go," I muttered.

Strutting out in ripped jeans and a tight white tank top, Baagii offered his hand to Ammon, who happily announced, "Meet our new guide."

Anything Goes
30

"What was his name again?" Ammon shouted over the engine as he nodded towards the driver. "Has anyone talked to him yet?"

"I'm not sure," I shrugged. I hadn't heard him speak even once. The man behind the wheel came across as a man of few words, but always boasted a big smile. He wasn't bad looking, either.

"His name's Bimbo!" Bree chimed in.

"Breanna!" Mom snapped.

"Wait, Mom, I actually think it was something kinda like that," Ammon said. "Go ask him," he finished, pushing me forward. Climbing over the bench and sitting on the hump between the driver and front passenger seats, I felt the heat of the engine beneath me as I asked him his name. Surprised by the question, he took his eyes completely off the road to face me. *Don't worry about the driving,* I thought sarcastically, but thankfully, there was actually nothing he could hit. I was quite sure he didn't speak English, but he could tell us his name, and it was Bimba. He put out his hand to shake mine. *Well, he's learned at least one of our customs,* I thought.

"Bimba?" I confirmed with a tilt of my head. He nodded and flashed another big smile. His eyes were like soft chocolate Hershey's Kisses.

"Bimba." I enjoyed tasting the word on my tongue.

He pointed to himself, gently tapping his chest with his index finger and again announced, "Bimba!" A moment of silence passed between us before we both laughed out loud. I held out a candy, one of many we'd brought from the capital. Using his knees to drive, he took it and began fumbling and tugging at the corners of the wrapper with his huge hands, his head cocked like a curious bird as he glanced at me, and then back at it. Before his frustration led to the candy being launched out the window, I reached out to help. Opening it gently with my teeth, I handed it to him unwrapped this time.

Jumping onto the backseat bench, I told them, "It's Bimba."

"Isn't that, like, the name of the warthog in Lion King?" Ammon asked.

"PUMBA!?" Bree said, shocked that he's got it wrong.

"No, no. Imba, Bimba, something," he continued, waving his hand vaguely.

"You mean *Simba*," I suggested. Bree was dumbstruck by the fact that Ammon wasn't up on his Lion King character names.

"Yah! You know what I mean, dork," Ammon played it cool. As I nestled back in my seat, I noted again that the woven fabric was spewing dust everywhere. As usual, all the windows were open to catch the breeze. The wind was warm to the touch, but the movement of the air did cool us somewhat.

We travelled across a really remote section, surrounded by nothing. No pollution, or buildings, or people, or power lines. Not a single telephone pole in sight, not even a road! Nothing but beauty, oddly enough. *Ulaanbaatar* had been replaced by open fields and rolling hills very suddenly, vanishing as quickly as it had risen up out of the dust. I was relieved that the northern part of the country wasn't exactly the same as the desert steppes we'd seen in the south.

Maybe it isn't an African Safari with warthogs and lions, but Mongolia sure has its share of semi-wild beasts running around, I reflected, but then I uttered my next thought rather a little louder than I'd intended. "Knowing these guys, they will probably end up dragging me across Africa!"

"Oh, that would be fun. Can't we go there?" Mom said, looking to Ammon.

"Just let me get us to India first," Ammon said, not for the first time.

"I should really learn to shut my mouth sometimes!" I said, annoyed at the prospect of adding yet another destination to our already lengthy itinerary.

Tiny flowers, like the offspring of the sun painted over the shallow hills, displayed brilliant oranges, yellows, and reds across endless stretches of endless fields. Infinite puffs of clouds floated like bubbling cotton, and it was as clear as the horizon why Mongolia is referred to as "the land of the big blue sky." There was almost nothing distracting one's eyes from its massive splendour.

From the moment we first stepped into our old Russian van and joined the small convoy, I knew we'd be in for an exciting two weeks. A Scottish/English couple named Tom and Sarah, a single Dutch woman, Noortje, and their interpreter, Baagii, drove along beside us in a separate jeep. The moment we met Noortje, she had immediately set the record straight, saying, "I am from the Netherlands; Holland is not a country but only a region of the Netherlands." I'd heard of neither the Netherlands nor Holland, and couldn't have found either of them on a map to save my life, but for whatever reason, she wanted to make that very clear to us. We also thought it a bit odd that Tom and Sarah had chosen to travel through Mongolia, given that they were vegetarians.

"I mean, why would they visit a country where the staple food is mutton?" Ammon had wondered after our first group lunch. Because mutton formed such a large part of the country's traditional cuisine, all the locals could manage to offer them in its place was thin slices of raw carrot and plain rice. Not eating mutton in Mongolia is roughly equivalent to reading a book without turning the pages. At the end of our two weeks together, we were impressed that Sarah remained a meat virgin, though Tom had given it up and, in desperation, eaten the mutton we were served so often.

Many hours later, just as we were beginning to wonder when we'd ever get a break from the constant bumping, we started to slow down. Three men sat crossed-legged in the open grasslands just ahead. One stood and raised an open palm to signal us to stop as we approached. We saw the familiar red, octagon-shaped stop sign displaying not so familiar Cyrillic symbols at the corner of two intersecting dirt tracks that created the only crossroads we had seen in over six hours. The other two men scrambled up from the ground, shook off the dust from their clothes, and presented themselves in a most professional, serious manner. They made a few stern gestures and barked commands at Bimba.

"What`s happening?" I asked from my window to Baagii who'd jumped out of his jeep.

"He is police," he said, dropping his aviator sunglasses into place.

"Seriously?" Bree said, scuttling up from the back seat to look at him.

"Of course," Baagii laughed. I was sure he was checking Bree out thoroughly behind his shades, and I did the same with these so-called cops. The first man's military cap tilted to one side of his head was the only sign of officialdom we saw; he was otherwise dressed in very plain clothing. He maintained a very serious stance, but not with a "know-it-all," power-trip kind of attitude. Rather, he looked as if he were merely playing a role. He stepped to the side and directed both drivers to pull over. The other two cops acted as if they were rookie football players who had finally been called off the bench to play in their very first game.

Who would think to set up a checkpoint miles and miles from any form of life, out in the middle of nowhere? Surely, they could only expect a dozen or so cars in an eight-hour shift, and that's assuming they even have shifts!

"What is he doing?" I asked Baagii, who was walking alongside our van.

"They ask him why he stops in the middle of the road and tell him he must pull over or he'll block the traffic." The first cop's attempt to prevent us from blocking the completely non-existent traffic was so ludicrous that it did nothing to clear up my confusion, but he seemed very proud of himself as he giggled and slapped Bimba on the back the moment he stepped out of the van. Baagii laughed right along with him, sporting a big, toothy grin. I could only shake my head. *Maybe the reason they're so anxious to make a kafuffle is to distract themselves from sheer boredom. Who assigns these guys?* I wondered. *Like actually, really, who is the person in charge? And where is the police station?* Everything was one big mystery, even with a translator along.

Once they'd all shared a good laugh, one of the officials walked over to their little pink-tarped shelter and came back with a hot pot of tea. The two drivers, the three policemen, and Baagii sat together in the dry grass to have a little chat, with not so much as a mat to sit on. I tried to imagine what they might talk about. *"So how is Billy Bob, and that guy who had that ugly goat? Oh man, and remember that kid who kept falling off his horse? Like, who does that?"* After their short tea break, we continued our journey, the police not having accomplished much of anything that I could see.

But maybe they were just being friendly. Everyone in Mongolia seemed to approach one another like long-lost friends pleased to have the chance to catch up. That was the norm when driving. Everybody waved to oncoming vehicles. They'd often stop to say hello and have a quick chat in the middle of the road before carrying on. Perhaps because they are so few in number, they really stick together and look out for one another, almost like family.

Faint dirt trails often branched off into several forks veering off into the distance, making it nearly impossible to navigate. It was now obvious why Ammon had broken down and paid for a guided tour, something that puzzled me before we started off across Northern Mongolia. There couldn't have been another explanation for spending our cash on a tour, although a couple of young, carefree drivers and torn up Russian 4x4s were a far cry from the GGTs (Grandma Glayde Tours) our grandmother took regularly. We had coined that nickname to describe the kind of tours where old folks pour out of their big, air-conditioned buses, their overly large, protective hats and glasses both secured by strings around their necks. A GGT could actually be a somewhat bearable way to travel, despite Ammon's insistence that they were mere vacations and not genuine travel. "Travel is not *meant* to be comfortable!" he'd say, and he'd made that crystal clear throughout our journey thus far.

With no GPS, maps, or road signs, it was a wonder our drivers had any idea at all where they were going. As far as I could tell, a local transport system did not exist. Even in the city, taxi drivers were just local citizens moonlighting to make a few extra bucks. Mongolian taxis could be anything from small Toyotas driven by clean-shaven men to a mother driving a station wagon, her children in tow. A bus stop in the countryside seemed a more than slightly farfetched notion. But then I remembered those local families departing from the train, burdened by sacks and taking off on foot into the emptiness. I wondered where they went. *How can they tell that a certain bump or rock is going to lead them somewhere that was still miles away? Had they mastered the art of teleporting, perhaps?* We spotted the occasional group of children along the way, playing in the fields with a sibling or two and often accompanied by a herd of goats. The eldest of these young shepherds seemed to be around ten years of age, and they wielded little sticks to control their family's livestock. We'd wonder every time we saw them how they found their way around and where their homes were? They never seemed troubled or upset, although we could never see *anything* for miles and miles. The children wore familiar-looking pants and t-shirts, and the girls most often had braided hair, wisps of which hung loose in their faces after what appeared to be a day of rough, robust playing. We saw no toys aside from their stacks of rocks, but they all smiled as we passed, their round, sienna faces smudged with dirt. Everyone seemed to be relaxed and carefree.

"Whoa! Maybe they're, like, people who live underground and come up out of the quicksand every once in a while," Bree let her imagination run wild.

"Nice theory," Ammon said. But it seemed Bree's conjecture could almost be true. We'd stopped at a very small sand dune and found a group of children ranging in age from four to thirteen with no animals, cars, bicycles, homes, or parents to be seen. Suddenly the random stop signs in the flat plains didn't seem so random after all. *Perhaps the expected is actually the unexpected in this strange land?*

Whatever the case, the faster and rougher the ride got, the bigger Bimba's smile seemed to become. Every once in a while, he howled with delight, and more and more often, he turned in his seat to check

whether he'd yet managed to splatter his passengers against the ceiling. The thought of this exaggerated cartoon buggy with socks, bras,
and t-shirts spewing out of the creases of the suitcases in the open
trunk made me laugh nervously. Luckily, though, my luggage was in
no way, shape or form a fragile little suitcase; it was a strong, bulky
pack that had yet to see enough wear and tear. *I hope you're having fun!*
I thought, glancing into the back where the rest of the family were
bouncing about, but I was glad my pack was starting to look like a real
traveler at last. It had built up some calluses and a fine coating of dirt.
I felt totally ridiculous meeting people who had flag patches sewn to
bags dirty enough to send germs screaming for the hills. One Belgian
couple we'd met on our three-day cruise down the Yangzi River had
been out for seven months already. *Seven months!?!* Their exploits made
our measly seven *weeks* seem insignificant, and we quickly dubbed
them our idols. *And all I've got is a lame sprinkle of dirt,* I'd think, realizing other backpackers would rightfully consider that pretty pathetic.

My hair was blowing and twisting in the whirlwind that whooshed
past my dry cheeks. Out of nowhere, a cloud of winged bugs appeared, and I had to tuck my head back into the 4x4. The calm air
caressed me as I shut my window and looked wide-eyed at all the
hovering bugs, their little wings flapping steadily against the glass. It
was as if we weren't moving at all.

"So what is Jiminy Cricket anyway? A grasshopper!?" Ammon
teased at one point when the bugs reminded him of one of Bree's
classic misinterpretations.

We continued to fight to stay upright as we rode roughshod
through forested patches lined with rivers and streams, occasionally
coming close to tipping sideways in a river or getting stuck in a crater
of mud. We stopped often to analyze different challenging passages
or to test how deep the rivers' waters were. The 4x4s turned out to
be a real godsend.

We had a few opportunities to slip off into wooded areas to pee
while the men were occupied with their trucks. And while the experts
studied the best way to navigate a river crossing, we washed ourselves
off a bit and cooled the back of our necks to relieve the intense heat.

"I'm so dirty! Do you think they have showers inside those little tents?" I asked.

"You mean, inside a ger? You'll find out tonight!" Ammon said, as he knelt by the river to fill our empty water bottle. The impossibility of getting an affirmative answer came to me the second after I voiced the silly question. *Of course there isn't a shower. How could I be so naïve?!*

When we walked into our very first traditional ger, I half-asked, half-stated, "This is *really* what they live in?" Without warning, the memory of the five-bedroom apartment we'd looked at on our last house hunt came to mind. I remembered how much I'd whined and bitched over the notion of moving into an apartment. I detested Mom for it, insisting I'd rather move out than live with hundreds of people in the same building and possibly even have to share a washing machine. *Disgusting!* I'd thought. *I won't even be able to say "come hang out at my house." What would I say? "Let's go to my apartment?!" Nobody will want to be my friend. Only homeless people live in apartments!* I could remember my feelings about it as if it were yesterday. I still had never lived in an apartment, but when I stepped into that ger, the memory of how skewed my perceptions had been shamed me.

My first visit to a local Mongolian home was a bit shocking. The ger was completely open inside, consisting of just one big, round room that held a sink, a colourful dresser, four metal-framed beds lining the felt walls, and a fireplace/stove in the middle. The roof was supported by reddish-orange poles in the traditional Mongolian style.

"So wait, how *do* they shower, then?" I asked, coming slightly out of my daze. There was no plumbing that we could see, only an up-side-down bottle of water mounted over the sink.

"Probably from the same place where they got the water to fill that sink over there," Mom said, pointing at the hobbit-sized hand basin in the corner. "From a well or something."

"This place looks like a fat teepee!" Bree said, really feeling the change in atmosphere. I sat on one of the simple metal beds placed along the wall and watched the flames in the tiny stove that had been lit before we'd arrived. The skinny, black chimney poked out of a hole in the circular ceiling. I enjoyed feeling its warmth.

"Very good! Strong built houses, but very light. Easy to take apart and rebuild," Baagii told us as he crouched to add more wood to the little black stove. It would get significantly colder as the night wore on.

"How long would it take to assemble one of these gers, then, if they're nomadic and moving all the time?" Mom asked him.

"It only takes one to three hours to build," Baagii told her, turning on his heels to face us after placing the last stick in the smoky fire.

"Wow, that's quick! Can you imagine being able to pack your whole house onto the backs of a few camels?" Mom reminded us about seeing a nomadic family in travel mode a few hours before. They had been transporting their ger on a couple of camels loaded with the orangey-red support poles and the ger's felt cover. Horses, goats, sheep, and a couple of dogs had trailed along behind them.

"So those camels with all that stuff... that was a ger?" Bree asked, finally piecing it together.

"I think it's so cute! I want to take one home," Mom said, excited by the prospect. *Geez, I should've settled for the apartment!*

"Cute? Sure, but our bathrooms were almost as big as this," I said, noting the whole five bits of furniture.

"So you should be grateful!" Mom and Ammon chimed in together. *I hate it when they pull that grateful, hippy-era stuff.* I thought, resisting their forceful tone. *I'll draw my own conclusions, thank you very much!*

That night I lay on my stomach on the colourful woollen rug explaining the day in my journal, even though it was hard to write when there was so much conversation going on around me.

June 28ᵗʰ, 2005, I always started neatly at the top left-hand side with the date. The top right was for the day count – *Day 55*. Only three hundred and ten days left. I wasn't aware of any actual return date, but a year was what I had decided to use for the countdown.

Noortje, the Dutch gal, was a writer, and she also kept a diary. I really admired how neat and precise her writing was.

"What kind of paper is that?" I asked her that night.

"It's just graph paper," she said matter-of-factly.

"Wow." I leaned over to Mom lying on her bed and said, "I need some of that." Graph paper was much better suited to my particularly tiny handwriting. I hated how my writing looked on paper with regularly sized spacing.

Earlier that day we had stopped for lunch in a town which was like a very large camp of round gers, some surrounded by simple wooden fences. The town that stood out most in my mind was called "Moron." I made sure to note that in my journal, along with Bree's immediate reaction to its moniker.

"So this is where all the mongoloids and morons came from!?" she'd exclaimed.

"Breanna!" Mom scolded.

"I don't get it, though," I'd been sincerely confused, "Why are those words used as insults when the people here are so nice?!" *I'll think twice before I use those words again, that's for sure!*

After I wrote *Visited:* at the top of the page between the date and the day count, I asked Ammon, "What was the name of this place again?" We were staying just outside the grounds of an old Buddhist monastery that was once one of the three most important in Mongolia. The monastery was surrounded by a few gers, some for the locals living there and some for visitors. Baagii explained that Buddhism was brought to Mongolia by the Chinese when they ruled the country.

"Amarbayasgalant Khild," Ammon answered very slowly, so as not to leave any letters out.

"Wow! That's so long?! Why would they need such a long name?" Bree asked. Given how small the villages we'd passed through were, they'd sure had long and important sounding names.

"I bet it's the first letter of everyone's name in the village starting from oldest to youngest." I suggested. Baagii laughed at this idea.

"Can you spell it for me?" I asked, hoping to record it before another conversational tangent started, but it was already too late.

"What kind of grand name is amambbdjakilt anyway?!" Bree jumped in, to my dismay.

"Amarbayasgalant Khild," Ammon repeated.

"Like I said, amammaaKILT. Oh, and I want to go to Scotland and see the men in kilts!" she continued.

"What kind of random---?!" I blurted.

"Yah, yah. That won't be for a while!" Ammon said, already stressed enough by the task of negotiating our passage through the next country on our itinerary.

"Yah! Why don't we go to Europe?" I wanted to visit all the blue-eyed hotties I imagined might be waiting for me there.

"Oh man! There's a lot more to it than just 'let's go to Europe'. It's not like you can just walk over there, you know. There is a LOT of planning involved!"

"Hey, yah. That would be fun!" Mom said. "But I thought we were going to Africa!"

"Nooo!" I objected.

"Why don't we all just enjoy where we are for now?" Ammon fussed.

"I am. It's great! I just want to see *everything* now," Mom exclaimed, reminding me of a deer that had just spotted the first tips of green grass sprouting up after a long white winter. Ammon cupped his forehead in his hand and shook his head ruefully.

"Aye, yie, yie! You guys are nuts," he groaned.

"You mean *those* guys. I'm the only normal one here," I said defensively.

"Could we go overland to Egypt?" Bree asked.

"Egypt? EGYPT?! How does Egypt even come in to this? Do you realize that would involve places like Iran, Syria, Afghanistan---" he tried to explain before I cut him off.

"Whoa! Now *that* would be something worth talking about," I said, surprising even myself.

"I wonder what kind of things we'd see there. What would the culture be like? What kind of architecture do they have?" Mom pondered those and other possibilities.

"Let's just get to where we're going first," Ammon said again, but started pulling his map out nonetheless and forcing my journal to the side.

"Sky would completely kill us!" I said.

We hovered around the tiny world map at the front of his guidebook by candlelight that flickered on our faces as we came up with all sorts of wild ideas and dreams, none of which had originally been my dreams.

With my journal lying neglected beside me, I continued to reflect upon the day. I stretched out as best I could on my short bed. So much had happened in the last twenty-four hours that I'd become exhausted to the point of restlessness, like when you lose your appetite after being hungry for too long.

The monastery's incense and candles had been overpowering, but as with most of the monasteries we'd visited, I'd rather liked it. In a strange sense, it had made me feel somewhat nostalgic for the Chinese monasteries we'd stayed in. It was as though the thick, smoky air was filled with spirits that surrounded me and I was inhaling them, welcoming them in one by one. I just hoped they were good spirits.

With the day's sights and smells still vividly real, thoughts poured in a mile a minute. I thought about whether the monastery had produced the smoky candles in our ger. *Did they get them from China like most of the world probably does? Or does their deep-seated dislike for each other run deep enough to prevent that kind of trade?* I wondered who brought them all the way from the capital. *Was there some nomadic candle maker who carried his wax on camels and set out on voyages like the uncomfortable, ten-hour trek we'd just made to deliver his supplies? Then again, maybe the monastery makes its own candles. How would you do that? Is it like bees' wax? What the heck, where does wax come from, anyway? Do they even have bees here? They must,* I concluded. *They have humongous fields of wild flowers. But does that mean there HAVE to be bees if there are flowers?*

On and on my mind wandered until I eventually passed out from sheer exhaustion. I always found it both unnerving and fascinating that I could never remember the very last thought I had before falling asleep. *At what moment did sleep happen? Did those thoughts pass through into my sleep and become dreams? Or was I awake the whole time in a different universe?* This was not the kind of thing this trip was likely to teach me, but I sure was learning about a whole lot of other mind-boggling stuff.

Where Nomads Roam
31

*B*ree spent the next few days walking with a slightly different tilt than usual and just a bit too much "wiggle wobble" for my liking. *That hair flinging has got to stop, and that eye twitching, too! Do all cultures find winking attractive?* While we played cards in the evenings, Bree would often take herself off to a corner and pluck her eyebrows, despite the dim lighting. *I wonder why?* I'd think sarcastically. Undoubtedly, she was as frustrated by my scowls as I was by her not-so-subtle flirting.

We hadn't seen Baagii much the first day, which was fine by me. We'd decided on the second day that it was only fair for us to pay half the price for Baagii's service so we could more legitimately pick his brain, much to Ammon's satisfaction. This also meant that he would travel with us during the day, because our van was bigger. This put him and Bree in even closer proximity, and drove me even crazier. Bree was thrilled with the new arrangement, and I could tell she was expecting more than just information for the extra cost. There was no escaping the two of them as they were tossed around in the back giggling. At the moment, she was hanging from her waist out the window, licking the air with uncontrolled excitement like a full-cheeked, howling dog.

"Are you SURE they didn't film *Lord of the Rings* here?!" she shouted up to Ammon, momentarily pulling her head in from the window.

"Definitely not! It was New Zealand," he responded immediately. He would know, too, as it is his favourite movie of all time. Maybe not, I thought, but as our vehicles chased each other up and over the hillsides in a kind of dance, I did feel a bit like I was in an adventure film. The military jeep, camouflaged and worn, raced alongside us in the meadows, stirring up dust in a long, trailing parachute.

Mother Nature created a cloud masterpiece in the sky, the biggest easel known to man; God used whipped cream instead of paint to show just how happy He was. Despite the burn I could see developing from suspending my arms through the open window to take photos, I could not put our little Nikon down. There was nothing to mar the landscape in all directions and for miles after that, and then a herd of wild horses would emerge, larger than I ever dreamt was possible. They roamed free and had all the space horses were born to explore. This land was truly a horse's paradise.

"Holy COW! I can't believe how many there are!" Bree shouted from the back.

"This isn't cows. That is horse!" Baagii corrected her exclamation.

"Yah, I know, but it really does look like cattle," she shouted again over the many other competing sounds. It was always loud, with the rustling wind fighting the noise of the engine for supremacy.

"They're beautiful," Mom said. Lavish and vibrant, they ran in herds across the grassland or clustered by small lakes, completely free of human interference. The colts played carelessly but always stayed close to their mothers for protection. When they ran, their long manes whipped in the wind and their elegant tails flapped in their wake. It was hard to tell if they were running with or from us.

The natural beauty of Mongolia acted like a super drug to calm my typical string of worries. *What if we break down way out here? My gosh, we'd never be saved. How on earth would we find a gas station?* The sun was suspended before me like a hypnotist's pendant, and my concerns faded away, replaced by pure awe. With the wild horses galloping in the distance, it was easy to fantasize that, in the case of a breakdown; I could just leap onto one of those elegant beasts and ride to safety.

I closed my eyes and imagined I was flying atop a horse that had the wings of an angel, as white and delicate as powdered sugar. We'd chase our shadow over the rolling hills and across this vast land. The horse's giant, outstretched wings would glisten at my sides like the trickling streams we'd soar over.

"How many must there be?" Bree's voice brought me back to the present reality.

"In that herd? At least a hundred," Mom said.

"Horses are the pride of Mongolia, and apparently there are a hundred different ways to say horse in Mongolian," Ammon said, pleased to have Baagii nearby to confirm his statement.

"Yes! Every man has ten horses. They are one with their horses. Some have three hundred," Baagii added. Mongolia is one of the last places on earth where wild horses exist, but I knew the horses we saw were not truly wild. Though Mongolian herds roamed freely without saddles and grazed without fences, I knew that somehow, somewhere out there, someone owned them.

Even the horses seemed to know they were special and loved. Occasionally, a single cement trough used by shepherds tending to their thirsty flocks appeared in the midst of the expansive landscape. At one watering hole where we'd stopped to help haul water using the rope and bucket attached to the heavy cement lid covering the fresh, cool water source, I witnessed a telling demonstration that horses were at the top of the livestock pyramid. Hundreds of sheep and goats were crowded around this trough before the water was even poured, the goats ramming each other with their horns as they fought for position. As if it were simply the natural order of things here, all the animals, even the larger camels, gave up their places to the half-a-dozen short, husky horses when they came butting in late for their drink. The horses just appeared to control the mob.

Baagii then told us a long-held Mongolian saying: "The more livestock, the better your lifestyle will be." *I can't imagine how that's possible. Ten goats won't give you a flushing toilet or make electricity suddenly appear. But at least they can be proud of their goats, so I guess they're not that different from me,* I thought as I quickly related travelers' competitions and my pride in the worn appearance of my big backpack to the pride they took from owning livestock. *Except, at least they have a home. I don't even have one of those funny little tents. They've got all that PLUS a really big backyard!*

I knew we had some money in the bank, but in our world, that was worth nothing without a house and a car. *How will we ever fit back into society?* We certainly didn't have enough to buy a house, so now I'm the equivalent of a nomadic Mongolian, but with no horse. I felt I could relate to how they moved from place to place. "Home is where the backpack is," was Mom's saying, or maybe it was Ammon's. *If only these friendly folk knew that when I spent a night in their home, it was literally my home, too.*

As we stopped beside a white ger, the guard dogs rushed over to inspect us. Baagii jumped out of the van shouting "nokhoi khor! nokhoi khor!" This common greeting translates roughly to "hold the dogs."

"Directions again?" I half asked, half joked as we made another of many quick stops to make sure we were still generally headed in the right direction.

"Could you blame them?" Mom said, watching from the back window as Baagii was greeted warmly.

When he returned, Baagii asked, "Do you want to try our local drink *airag?*" holding out a plastic bottle full of white liquid. "It's mare's milk."

"*Horse* milk?" Mom asked curiously.

"Yah, I do! That sounds cool!" Ammon was always happy to sample new and bizarre foods.

"Did it come straight out of that horse!?" Bree asked pointing to a beige mare nearby with a suckling colt. I couldn't tell if she asked in an intrigued or disgusted way. Baagii only smiled and laughed. "OOOooh, that is sour! Why is it so sour?!" Bree cringed after pressing the bottle to her lips.

"It's fermented," Mom said, her mouth twisting, too, when she tried it.

"What does that mean?" Bree said, tilting her head back for a second try.

"It's like wine. As it rots, it changes to alcohol," she explained. Bree grasped her throat as if she'd been poisoned when she heard that. I giggled as I watched her almost spit it out onto the seat in front of her and down Bimba's neck. Bree had drunk endless amounts of the green tea we were served in China before we told her it was caffeinated. She had choked then, too, and sworn not to drink any more of the evil beverage. Of course, with the teapot going around our table at every meal, her resolve didn't last long, and she often lamented her state, "See? It's too late for me now. I'm doomed. I don't want to drink it, but I do anyway. I'm addicted to the caffeine, and I hate myself for it!"

We got the same effect when we told her she was drinking alcohol. You'd think we'd killed her. Her reaction was a bit extreme, perhaps, but what isn't extreme about that girl? "I can't believe you drink that stuff?!" she said to Baagii disgustedly. He made no response other than to pass it sheepishly to Bimba, who took it happily.

Ammon and Mom looked at each other as safety issues occurred to them both simultaneously. In the end, they simply accepted it with a shrug. Drunk driving couldn't be much of a problem when there was nothing to hit as far as the eye could see. I thought it should be fine as long as we didn't meet another road block or stop sign. Thinking back on it, though, those cops had all looked a bit happy themselves. I wonder if they had had their own big, white bottle. Then again, I wondered if drunk driving even mattered here.

The bumps and the rigid earth didn't prevent Bimba, drunk or not, from flooring the gas pedal to hit our maximum speed of 50km/h (31mph). I could tell he loved his work from the ever-increasing size of his grin as we hit bumps harder and harder. Bimba also played chicken with anyone who passed us on the "road." The closer he came to causing a collision, the funnier he seemed to find it. In one such incident, a motorcycle took him up on the challenge and drove straight at us, but Bimba wasn't about to lose that game. Thankfully, the motorcycle swerved at the last second. He and his rider were thrown from their seats and landed on their butts in the dust storm that trailed in our wake. As I looked out the rear window, I could just barely make out the passenger sitting stunned in the sand while his friend smacked the ground, unable to contain his laughter.

The daily rides were long, averaging about ten hours. As soon as we quit for the night, the two drivers would jump under their trucks and start the necessary hours of repairs. I was sure most of the damage could've been prevented if they hadn't driven like maniacs all day long. We didn't see them often in the evenings; for all we knew, they slept underneath their trucks.

Our ride became progressively bumpier forcing us to hold onto our seats and flip-flops. The heat and constant shaking made Baagii's small barrel of rancid horse milk, which was stashed in the back, hiss threateningly. The full bottle of the fizzy drink he held in his hands was also on the verge of exploding. Sensing a prime opportunity, Bimba purposely hit a large bump and in the blink of an eye, Baagii was wearing what he was drinking. Bimba roared with delight at his success.

Just then Bree shouted "What's that up ahead!?" and poor soggy Baagii was old news.

"It's an ovoo," he answered, looking like a drowned cat in his wet seat.

"A what now!?" I asked. Because there was nothing around but the grassy rolling hills, we could see it from a long way off. Our very first ovoo was a rock cairn with threads of silky blue scarves tethered to a stick protruding upwards from the centre.

"You must always go around clockwise three times," Baagii explained as he jumped out, shaking his wet hands to dry them. "For a safe journey. It's like a shrine and it is symbolic of the open sky and *Tengger*, the sky spirit Genghis Khan prayed to before he came to power. Also makes good reference point," he added, admitting that he knew this ovoo.

Having been crammed for so many hours in the car, Bree got excited and circled it a few times like some kind of maniac. Then she cried, "OH NO! Baagii, I lost count, I think I went four times!"

"Then you cannot stop. You have to go twice more. You can do six if you want. As long as it is by threes, it is okay."

"Geez, Bree. You would be the one to curse our trip!" Ammon said.

Once Baagii'd told us more about their history, we realized this was a lot more than just a big pile of rocks. An ovoo is a traditional shaman pile started because someone is ill or wants a wish granted. Passers-by continue to pile things on top, generally rocks or wood, and over time, it becomes a massive mound. It felt as if the land had a magnetic force that collects and hoards bits and pieces in one place, the way autumn winds gather piles of crunchy leaves on a doorstep.

"People leave offerings here, anything from money to milk to sweets. Vodka is sacred," Baagii went on to explain.

"I could imagine that vodka must seem holy after all that horse milk," Ammon said.

"I can still taste the hay in it!" I said.

"Look at this!" Bree came from around the back of the ovoo after finishing her last round, hobbling on a single crutch she'd picked from the pile.

"Oh no, no, no!" Baagii said.

"What are you doing?! You should respect it. Aiy, yai, yai!" Ammon groaned.

"Some dead dude is going to come after you," I said, horrified.

"No, they put it there because he healed," Baagii laughed, "not because he died."

In some ways, the occasional animal skulls resting nearby reminded me of an abandoned sacrificial site where someone may have been strung up to feed the vultures. I imagined that the torn blue pieces of silk waving in the breeze were remnants of abandoned bodies. But in its own way, it was majestic.

Walking around it the first time felt a bit silly, but I began to feel much more solemn by the third time as I inspected the simple treasures left behind more closely. It was like making a pact with many unseen people, holding hands in another place and another time in a sort of uniting as I tried to connect with each person who'd traveled past here. *Where were they headed? What's the story behind the crutch, and where did it come from? Had they come by camel? On foot? How long has it stood here? How many generations have met at this spot to share their faith and wor-*

ship? I came to understand the beauty of something that I had, at first, simply thought of as being a bit silly, and the experience reaffirmed for me how special Mongolia was.

From Sheep to Mutton
32

"Bree. Bree! I have to pee."

"Well, go then! What are you waiting for?"

"Eerrgg," I growled, stomping my foot. Searching my brain for a good excuse, I finally remembered the one that should do the trick. "Don't forget Travel Rule #3!" and then whisper/shouted, "Buddy System!"

"Oh man, you are such a wimp," she said, directing a charming smile at the shirtless boys who were all hammering away halfway under their trucks.

"What are you doing?! Stop being so flirty!" I tugged on her shoulder to pull her in towards me.

"I'm not doing anything. I'm allowed to do what I want," she said, pushing me away. "Mom says I have to be independent and not hang on to Fernando," she said flustered.

"Right. Does *he* know that?" I asked.

"Yah, of course!"

"Does he really?" I pressed.

"No, well, I dunno. Whatever! I'm allowed to do what I want," she repeated, unsure of herself.

"I just hope you know what you're doing." I knew she still cared about Fernando, why else would she write him long letters every other night? I knew that she even cried herself to sleep some nights, but her hormones were raging, and Baagii was a welcome distraction. Then again, perhaps I was just jealous. If so, I certainly wasn't about to admit it.

Before I knew it, we were sifting through the bushes to find a good log to sit on or hide behind, remembering to keep a watchful eye on the camp below to make sure we didn't stray too far and lose our way. I was beginning to forget what electricity or door handles or light switches felt like. Our potty stops had faded to nothing more than door-less, wall-less outhouses provided by nature. But I was surprised to find myself preferring the outdoors over the disgusting holes we'd used in China.

It was not a dense forest, by any means, and it was as dry as most of the land through which we'd travelled. Bree was a few metres ahead of me, as always, manoeuvring through the brush like she belonged there and letting the branches snap back in my face.

"Gosh dang it! Stop that!" I said, lifting a hand to the scratch on my cheek.

"Well, if you'd keep up!" She retaliated before taking a sharp right under a hanging bough. "Okay! This is a good spot. Now go! Nobody can see you."

"Oh, man! I can still see them," I said, beginning to unsnap the button at my waist while I did the pee-pee dance. *I should really time it better than this and start hiking BEFORE I have to go this badly*, I thought, but I'd wanted Bree to escort me as usual, and so I had to wait until *she* was ready. To hurry her along, I often had to encourage her, subtly, of course, to drink more.

"Well, first, they aren't looking. Plus, they're out in the open, and we're not," Bree insisted, "not to mention the fact that we're looking down on them. Unless they're *trying* to see us, I guess."

"Okay, okay, okay!" I said, scooting out of my pants and squatting. Bree shook her head at me while she backed up to a thin tree trunk. I knew from her expression that she still couldn't understand why I was so anal about the whole thing. And I knew she was right. It was a good spot. After all, we had chosen to hike up the hill rather than use the guesthouse's outhouse again, largely because it was just a few wood planks hammered together over a shallow pit, but there were other reasons. Despite our continuous efforts to chase the goats away before using it, they were insanely persistent and always crept back. They'd nibble at the slat walls so vigorously that I was afraid it would collapse right on top of me while I was so vulnerable. I reluctantly had to use my nose-plugging hand to cuff the animals through the wide openings between the slats. Clouds of dust rose every time I smacked their hindquarters. One even reared up and threatened to kick me, and I could only pray it would change its mind. I flicked a young one in the nose and it jolted reflexively to the side, catching another in the belly with its short, stubby horns. Reflexively cringing and doing my best to hide behind the narrow slats, I was afraid I might start a stampede!

This could only happen in a Donald Duck cartoon. One kick out of that guy, I thought, as I watched the biggest of the six glaring through at me with dark golden eyes*, and this whole thing is going down. Ker-splat! And I'll be here squatting in the middle of an open field – again.* To avoid the absurdity of being caught between an open cesspit and a collapsed shack, we'd headed for the forest.

The fact that the sun didn't set until after ten o'clock was annoying, frankly, since darkness offered the best privacy available. And oh, how blissfully, sinfully dark it could get on a moonless night. The stars were like a trillion pieces of shattered glass sparkling in the sky making the heavens sing. It was truly the earth beneath and the speckled sky above. There was nothing in-between, and it felt almost as if I, myself, did not exist.

During our daily drives, the toilet issue proved to be even more of a challenge. We would make special stops in an occasional "town" and find a single gas station where there'd be a three-sided outhouse. For some unexplained reason, the opening always faced into whatever traffic there might be. More often than not, the inadequate wood structures where we could relieve ourselves were just thin planks over a big open pit, similar to the guest house latrine just described. At one roadside pit stop, we were lucky enough to find the edge of a crag to climb down into that offered far more privacy than squatting behind the van's large back tires. As we hung onto the roots and the earth on the side of the cliff, *it* splashed down the rocks in a waterfall-like whoosh.

Bree had nearly startled me into falling to my death when she yelped, "Ow, Ow, Ow!" while rubbing her rear and trying to scoot over, finally balancing herself on the tiny mossy ridge.

"It bit my butt! Ow, Ow," she'd continued.

"What?! What bit you?" I'd jumped.

"The stinging nettle, ooooh!" and she'd started to laugh. When she was done, she turned and showed me her startlingly white bum and the red rash that was already spreading across her left cheek.

"Just don't fall off, you two!" Mom had shouted down at us upon hearing the commotion.

My final reflection on the subject of available toilet facilities was that Bree was right. These bushes were ideal, given that they were, at a minimum, free of goats, stinging nettle, traffic, and stink. By the time we started making our way back down the hill to the lone wooden house, we could see a long trail of dust heading in our direction.

"It looks like Ammon's back. Let's go see if they caught anything!" Bree said, picking up the pace.

"Nope! Nothing," he said, as we approached the idling motor-cycle. "Those sheep are smarter than they look, I guess!"

"So, what now?" I asked, my stomach already starting to rumble.

"I think they're going to go out and try again later," he told us. *Nothing is reliable here, why should the animals be any different?* I thought, disappointed that the wait for dinner would be longer than expected. Despite having half a dozen small cows and a pen full of goats, sheep was on tonight's menu, so they would go out again in search of their roving herd. I wondered when mutton *wasn't* on the menu, but I pretty much knew the answer to that question.

The hunters had had some success the night before, though, and treated us to roasted wild gopher. There was very little meat on the small rodents, hardly enough to fill my belly, but my taste buds appreciated the change from mutton. Another day, we'd bought smoked fish from a "side of the road" vendor at a nearby lake, and I went from being a fish-hater to a fish-lover the moment I tasted it. *That gopher and fish were some of the best food I've ever eaten,* I thought, practically salivating as I recalled those meals. *I swear that gopher was the most flavorful, tender meat I've ever tried. I'm sure it was good, even by western standards!*

But when I stopped to think more about it, I realized how it would sound back home. *"Hey guys, come try some of this roasted gopher!"* I imagined myself grabbing one out of the oven. *"And how would you like a rat to go with it?" That would never fly! Next thing I know, I'll be the one carrying a bag full of duck tongues and chewing a baby chicken's head on a skewer.*

Tonight our accommodation was not a ger but a wooden shelter with a couple of rooms. Our family shared a room with four metal-framed beds, the ceilings so low that Ammon was forced to lower his head in order to stand. We were only staying one night. In the morning, we'd move on to Kovsgol Lake and then continue to White Lake. We planned to spend a couple of days at each to do some exploring on horseback – finally!

While we waited for our dinner to be caught, we entertained ourselves with the rest of the local family's livestock. Baagii was happy to join us on our "day-at-the-farm" adventures. A young boy led us around back to the shed. Inside was a wired kennel from which a trapped puppy whined. When the wooden door creaked open, I could see it had blue eyes and dark fur, and it wagged its tail uncontrollably. He looked so happy to see daylight, but my heart wept to see it gnawing at the wires and reaching desperately through the cracks.

"Why don't they just let him go?" Bree asked when we heard it was not a pet, but a young wolf that they'd caught recently after they'd had to kill its mother.

With Baagii translating, the boy told the story. "His mother, she eat our herds! Soon, he will eat them too if we let him go. We must kill him, or he kill them." With that, he'd pointed to the tiny, unsecured pig pen where a huge sow lay grunting on her side. The eight or so piglets running around in and out of the pen didn't stray far from their mother's teats. Given Mongolia's harsh seasons (ranging from -40 to +40°C [-40 to +104°F]), I knew that any loss of livestock could be devastating. He didn't need to finish for me to know that the logical extension of his argument would eventually be, *"He kill us."* Compassion for the baby wolf was a luxury these people could not afford.

"Time for milk," Baagii said to lighten the mood. He smiled broadly and handed Ammon an old, beat-up pail.

We made our way towards the cows in the open field, past the calves locked in wooden pens where they would remain until the humans were finished harvesting the "easy" milk. The first cow we were led to was definitely on the scrawny side, and I wondered how much milk we could take out of such a beast and still leave enough for the poor calf to suck dry.

After I'd learned by watching everyone else struggle with the task, I cautiously took a seat on the short stool next to a cow with brown and white colouring. I couldn't help but notice that her back legs were tied together to prevent her from getting away or kicking us. *That tiny rope is not going to help me if I am sitting almost underneath this refrigerator of an animal when she decides she's sick of being pulled and tugged at.* I'd never been so close to a cow before. She was soft, and I really wanted to snuggle her, but instead, I reached underneath and concentrated on how I was going to extract her milk. It wasn't until the moment I clutched the warm, firm teats in my fists that I thought, *Oh my gosh, is this awkward or what? I'm touching nipples!* I struggled with them until I heard the rewarding sound of milk splashing into the tin pail. The discomfort quickly dissolved into satisfaction, which just as rapidly turned into guilt as the baby calf came rushing from its pen towards us. Nudging me away impatiently, it nuzzled the small swell. My fingers felt wet and sticky from both milk and the calf's wagging tongue.

Not far behind the youngster, an old woman wearing a long skirt and woollen shirt, presumably the wife and mother of the farm, hobbled after the calf carrying a bucket in the crook of her arm, milk overflowing from the rim. Taking notice of our nearly empty pail, she shouted a few abrupt words and waved her hand at us in amused disbelief. Clearly, she had already milked all the other cows and was distinctly humoured by our "accomplishments". Between giggles, Baagii managed to explain what she'd said. "Eight people and *this* is what you get?!"

I leaned forward awkwardly to get a look inside our pail and felt a flush creep up my cheeks. We had maybe two inches in the bottom. The woman replaced me on the seat and quickly clutched the organic milk dispensers. The milk squirted out under the force of her powerful fingers as if someone had turned on two fire hoses. Within minutes, the pail was more than half full.

While we were thus engaged, her husband had finally been able to fetch our dinner. A limp, trussed-up sheep hung from the back of his motorbike. The sheep's pinkish grey tongue dangled from its mouth. I could see that it was already scared half to death, and my heart contracted again. I knew what was about to happen so it wasn't as shocking as the bird I'd seen killed in Longji, but it was no less upsetting.

The man had a little black moustache and he wore a blue baseball cap with a big, dark coat. He went straight to work, untying the animal and letting it fall flat on the ground. Barely able to right itself, the terrified animal did not have the will to escape, so no restraints were needed. The man brought a pink tarp from inside the house, rolled it out, and promptly threw the sheep on its back onto the tarp.

Baagii explained the procedure as the man went about his chore, completely unfazed by our presence. He pressed a small, sharp knife into the skin just below the sternum and sliced downwards, making a gap barely big enough to slip his bare hand through. Reaching in halfway to his elbow, he "unplugged" the heart artery so the sheep would slowly bleed to death. In Mongolia, this efficient, clean slaughtering method keeps all the blood neatly contained within the body. I was wondering just how long it would take to bleed to death when the man immediately pulled up one of the legs to start the skinning process. Although I was envisioning its eyes rolling around like marbles in its head, the sheep did not utter a sound as the hide, starting from the ankles, was pulled away from the body. It was done much like you might peel a banana.

Bree was already sitting on the ground with her back against the tire of the truck. Her head hung nauseously between her legs. She groaned more than the sheep ever had. The others laughed at her weak stomach and the twisted faces she was making. I felt the same, but was not about to admit it and suffer their derision, too. By the time he was working on the third leg, my stomach was a wiggly nest of worms. I pretended to be strong and immune to what was happening, but though I kept my eyes surreptitiously on something else, I could not block the sound of crunching bone as he broke the legs at the knee. *I have to get out of here. I need to get a breath of air.* My head was spinning and I was overwhelmed by this new feeling. *How can I be reacting like this? How can seeing something make you feel so lightheaded?!* I was confused. *I'm not ill. It's all mental, but I sure as heck am physically feeling this. This is NOT my imagination.* As specks of black entered my field of vision, I casually made my way back to the dwelling to "get a drink."

The room was dark when I entered, and I had to pause to let my eyes adjust to the dim lighting. The thick smell of sheep's wool flipped my insides all over again but I was relieved to find Noortje and Sarah there. They both preferred not to witness the gruesome event. An older daughter in the Mongol family, probably around thirteen or so, was preparing noodles for dinner in the squishy kitchen. She kneaded the pale dough and then sliced and rolled it into very lumpy, uneven strips. It was not about presentation as much as it was about just getting it shaped into pieces that could be thrown into the soup. *I guess it all looks the same at the other end, anyway.*

I didn't want to be gone too long and attract suspicion about my absence. Having reached a somewhat more sober condition, I walked myself back outside. The youngest girl, who was about six years old and too young for other chores, took an interest in the gutting. She squatted next to her father, her head nearly inside the hollow belly of the sheep which was now split open from neck to groin. She was hunched over and ever so silent, fully attentive to the process as he dissected all the organs and intestines into three different buckets. The man carefully removed the gallbladder, ensuring that he kept it fully intact so as not to damage the rest of the organs. Except for the gallbladder, every single part was used. Even the blood was scooped out to make sausages.

Once he'd peeled the skin from the ribs and hindquarters and bared the red muscles beneath, the wife came to retrieve the meat. The sheep was eventually reduced to nothing but a clean pelt which was hung inside the small dwelling. Later it would be tanned and either sold or used to furnish their home.

The little girl ran off to play when her father stood to fold up the perfectly clean pink tarp and go inside. One day this business of handling the meat with her bare hands and stringing it up inside would be her responsibility. *It's good for them to be exposed to it so young.*

The carcass was hanging in one piece from the low support beam in the kitchen. The mother stood at the small counter near the stove making dinner. She sliced bits of neck meat from the carcass and threw it into the soup pot together with the older daughter's doughy noodles. The slaughtered corpse hanging nearby did nothing for my appetite, but I was too hungry to skip dinner. I waited cross-legged on the colourful wool rug, my belly twisting with hunger and un-certainty as I remembered my very first taste of mutton back at the Mongolian border. Khongorzul, the lady who travelled with us on both the overnight bus and the train, had promised us the best soup of our lives.

"C'mon. You come with me. I get you some real Mongolian soup," she had said. "This is REAL soup. *Mongolian* soup," she went on, in-ferring that it was far superior to the "awful" Chinese food we'd been enjoying. Lipton's instant chicken noodle soup immediately came to mind, the kind that we couldn't possibly dream of getting here but I was hopeful nonetheless. The bowls we were served contained a thin broth with an oily film on top. Careful not to insult her favourite Mongolian dish, we hesitantly asked if we were supposed to take out the floating, white chunks.

"NO! That is best part. Very healthy," she insisted before scoop-ing one up on her spoon and happily shoving the blob in her mouth. *Oh man!* I was not in the mood to sample dead animal soup, and fatty, greasy soup at that! It was dreadful, to say the least, and a rather un-nerving introduction to the country where I would spend a whole month. *I can't even believe someone could eat this. I heard these Mongolians had a sense of humour. Maybe she's pulling my leg?* But no. Though I desperately wished she had been, she continued to slurp passionately until the bowl was empty.

"This isn't too bad!" Bree'd said.

"Oh yah? Just wait a few more days and we'll see what you think of it then," Ammon predicted, scowling at his bowl when Khongorzul had gone off to the bathroom. The mere *word* mutton had always pro-jected the image of a skinny, old sheep wrapped up in dirty grey wool hanging in matted clumps and dying in a muddy ditch. Upon actually tasting it in that horrid soup, my worst suspicions were confirmed.

After this introductory meal, I realized that the food was as horrible as I'd heard, but that obviously, the locals didn't share my assessment. They thought it was divine, and no matter how distasteful I found the food, I knew there was no need to feel sympathy for them. Taste is a relative, cultural matter – we mostly like the kind of food we ate as children. *Besides, they would probably find my chicken noodle soup disgusting.* I could appreciate her being completely content with, and proud of, her country's cuisine, but it was not for me. *No, thank you very much!*

From the time of our first introduction to traditional Mongolian food, Bree was still eating her fair share at every meal, while Mom and I learned to surreptitiously shovel most of our meals into Ammon's bowl. He'd glare at me out of the corner of his eyes whenever I did it, as he only ate to avoid losing weight from a physique which had always resembled something of a stick bug.

While we waited for tonight's sheep noodle soup to cook, Baagii taught us some more customs as vegetarians Tom and Sarah munched on their packaged cookies. For example, in Mongolian culture it is unacceptable to refuse anything that is offered. It is obligatory to take at least a sample, no matter what it is.

"Please, Baagii, no! Don't let them bring us the eyeballs," Bree pleaded, squeezing his arm tight, knowing that sheep's eyeballs and their large fatty tails were considered delicacies and were therefore usually offered to honoured guests. Mongolian sheep store fat in their tails to help them survive the harsh terrain the same way camels store it in their humps. He smiled and I saw Bree melt a little more than the heat warranted. Because Baagii had lived in the United States for a couple of years in his early twenties, he could appreciate how revolting eating eyeballs was in our culture. Though I'm sure he'd amused himself many times observing the reactions of other vulnerable guests, he obviously had a soft spot for Bree.

When he said, "Okay, I won't," she fell even deeper into whatever spell she was well on her way to succumbing to. We were grateful never to have been tested by such delicacies. The main snacks offered to us were comparatively bearable. The sour goat milk biscuits they loved tasted a bit like vitamin C rocks. I might have enjoyed them had they not been streaked with dark goat hairs. The yoghurt, which was equally sour and hairy, was homemade in an old, stained bucket. With China's to-die-for yoghurt still fresh in my mind, this Mongolian version fell completely on the opposite end of the spectrum. Nearly every night, though, these same "munchies" returned to haunt us.

As non-drinkers, we were relieved to learn that when offered an alcoholic beverage such as vodka or airag (fermented horse milk), we could avoid offending anyone by simply touching our lips to the mug before returning it. The key seemed to be more the act of acceptance rather than the consumption of the drink. This was a much easier challenge to avoid than those faced by the vegetarians in our group.

Baagii informed us that the most important custom to remember was that an empty bowl meant you were still hungry, and that simply covering the bowl with your hand signified that no refills were needed. Of course, we learned this the hard way. We'd been representing ourselves according to Canadian manners, and we'd choke down every last bite only to be shocked when our bowls were then refilled immediately. I would've been ever so appreciative had Baagii mentioned this little tradition sooner and saved me the trouble of consuming all those extra chunks of white, gristly lard.

Baagii also explained how important it was to symbolically support the right hand with the left when offering or accepting anything. Accepting food with the left hand was a big no-no.

"I can only imagine why," Ammon said suggestively.

"What do you mean? Why?" I asked, falling into his trap.

"Have you seen a toilet?" he asked.

"I guess, if you could call them that," I began, wondering how the two were connected.

"How 'bout TP?"

"Oh NO! They don't really!" I choked.

"Yep," he smirked, pleased by the expression on my face when I realized the duties of the left hand. When accepting my soup bowl from our local hostess, I tried but failed to not look at *her* left hand supporting the right arm. I rustled up a smile and held out my right hand to receive it.

I could all too easily imagine that my dinner had only that morning roamed free in his flock. His brothers and sisters were still out there with their fat, bulging tails which floated up and down like a school of jellyfish whenever they ran. I found it really disgusting when bits of tail lard bobbed up and down in my soup like buoys in the salty liquid, but hunger was hunger, and I actually enjoyed the soup's bits of neck meat. I couldn't help but marvel over the swift transformation from living creature to food as I scooped the last piece of it onto my spoon.

Mongol Ferrari
33

" *A* Mongol without a horse is like a bird without the wings," Baagii said softly and directly into the ears of the black stallion. "A traditional saying," he explained as he stroked the horse's nose before leisurely climbing on. We'd woken to see horses outside our ger munching away on the short, tough grass. Their hides twitched and their tails flicked the few flies away.

This was one of Tom's first real horse rides. I smiled upon hearing him talking about horses he'd ridden in circles at fairs. Noortje and Sarah had both passed on riding with us, and I admired Tom's spunk. Baagii noticed Tom's hesitation as he awkwardly stepped closer to his designated horse and asked if he was scared.

"Not so much scared," he explained as he timidly petted the creature, "but worried that I'm going to make a total ass of myself!" *I'd be worried, too, with all these six year olds riding around like pros. Mongolians must learn to ride before they can walk, and it's obvious that they really love their horses,* I thought, thinking back on twenty-odd mounted kids between the ages of six and ten we'd seen practising for the Nadaam Festival. We'd found ourselves driving in the midst of them as they raced across a vast plain like warriors off to battle decorated with multicoloured ribbons braided into their hair. They'd woven their tiny hands into their horse's manes as they rode bareback, fitting snugly into the base of their mounts' moist necks. The sight of the galloping animals' strong, rippling muscles was, for me, a highlight of the two week excursion.

As I watched this fully grown man, Tom, trying to decide where the reins belonged and how his feet should fit in the stirrups, I was grateful that I would not be the most inexperienced rider today. I had learned to be comfortable in a saddle during the frequent horseback riding excursions our family had run for the ESL students. I was, however, a bit worried about our lack of a guide, but I knew better than to think about that. Our horseback riding tours of Canada's vast meadows and forests had also taught me that horses always use their innate sense of direction to find their way home.

On family vacations, we'd go to the Flying U, one of the biggest ranches in B.C. This was the one vacation Dad always skipped, owing to his general fear of horses. I could still hear his defensive explanation. "I'm not afraid of horses! I just don't *like* them, especially when they're hell-bent on running at full speed into the lowest hanging branch of the only tree in an open field. I like riding but unfortunately, you need a horse to do it." Dad claimed he had enough negative experiences as a child on horseback to write a novel and reveal horses' secret agenda to the world. Although I did feel a certain healthy degree of caution around horses, I couldn't agree with him.

The stiff, wooden saddles had no padding, and they were placed high up on the shoulder blades. Mongolian horses are very small and stocky, but I quickly learned not to judge a book by its cover. Initially, I had even been hesitant to sit on one for fear of breaking what appeared to be a fragile back. I could hardly stand to watch Ammon, envisioning that once mounted, his toes would come within inches of skimming the ground.

I felt the beast's power beneath me as I swayed side to side with its movement. His rich and distinctive reddish-orange coat made him a real beauty. Leaning forward I patted his soft neck, instinctively smelling my hand afterwards. I liked its wholesome and grainy, hay-like smell. *We were meant for each other, you and me, even though I started out prejudging you, just like all those people at home who told us we wouldn't last out here.* I was already well into my second month on the road, and I now knew we would not only survive, but thrive.

"He's so toned. He's the hottest cowboy I ever saw – EVER!" I heard Bree rhapsodizing about Baagii as she rode up beside me.

Halfway through the day, he had conveniently taken off his shirt and exposed the beads of sweat crawling down his back. He literally glistened in the sun and melted my poor sister's heart. You could sense that his skin was as soft as rose petals. She trotted off to get closer to him, and my horse followed instinctively.

"He looks like a little boy," I said. "He doesn't even have a single strand of hair on his chest."

"I know!!" Bree said, practically falling off her horse and landing in the puddle of drool she'd made. "That's the best part about it! And he doesn't have even ONE zit."

"Oh, brother! I bet he doesn't even have armpit hair," I said.

"Good! That's gross, anyway!" she said, looking over at me disgustedly.

"No, *that* is the best part!" I said, before kicking my heels into the horse's sides and taking off. Bree shouted happily and laughed as we both broke from a walk into a canter and rode side by side.

I couldn't believe these creatures' speed and strength! Any Canadian horse would've been foaming at the mouth if pushed this hard, but this guy hardly even broke a sweat. Just when I thought he had hit his max, we'd shift into yet a faster gear and cut through the land like a heat-seeking rocket.

Looking skyward with my arms outstretched, I inhaled deeply and filled my lungs with the freshest of air. I didn't exhale for as long as possible, wanting to fill myself with the moment and never let it go. Even if I gave my siblings a three-second head start, I'd still catch up to and then fly past them! Despite its small size, I'd never before been on such a high-spirited speed demon.

Once again, history was coming to life, this time with the wind gripping my hair. Suddenly I felt like I could've been part of Genghis Khan's Mongolian Horde, shaking the earth as it stampeded across Asia on horseback in the thirteenth century. It didn't surprise me that the Mongols ventured so far west if their horses were anything like these. The captivating splurge of blue sky above came right down to the tips of the earth, meeting the green of the rolling grasslands. The Mongols timeless adventures had led them all the way to Turkey and beyond, where they forged an empire of unforgettable strength and changed history forever.

After a good hard run, Bree finally slowed to a walk beside me.

"What is wrong with you?! Didn't you hear me yelling at you to stop? You're such a jerk, Bree," I barked.

"What? Why?! That was awesome!"

"I was trying to stop the horse and then you came flying up past me, so of course, mine took off after yours."

"Well soooorry! Hrmph!"

"I just wanted to fix this killer wedgy! Seriously! It's the worst I've ever had!" I said, reaching down and dislodging what felt like two metres of fabric from between my cheeks.

"Wow! This is gorgeous," I heard Mom gasp as she looked out over Lake Khovsgol.

"Mom, what's the matter with you? Didn't you hear Savannah has a wedgy!?" Bree teased.

"Shut up! I'm never telling you anything anymore."

Ignoring our squabbling, Baagii told us more about the beautiful lake. "This lake holds seventy percent of Mongolia's fresh water. That's half a percent of the entire world's fresh water." *I wonder what percentage of this underwear is still in one piece?* "It's so clean the people drink straight out of it. No treatment needed." *Maybe not, but I'll need treatment once I see what kind of damage this wooden saddle did. Bree will be picking the slivers out later!*

Once that issue was finally settled, I took a look and agreed wholeheartedly with Mom. The lake was stunningly clear, so clear that the shape and colour of every individual pebble was visible. It invited us for a much needed dip, though I felt guilty about dirtying such pure, clean water.

"It's so beautiful! It sure would be nice to live here," Mom said.

"But you'd definitely need a horse. How much would it cost to buy one?" Bree asked.

"At least two hundred thousand togrog," Baagii answered.

"About two hundred bucks, then." Ammon quickly calculated.

"I'd buy mine! I bet he'd compete in the big festival," I boasted as we trotted along. "In fact, we should race him in it ourselves!"

"How much longer are you staying in Mongolia? Will you still be here for the Nadaam Festival?" Baagii asked.

"Yah, for sure! That was one of the main reasons we came. We'll be here another week after that because we're planning to go on another tour to the Gobi Desert. But it's so expensive," Ammon said, though I knew we were only paying twenty-two dollars a person per day for everything.

"Especially with four people," Mom threw in.

"Yah. The hotel, they charge a lot for commission and have to pay everyone. That is true," Baagii agreed, unfastening his saddle bag and taking a swig of warm water.

"I just wish there was another way to see the country, but it seems like it's nearly impossible without a public transport system," Ammon said, eyeing the emptiness around us.

"Yes, that is also true, but it is not impossible to get around, really. You just have to know where you want to go. And I know where you want to go."

Ammon paused to analyze this remark before asking, "What are you suggesting?"

"Well, I know the sights, the area, and what to do. So maybe," he stopped to think as he offered the water to Bree, "I have a friend who has a car, maybe we just bypass the hotel commission, then you don't pay for a whole tour price. We go, you know, kind of, like, as friends," he said, and I caught the way he subtly glanced at Bree.

"Really, you think you know someone? Well, of course we would pay for fuel and his expenses," Mom said.

"Yah, he has a van and can speak English too. He's a really cool guy! And then I can come. Would be fun. I have to see if I have time off my other job, my radio job. I can translate for you, but only as a friend, no money. When we get back I ask my friend. Don't reserve anything with the company until I talk to him. And, you know, my boss, he can't know."

"Of course. We will just wait for you," Ammon said, with a reassuring smile.

"But you're coming to the festival too, aren't you?" Bree asked anxiously. He smiled his charming smile at her and winked before he purposely made his aviators fall from his thick hairline to cover his eyes. Tom had already stopped up ahead, unsaddling for a lunch break on a hill overlooking the gorgeous, multi-coloured lake. The edges of the waters were so green it almost glowed, and rings of all shades of blue faded into the centre.

Directing the horses with a slight, confident squeeze of the thighs, we sped up to meet him.

A few days later, we were situated by a different beautiful lake and we'd just returned from another six hours of hard riding. Bree and I hobbled our bow-legged way up a grassy hill behind our ger. My bladder was fit to burst by the time we climbed to where the rickety wooden structure called a toilet stood.

"Where's the T.P.?" Bree asked as she stepped into the door-less shack.

"You have it," I told her confidently.

"No, I don't. I told you to bring it," she scowled.

"When did you ever say that? That's your job! Everybody knows it. You always have some stashed away."

"You *always* forget. Ugh!! Now you have to go back and get it," Bree said, gesturing down the hill towards the seven white gers settled next to the vast waters of White Lake. She sounded as irritated about it as if she herself had to retrieve it.

"Just go and get it? It's like a ten-minute walk each way, and this is a steep hill. You're the fit one. You do it," I retaliated.

"Nope. You need the exercise, so you should go."

"Oh Bree, c'mon! I'll pee myself if I do." I started to whine, 'cause I already knew I was going to lose the argument once again.

"Just like that time with the berries. I can't trust you with *anything!*" she carried on, starting to get angry as she remembered something I

did when I must have been all of six years old. She'd made me walk
four blocks home carrying a bowling-ball-sized batch of fresh, juicy
blackberries tucked up in my white t-shirt. She had picked them for
hours from the school ground's forested area, climbing in and out
of the thorns and vines and dropping handful after handful into my
outstretched shirt. My arms were tired from holding the load before
we'd even started the long walk home.

I nearly wet my pants when she'd finally turned around in our driveway and shrieked at me, "WHERE ARE ALL THE BERRIES!?!?"

Dazed and exhausted from having run all the way home to keep
up with her nine-year-old pace, I'd looked down in a panic at the red-
stained shirt that was completely soaked and sticking to my belly. A
quick glance behind me revealed only a bare sidewalk. *Where did all
those berries go?* She'd marched us at least two blocks back to search for
them to no avail. Just short of getting beaten into blackberry pulp
myself, we returned home completely empty handed.

"I spent hours in those thorn bushes and if it weren't for---" she
was saying.

"Okay, okay, okay!" I said, cutting her off mid-sentence. I'd been
subjected to this guilt trip a hundred times already, and would rather
spend the next twenty minutes walking than being yelled at. Before
I left for the toilet paper, though, I negotiated a fifteen-minute neck
massage in return.

"And bring the camera, too!" she shouted after me. It was getting
late and the early evening fires' smoke was starting to drift out of the
chimneys protruding from the centre of each roof. Aside from a few
white gers dotting the shoreline, the landscape was completely free of
any evidence of human habitation.

I made it back to Bree at the toilet, which was halfway up the
grassy green hill. After taking care of business, we decided to go to
the top to see the view, since we were already nearly there. We skipped
from rock to jagged rock along the rim, scratching our legs as we
went, until we reached a point that had a hundred and eighty degree
view of the distant mountains that enclosed the crystal waters. As we
sat in that tranquil spot at the summit, we reminisced about our many
mutual friends and loved ones and talked about our sad goodbyes

and painful last words. As I received my promised massage, she told me the details of her parting from Fernando, the boy she'd dated for more than a year. I remembered her waving out the window of our van as we headed to Seattle, absolutely crying her heart out.

"Do you think our friends ever think of us?" I asked her as she dug her thumbs deep into my neck.

"Are you kidding me? Of course! We gave them the best time. Like, sure, we didn't always wear the latest popular fashions or buy the newest gadgets, but who cares? We didn't need to spend money to have a blast. They'll remember our fun times more than some stupid shoes they bought at the mall."

"I miss spending nights under the stars on the roof," I said, cringing as her grip on the scruff of my neck intensified. "Ouch! Ouch! That kills! Go easy on me."

"Oh shut up. You asked for a massage," she said, maintaining her grip. "Plus, you're all knotted up. You need this. And remember the scooters? That was such an awesome invention," Bree said. Shortening the scooters' handlebars to the lowest possible setting and then securing milk crates onto them with bungee cords, we'd assembled our own little Mario karts and rode them down the streets of our mountainside neighbourhood.

"Oh, the faces they made when they saw us coming!" I laughed. "I can't even count how many shoes I burned through braking on the pavement."

"Remember soaping up the trampoline on a rainy day?"

"Or chasing the rabbits when they escaped onto the neighbour's front lawn?"

"Yah. Good times," we declared in unison, and then we both sighed.

"Believe it or not, I even miss our magic drinks," I said. We'd developed a game to see who could drink the most semi-noxious ingredients without getting sick. We'd take turns going into the kitchen and secretly adding strange items to the mix before blending it up again. In the end, we'd have a concoction of mustard, soya sauce, egg, mayonnaise, cheese, and/or Tabasco sauce, etc. Somebody once even threw in dog food.

"Those were disgusting!!" Bree said, and I could feel her body shaking at the memory.

"But so fun!"

"And I still can't believe we jumped off the roof into the pool," Bree added, shaking her head in disbelief.

"That was sooo bad!" I agreed. I could never work up enough courage to try the blind, two-story-high, running jump over concrete before landing in the safety of our swimming pool. Just watching my best friend and sister do it made my heart pound.

After a moment of silence, Bree said, "Seriously, they will never forget those times." And I had to agree. *I was so caught up with money then, trying to keep up and still always feeling like I wasn't good enough, but maybe I contributed something to the social mix after all.*

We fell into silence as the sun set before us. I had watched it sink and disappear countless times. I often felt it was the only thing connecting me to the other side of the world. Even the hill I sat on wasn't connected because of the massive oceans that separated us like parallel lines that never met. Whenever I saw the moon, as distant as it was, I knew that the sun had left to greet my friends in the morning. Sometimes I'd wish they could know I had sent it over.

"What are we gonna do without you here?" I remembered my friends saying days before I was to board the plane. *"I just don't believe it,"* another had said. *"What will Terri do without you? I don't think I've ever seen you two apart."* Her twin brother, Tyee, had added, *"You guys are inseparable."* I found that quite flattering, coming from someone who'd shared a womb with her.

I'd stayed the final two weeks at Terri's, which made it easier for everyone. During those final days, my grandmother's house was full with the rest of the family crashing on all available beds and couches once we'd moved out of our house. When stress and the fear of leaving kept me awake, I'd often sit up and watch Terri sleep, thinking about how very much I would miss her.

When Bree stood up to leave, I told her, "I'm just going to stay a little longer. I'll be down in a few minutes."

"Suit yourself," and she leapt over the rocks and down the steep, grassy hill. The rich oranges and reds reflected from the sky like fire, and I realized that one day, years from now, I'd probably be sitting at home reminiscing about this precious time I'd shared with my sister. Even now, watching her get smaller and smaller as she walked down the hill, I could actually feel her absence. I was alone. *One day she won't be there, either. She was right here by my side, like Terri always was, and just like her, she'll be gone.* I would miss her just as much as I missed Terri now if we were apart.

The setting sun still hugged the water, transforming it into what looked like a huge pool of orange juice. It would be pitch dark soon, but with only two lights shining below, I would find my way back as easily as a moth to a flame.

It was always hardest when night fell. In contrast to the eventful days, at night I often felt like a lost little girl (sometimes literally lost, but usually just emotionally), and I was lonely. I felt trapped within the group and by our remote surroundings and the lack of the kind of facilities I was used to. I needed my own room to escape to when my Gemini moods started swinging. And it was scary seeing only an endless road that led to who knew what. As hard as I tried, I could not see the light at the end of the tunnel. But mostly, all this came down to a simple case of gut-wrenching, debilitating homesickness. It was initially harder than usual to clearly identify what it was because I'd always related homesickness with missing Mom, and she was right here.

But as I sat there enjoying the peaceful solitude, I gradually came to understand, perhaps for the first time, just how miniscule and positively young I really was. All of my demands and know-it-all attitude seemed to recede into the darkest corners of the lake, and my pathetic fifteen years on this earth seemed incredibly insignificant. But rather than feeling remorsefully unimportant, sincere gratitude and appreciation washed over me, and I finally pushed through that barrier of stubbornness I'd always carried to see a new reality, one where I was unbelievably blessed by all the wonderful, positive things in my life. It was more than just an abstract concept, as if all the colours of the spectrum simultaneously blended into a white light that burst through my soul. I felt as pure as the crystal waters below, and I knew that, despite my age, my inexperience, and the minimal impact

I had made on the world thus far, I would no longer be able to resist or ignore this new comprehension of my place in it.

After just two short months of travel, I felt a huge shift occurring. I'd already become a different and, in some respects, a better person. I was learning how to be in the world without portraying myself as someone with a seemingly callous nature, or hiding behind the protective laughter and constant jokes I'd always felt I needed. It was like looking directly into my soul, and I saw more of my potential. I was calm and serious, in a state as close to meditation as I'd ever been. There was no one from whom I needed to hide my emotions and no need to be on guard as a welcome maturity seemed to slide down into my chest like molten lava and find a place to settle. Was it there to stay?

Recharge
34

When I walked into the grungy hostel in *Ulaanbaatar* the second time, I welcomed the sight of the dark dorm room with its twenty unwashed beds. I was even excited by the tiny drizzle of a shower located down the unlit hallway in the back. It somehow didn't seem so dreary anymore. I saw a half-naked brunette guy, probably in his early twenties, sweating in the bed that had once been mine. Ammon's former bed was not occupied so he promptly reclaimed it. The little yellow post-it notes Sandra had given us, each marked with a date and a smiley face, were still stuck to the wall from when Ammon had pulled that day's note off and stuck it near wherever he was sleeping. Nothing had changed; the place not only felt dirty, it *was* dirty. Even the air felt like the same stale air I'd breathed two weeks earlier. As I threw my daypack on a bed to claim it, I peeked at the guy sleeping in my old one and wondered who else had slept in this bed? *Had he been fat? Hairy, perhaps?* I wiped the sheets down, keeping an eye out for curly back hairs, in particular.

But despite the filth and wondering why we couldn't afford a more luxurious hotel for $5 a night, it had a cozy, home-like effect on me. It was a familiar place, something I recognized, and I found myself craving that feeling more often lately. Plus, I knew exactly where and how to get on the Internet here.

I was disappointed when I opened up my email to find only four new messages. *Two whole weeks, and that's all I got?* My heart sank as I glanced over at the sixteen Bree had in her inbox.

I opened my inbox and read a short one from Terri telling me that nothing much was going on, but I didn't believe her. *How could she say that? She at least has a comfy bed and a hot shower. She has the whole world at her feet!* I couldn't help but feel stressed over her choice of friends since I'd left. She had started to hang out with the partying type, and I was worried, threatened, and perhaps even a bit jealous.

There was one piece of junk mail, which I hate as much as the next person, and another was an informative one from Grandma about home that asked lots of questions. My heart fluttered when I saw that the last one was from Grady, particularly when I glanced over to Bree's screen and saw that she had not received one from him. I couldn't believe he'd written and it made me blush. He was *her* friend, after all. My smile widened as I considered reasons why he might have written to me.

It was also really nice to finally be able to check the blog again and read the comments, since it had been blocked in China. There were a few more there which also cheered me up.

> ***hey family!!!*
> *omg it sounds like*
> *you guys are having a*
> *blast:(...i'm sooo jealous:(...*
> *I wish i was with you guys....*
> *i miss you guys tons*
> *luv your sis/daughter*
> *Terri*

> *I've missed you guys.*
> *I wish I could see you*
> *when we land in Cherry*
> *Point, it sounds like there's*
> *going to be a lot of people*
> *waiting. Please be safe but*
> *have fun. I love you, Sky*

savannah i miss u like crazy!!!!
well i miss the whole family!!!
mom i need u!!!
luv your sis/daughter
Terri**

I did feel a degree of guilt and sadness, knowing how important we were in her life. After we left I was afraid she might feel as if she'd been neglected for the second time, since Terri and her twin brother had already been abandoned by their mother as infants. This had left her father a very busy single parent trying to juggle the needs of three kids under the age of four along with his crazy emergency room schedule. They were raised by this glorious man who, to the best of his ability, covered all the parental roles imaginable. Not wanting to ditch Terri we had initially invited her to join us on our one year excursion. Her dad had actually considered the invitation but decided against it on the basis of school being a priority. I often dreamed of what it would've been like if she had come but I knew her dad had a valid argument.

I finally managed to get onto Microsoft Network (MSN) and have a live chat, which was very exciting. I started up a conversation with a guy from school, Tony, though I honestly couldn't recall how I'd got him on my contact list. He was someone I had never really talked to, likely because he was more popular than me. When he said I was the luckiest person he'd ever known, I was amazed that my own peers, even guys I never had the courage to talk to, were not only acknowledging my presence but complimenting me because of this trip! I couldn't believe it.

I worked up a sweat just sitting in the small, stuffy Internet hut for an hour, so I took a cold shower and then sat quietly with my thoughts.

"Don't get too comfy, Savannah. We're only staying three days for the festival, then we're out of here," Ammon said when he saw me grinning. Though I was happy to be clean again and comforted a bit by being in a familiar place, it was the thought of Grady's email that accounted for the smile on my face.

The next morning, Baagii joined us as we headed out to watch the Naadam Festival's opening ceremonies that included horses, ballroom dancing, and rap music. Sukhbaatar Square was full of onlookers as nine men, dressed in dazzling red and blue, super-hero-looking outfits and holding sacred horse tails, assembled in front of their horses and then mounted to parade around the city.

Bree managed to trip over someone in the commotion and Baagii rushed over and gave her a strange look.

"What?!" she asked.

"You have to shake his hand!" he said, turning her so she faced the man waiting patiently behind her.

"What do you mean?"

As he led her by the elbow, he explained quietly in her ear, "It is custom. If you kick someone's foot you *have* to shake their hand."

"Okay!" She laughed and did as she was told. "If I had known that, I'd have kicked yours ages ago!" That lame comment started them both giggling away.

Suddenly I saw two familiar faces in the crowd. "Hey, there's Tom and Sarah!" I said, pointing.

"Oh, hey! Small world," Tom greeted us. You can't imagine how cool it feels to be in a totally different country and bump into people you know, just like you might casually run into a neighbour at a mall back home.

"There's a guy who just got robbed. You should watch your stuff," they informed us.

"Yah, we heard some similar stories at our hostel," Ammon responded. At that time, Ammon had told us that it shouldn't change our opinion of the local people, that thieves are drawn to crowds anywhere in the world and every country has them. Mom reminded us that although our larger group would discourage theft, we still needed to stick together and watch each other's backs. The camera strap was always wrapped safely around one of our wrists.

As if the world isn't bad enough with people killing each other! Ammon seemed to read my mind and asked, "Hey, did you guys read about the bombs?"

"Bombs?!" Tom repeated, a bit stunned.

"Yah. A bunch exploded in the U.K. this week," Ammon confirmed with a remorseful nod.

"What? No! What happened? Was anyone hurt? Where did it happen?"

"On subways across the city and on a bus in Tavistock Square in London. A bunch of people died, about fifty or so. They're saying it was a terrorist attack." Ammon had read about it that morning on the Internet and told us, but it didn't affect me until I saw the shaken look on Tom's face.

"My sister takes that train to work every day! I have to get on the Web. Is there a place nearby? You guys enjoy the festival. We've gotta go check and see if everyone at home is alright!" Without waiting for a response, they rushed off.

International news stories were normally too distant to affect me, but seeing someone's personal reaction firsthand really hit home. It became much more real to me when I saw how directly he was affected by having family and friends to worry about. This was more than just headlines above photos; my desensitized emotions, which could hardly distinguish between "fake action movie" and reality, were newly awakened and I developed a whole new perspective.

It was hot when we arrived at the National Sports Stadium where the rest of the three-day festival was held. From the bleachers, we watched archery, wrestling, and horse-racing competitions. The wrestlers wore Speedo-like blue "underwear" and tiny red jackets, which essentially were just sleeves that left their chests fully exposed. The winner of each round performed a traditional, birdlike victory dance, prancing in circles with outstretched arms slowly flapping. The whole celebration passed as if in a dream and did not move me, perhaps because my mind was simply somewhere else again.

"Do you guys know why they have those outfits? With the tiny vests?" Ammon asked.

"Because they have to wear the first jacket they ever trained in?" Bree guessed.

"Not quite, Bree. But I know you'll love the answer. One year a woman won, but women aren't allowed to compete, so now, they bare their chests to make sure they are all men."

"I thought that's what the tiny little Speedos were for," Bree quipped as my mind wandered off again. *I can't believe Grady wrote me.* --- "just like sumo wrestlers" --- *Does he finally see me as something more than just "the little sister?"*

"Savannah, are you here at all? This is the biggest yearly festival in Mongolia! Why aren't you paying attention?" Ammon urged.

"I am! I heard the bums hanging out part!" I said defensively.

"That was Bree's contribution, and it was pretty useless, as usual. Did you hear what the nine sacred tails are all about?"

"Nope, missed that. Please tell me," I replied. *I wonder if he misses me. He SAID he missed me, but is that just being nice? I can't believe he wrote me. ME! Does that mean he cares? Or is he just being polite? But he didn't write Bree. That must mean he really does want to talk to me.*

When we'd changed schools a few years back, Grady had quickly become Bree's best guy friend. I vividly remembered the day she'd called upstairs to me, "Savannah, come down here! You've gotta talk to my buddy. He's so freaking funny!"

"I'm busy!!" I'd foolishly yelled back.

She came up at that point, took me by the wrist and said, "You can do that later. C'mon!"

I was a goner the moment I heard his voice on the phone. A strange, vague vision washed over me and I thought to myself, "I will marry him." I didn't know what he looked like. In fact, I knew nothing about him except that his name was Grady and that I loved him. When I saw him for the first time with his zits, crooked teeth, and big, wild hair, none of it mattered because, well, I was already hooked. I was twelve years old then, and at fifteen, my feelings hadn't changed. *But how to make him see?!* All my sibling's friends treated me like a bratty little sister – everyone but Grady, who made me feel like an equal.

On top of this, I couldn't believe that Tony, who I considered to be way out of my league socially, had said he was jealous of MY life!! Life was good!

The next day Bree returned to the hostel after spending time with Baagii and informed us that he was unable to get time off to come with us on the next adventure. She was, of course, sorely disappointed by this news. I found myself actually having mixed feelings. I had come to appreciate Baagii in the two weeks we'd all spent together touring the countryside, but I did like the idea of having my sister to myself again.

Fortunately, he had managed to arrange our next trip. That evening, a man with a big friendly smile stumbled out of a little silver minivan, and Baagii introduced Future, saying, "This is my good friend and your new driver! He is going with you to the Gobi Desert!"

Sand Traps and
Good Samaritans
35

"**W**hat? You do not trust me?" Future asked as Ammon buckled his seatbelt in the front passenger seat. *Oh yah, right,* I thought, as I slowly released my own, remembering Baagii's warning on the previous trip that in Mongolia, wearing a seatbelt is an insult to the driver. I hadn't really worn one since we left home; in fact, I'd hardy even seen one.

When we met Future, he'd invited us to come to his little apartment in the city. He was an affable guy, clean shaven and just a few years older than Ammon. He was larger in breadth and height than the average Mongol, who was, on average, a bit taller than the average Chinese.

"You are my first foreign guests ever in my house," he'd proudly announced, and we happily toasted that statement with either "Cheers!" or "Togtooyo!" That honour did nothing to calm my nerves about the journey we were about to take, but on the strength of Baagii's recommendation, we'd set off together into the Gobi Desert two days later.

"Are you sure this is a good idea?" I'd questioned the night before as we packed our few belongings.

"Yah, of course it is! It'll be fine," Ammon declared. "We've got a vehicle and the only way you get around this country, it seems, is by stopping for directions every time you get a chance. And Future speaks the language, so it's all good. What could go wrong?" I would've liked to have said, "How do we know he's not going to chop us into little pieces, or just leave us out there?" But I knew they would have none of that, and that I'd only end up looking like a wimp.

"This'll be great! And it's a lot cheaper than the last tour," Ammon bragged.

"Yah, by how much? A few cents?" I inquired.

"No, smarty. A couple bucks each, per day. That adds up, you know!"

The potential disadvantages of frugally downgrading to a minivan that didn't have four-wheel drive were waved off by the others. Despite their nonchalance, I could not help but worry that we were apparently the only people attempting to travel the countryside without it. Nonetheless, cheaper was cheaper, and money talks.

Future broke the ice to start us off on a positive note by asking if we'd like to hear him sing. We nodded, feeling both cautious and curious. He promptly inserted a compact disk, carefully adjusted the volume to his satisfaction, rolled down the windows and blew us away with the strength and clarity of his lovely voice. As an avid lover of classical music, I was impressed by his beautiful operatic baritone. We'd almost expected to hear the traditional throat singing commonly practiced in the homes we'd visited with Baagii.

"'Ulemjiin Chanar' is name. Is very famous in Mongol. Meaning is about beautiful woman and nature, deep meaning, is very philosophically," he explained. This friendly man turned out to have a lot more depth to his character than was evident originally. Obviously he could sing, but he was also graduating from medical school and could speak several languages: Mongolian, Russian, English, and Japanese.

His facility with languages reminded me of Dad, who had lived in Japan for two years and could communicate with our Japanese ESL students. Before long, we were showing off the few words we'd learned from him and from the students we hosted when we'd gathered around the dinner table.

Mom seemed lost in thought as she gazed out the window with her earphones on. *I wonder if she misses Dad?* I thought, my mind drifting again to Grady. I found myself dreaming to the music, wondering if Bree was missing Fernando and wondering if I'd ever have a chance with Grady, especially now that I wasn't even around. *Does Mom feel this same kind of longing? Or is she worrying about Sky?*

I studied her face, trying to read her thoughts. She was often quiet, but this time she seemed quiet in a different sort of way. Her face was inscrutable, so I gazed out the window at the vastness of the land, my attention diverted by my fears about having no GPS or experienced guide. I couldn't imagine how helpful Baagii's verbal directions could be to a guy who'd never even been to the 1.3million km² (500,000m²) Gobi desert. This was just one of the troubling details we'd learned after our departure. By the time we'd stopped for the tenth set of instructions on our first day out, I knew that Baagii had undoubtedly advised our apprentice guide to stop at every possible opportunity to ask for directions. *Because if you go even slightly off course, you'll be driving north instead of south*, I thought cynically.

We'd gotten off to a late start the first morning and soon began to doubt that we'd ever reach our intended destination. As night began to fall, Future stopped a solo man on his undersized but sturdy brown horse.

Following a quick chat, he returned to tell us, "He says it over that way, but it is getting late, and we should coming to his place and leaving in the morning." We followed the horseman and arrived fifteen minutes later at his few gers sitting beneath the wide-open, pastel sky.

We peeled ourselves out of the van and went inside. Ducking to avoid the drying meat strung up from the poles supporting the wood ceiling had become so routine that I barely even flinched at the sight, but the odour always got to me. Each day, I disliked it more and more. "Sheep" was present in clothing, shelter, and food, overwhelming the rest of my senses. I began to feel jealous of Future's self-assigned accommodation; the van's dust would seem less smothering than the overpowering smells destined to invade tonight's dreams.

After respectful handshakes and bows, we took seats anywhere we found room, whether it was a bed or the floor. There was not much to the simple home. They had the typical painted, wooden beds lined up against the walls, a simple fire stove in the centre, a tiny sink, a table surrounded by four small stools, and a small shrine for worship on one of two dressers. I consciously remembered to honour their custom of not turning my back to the sacred shrine except when exiting the ger.

Despite the fact that we had essentially taken over their home for the night and were both unexpected and unannounced, we couldn't have been more warmly welcomed. Future struck up an easy conversation with the man as his wife offered us what little they had to eat. Anticipating the family's dinner-time hospitality, I was mindful of a guest's guidelines. One of the hardest and sometimes scariest customs was that we could never refuse anything that was presented to us, and we could never be completely sure what might be offered.

Not surprisingly, we were served the standard appetizers: the infamous sour biscuits which were tough as nails; very sour yoghurt homemade in a big, yellowish-white pail; and of course, salty, milky tea. When I saw all of these things laid before me and passed around once again, I longed for Ulaanbaatar's wide selection of foods, and I still dearly missed the ever-present green tea and the amazing yoghurt we'd had in China. Mongolian tea was basically made by adding goat milk and a few teaspoons of salt to boiling water, plus the inevitable goat hairs which never failed to find their way into the soot-smeared kettle. Thank goodness custom didn't require us to finish each portion, only to taste everything, but I guess it boiled down to a case of "beggars can't be choosers." I did my part and nearly broke my tooth on yet another one of those sour biscuits. Sharing a few cups of fermented mare's milk, the two Mongolian men continued to laugh and talk over our mutton and rice dinner. Future told us that the man was the local ranger, but the ranger of what, exactly, I never did find out.

After the meal, Bree and I went outside, water bottles and toothbrushes in hand, and surreptitiously watched the nomads' evening routines. The ranger's sons were busy rounding up the goats for the night. I could hear their soft shouts as I brushed my teeth behind the ger, where the rocky earth was covered in animal droppings. Smelling the "sheepy" essence and feeling the soft, wet ooze of a fresh pile beneath my flip-flops, I tried not to connect this with the fuel for the fire that had heated the ger and cooked our dinner.

Returning to watch the shepherds a while longer, I saw the ranger's young daughter on her knees in the dirt with her arms wrapped around a younger goat's neck. He was mostly white with a brown patch over one eye, and his tail wagged like a puppy's. She sobbed and sobbed as she clung to him. It made me think of Harrison, and my heart hurt for her. I always tried hard to avoid thinking about him; it was just too painful. But with the cool air signalling the night's beginning and the stars slowly coming out, I had a hard time not feeling the weight of longing for him. I missed the softness and smell of his fur, and the way he'd sneeze when I puffed baby powder in his face. I wondered if I'd ever see him again.

Once I'd opened the door to those emotions, they came flooding back to haunt me as I remembered how the story had played out. Kathy took him home with her and returned only empty promises. As our departure date drew nearer, I'd grown increasingly anxious. After many unreturned phone calls, she finally confessed that she'd not been able to keep him because of her landlord's "one dog" rule. Naturally, she had chosen to keep her ugly Shiatsu over newcomer Harrison. Hoping to make the best of a difficult situation, though conveniently leaving me out of the loop, she'd completely changed our agreement and given him to her boyfriend, Dick. He'd turned out to be a philandering jerk who then gifted Harrison to his wife and their two teenaged sons. I had nothing more than a telephone number to work with after Kathy refused to ever talk to him again. Numerous calls to the aptly named Dick got me no closer to a final visit because he had lied to his wife about Harrison being an unloved, unwanted dog from the pound. He was probably afraid she would learn the truth if he involved me. Feeling like a ragdoll being tossed around, I made a final desperate attempt and called Janice, his wife. I explained our plans and assured her that I was not looking to take Harrison back, that I only wanted to say goodbye. After believing for a few days that I would finally get my final farewell, she'd called back to tell me that she thought it best if I never saw him again. Her words still burned like salt on an open wound.

I abandoned that train of thought to watch the Mongolian girl release her goat to join the herd being led into the corral. She promptly ran off, cradling her face in her hands. I sympathized with her and wished I could understand her language so I could hear her story.

Crawling into my bed that night I couldn't help but curse the fact that not one of the three adults involved, all of whom had children of their own, was willing to do what was necessary to allow a fourteen-year-old girl to see her beloved puppy one last time. I cried myself to sleep that night.

A van arrived in the morning and I watched the same young men bustling about. While Future was still inside with the man of the house, asking directions and thanking the family once more for their impromptu hospitality, we went over to investigate and found the men slaughtering the sheep and goats. They would most likely be taken to town and traded for some needed goods. Seven were already dead and lying belly-up on a long green tarp, waiting to be swung like sacks of dirt into the van. I felt compelled to search for a particular white goat, hoping he wasn't one of the dead. I found him squished in a pen, running left and right in synch with the others. He was slightly smaller than the rest and was being trampled as their agitated dance increased in intensity.

Unlike the timid sheep that practically rolled over and surrendered their lives, the goats did not go so willingly to their deaths. They had to be knocked out before their main artery was detached from their brave hearts. One by one, they were led from the pen and whacked over the head with a hammer. The job took two men, one to hold the goat between his legs and keep it steady while the other delivered a clean hit between the horns to crush the skull and knock it out.

Each goat was, in turn, hit, flipped, processed, and placed on the tarp until finally it was the turn of the white goat with the brown patch. As the daughter's predicament became clearer, I was relieved to see that she was not present. I'm sure it was better that way. Her goat's back hooves dug into the dirt but he couldn't get a grip and was inevitably dragged forward. He wrenched his head from side to side trying to free himself from the man's tight grasp on one of his stubby horns, again to no avail. Occasionally, it had taken several hits to do the job, so I was glad that he needed only one solid whack. His knees buckled and he hit the ground in a puff of dust. In that heartbeat, I ached at the realization that she would never, ever see him again.

As I looked back and waved goodbye to the nomadic family, I saw an aimless twister spinning in the emptiness of the dusty corral out of the corner of my eye. We weren't yet in the desert, but by the end of the second day, I could already see the scenery changing gradually from green to brown. We were running low on diesel fuel and had no clue where the nearest gas station was. Future, in authentic Mongolian fashion, maintained his carefree demeanour as if he were entirely unaware of any impending problems. The rest of us constantly watched the fuel gauge as the needle continued to fall. When the alarming red light first appeared, we all subconsciously held our breath, but Future poo-pooed our concern, saying, "My car, it goes way low. No worry!! You want to see canyon? We go to canyon. They saying is very beautiful. It's just somewhere here." A half-hour earlier, a few shepherds on a barren ridge had told us about a spectacular canyon we really should see, and Future was intent upon making sure we were satisfied tourists.

I wanted to believe he acted as happy-go-lucky as he did because he knew something we didn't, but I eventually decided that he was just plain crazy with respect to what was clearly a case of "the-nearly-empty-diesel-engine-in-the-middle-of-the-roadless- desert." It had evidently escaped him that if the car broke down, we would be something less than completely happy as we waited for someone on camelback to wander by and save us. The more likely rescue form of transportation would be a Russian van like Bimba's, stuffed to the rooftop with either families or dead sheep. Just such a van had driven up to the guest house where we were staying a few nights before as we were having dinner. A never-ending parade of people poured out; we stopped counting at thirty. The sheer number of people crammed into that van was unbelievable! After a quick stop to eat, they all piled back into the unfortunate vehicle and took off into the night. *Is he just completely oblivious? Or does he just not care what happens? Clearly, his priorities are mixed up.*

"No, no, Future. You know what? I think we're good. We can live without seeing the canyon," Ammon had finally said to prevent Future from venturing further and further off course and wasting more fuel hunting for it. Even when we were finally heading in a direction that was more likely to lead to a town, my heart fluttered with the same rhythm as the blinking, red fuel light.

At last, a small clump of "civilization" rose up out of the dust, and we spotted a lone gas station with two pumps. We had only a brief stretch left to go, but our relief was short-lived. Responding to the tires' resistance to a sand trap of sorts, Future stepped on the gas and only managed to dig us in deeper. *I'd have thought knowing how to drive in all kinds of sand would be the first thing taught in Mongolian driving lessons, but what do I know?* The tires sunk deeper into the trap and were eventually swallowed up. Future made a "tck, tck, tck" sound with his tongue, but seemed to have nothing more constructive to offer.

"At least we're in a town, though," Mom said as we climbed out to inspect the seriousness of our situation. I did feel better knowing we were that much less likely to starve, dehydrate, and wither away in the desert.

"Well, yah, but we're not out of danger yet," Ammon warned. I knew exactly what he meant. If our diesel ran out and left the tank dry and the van kaput, we'd become the four-Canadians-plus-one, itinerant, vagabond cabal. The recent image of the thirty hungry, dirty people spilling out of the van haunted me. I did not want us to be passengers number thirty-one through thirty-five bumping down the road on someone's lap for twenty hours. The town was surrounded by desert, and probably had no transportation or even Internet or a telephone to communicate with the outside world.

I was really missing Bimba and Baagii by this point. Our predicament made me appreciate how professional and comfortable the last tour had been. This time, we were not booked in or expected anywhere, and there was no tour operator sitting safely in Ulaanbaatar with the means to send out a search party if we didn't return. The only person who would notice we were missing was Baagii, so maybe we were lucky he couldn't get time off his radio job. On the other hand, if Baagii'd been in charge, I doubt we'd be in this predicament, but then again, I asked myself, *What do I know about travelling across a desert anyway?*

We could not judge exactly when the car's fuel would give out and were contemplating bringing diesel to it instead when Mom pointed at a couple of men who were making their way over. "Oh look! I think they're coming to help." All at once the ghost town came alive. Heads poked out of a tipped-over, metal shipping container and a few other unique forms of housing. Before we knew it, there were half-a-dozen men pushing the back of our car. Mom steered as the car popped out of the sand's grip, and we leapt aboard through the sliding door. The helpful local men cheered in our wake as we drove directly to the fuel pumps just ahead of us.

"Yah, is closed," Future said after a quick look around. "We have to find owner to fuelling pump." It was not good news, yet we were relieved to know that "closed" didn't necessarily mean a dead end here. Our tentative plan was to search through the concrete neigh-bourhood, but Future began shouting something repeatedly from the car.

"What is he yelling?! 'Gas station guy, we need fuel! Gas station guy! '?? Seriously," Bree laughed.

"Pretty much," Ammon replied. "The guy probably decided to close down early because it was slow."

"I can't imagine it ever gets busy. I'd go home, too," Mom said. "I bet only four people in this whole village own a car."

"And no doubt they all know where each other lives," Ammon added. With so few clients and no competition, the owner might as well sit at home and wait for work to come to him. We certainly need-ed him a lot more than he needed us.

It soon became apparent that Future's stationary shouting was not getting results, so we reverted to plan B. It was not too hard to locate the owner's low-rise apartment building by asking people in the small town where he lived, at which point, Future shouted some more, this time over a wooden fence towards the indicated building. A few minutes after a head poked from a window, the owner was roused from his bed, night cap and all, and came shuffling down the outer concrete stairs. Future threw him in our van and off we went, our headlights catching the wings of dancing bugs. This time, he was extra careful to avoid more sand traps.

The man went to work with no complaints. His eyes were dark, his skin a pale brown, and he sported a pronounced five o'clock shadow. Once we were refuelled and in the clear for another day's adventure, we drove the owner home and he waved us off. It wouldn't be the last time we'd have to do this. I wasn't quite sure where the week would lead, but I knew we had an interesting new friend along for the ride, posing as our guide.

I Know You
36

"**W**e've got to get going," Ammon was urging. "Where is Future? Doesn't he realize if we don't leave now, we're never going to make it? And you can't get anywhere in the dark. Like the ranger said, it's hard enough in the day. This guy is just fiddle-fartin' around like he's on a holiday or something."

"Well, that is kind of the mentality here, I think," Mom piped in. "Are you as tired as I am? I couldn't sleep through those dogs howling all night long!"

"We haven't even ordered breakfast yet!" Ammon growled and threw up his hands in exasperation. He must not have slept well, either. When Future strolled in a few minutes later, it was obvious that he was enjoying himself and didn't see any point in rushing.

"There has to be something to eat!" I demanded, not meaning to be heard.

"Yes, Little Savannah," Future said, walking over to translate the chalkboard menu on the wall. "There is mutton with rice, mutton soup, mutton---"

"I swear to the lords I am not eating another stinking bowl of that yucky, horrible – Argh!"

He laughed in response and simply said, "Little Savannah, this is good for you." *In comparison to what? Sand?* The thought of another soggy white dumpling stuffed with woolly old sheep made me sick.

At dinner the night before, I'd lost track of how many hairs I'd pulled from my bowl and teeth.

Most of the ten-seat restaurants we stopped in at little towns along the way had menus hanging on the wall. Each apparently offered a wide variety of choices, but they were invariably out of every item we ordered except for those based on mutton. All we ever got in response to Future's queries was head-shaking and an endless series of "noes," though every once in a while they'd have goulash, a delightful dish made with beef, noodles, and potatoes. Sometimes we had the added luxury of the local version of carrot salad, which was, quite literally, just shreds of carrot with a bit of vinegar and pepper for dressing.

"Oh dear, I guess there was no imagination put into that one," Mom had initially laughed at the small orange pile on her plate, but we ended up shovelling the salad down happily. It was delicious!

Just as in China, we never knew what we were going to get when we ordered. We were repeatedly surprised by Chinese versions of club sandwiches, French toast, and spaghetti bolognese. Ammon always shook his head at the strange versions of western food we were served as he enjoyed a fabulous Chinese dish for a quarter of the price. I found it hard to accept the fact that, as often as I might order a pizza, I wasn't going to get anything that came close to the favourite food I so dearly missed from home.

"Well, you're going to have to eat the mutton unless you want to walk back to Ulaanbaatar, 'cause it's not getting any better from here," Ammon impatiently hurried our discussion of our limited choices. "And you have six days left! So suck it up and get used to it!"

Nearer to Mongolia's capital city, meals often included at least a few standard vegetables, mainly carrots, onions, potatoes, and very occasionally, beets. Ammon was just telling me what I already knew; the further we ventured away from Ulaanbaatar, the fewer options there'd be.

Mom yawned and tried the gentle approach. "Savannah, these people have eaten it all their lives. It's not the end of the world if you have to eat it for a month," she said, trying to preserve her children's small remaining bits of sanity.

"Mom, dogs eat dog food their whole lives, too. It's hard to force them to go back to it once they get a taste of what human food is like. It's too late for me! I've already tasted real food. These guys don't have anything to compare it to, so how can they complain?" I objected, remembering Khongorzul and her satisfied smile as she enjoyed that horrible soup in the tiny border town before we took the sixteen-hour train ride to *Ulaanbaatar*.

"Okay fine. There's some chocolate in the car. Go eat that while it's still hard," Mom said. The days were scorching hot and they some-how got even hotter the further south we travelled, but the desert climate's relatively chilly nights gave the melted chocolate a chance to harden again.

All Bree had to say was a subdued, resigned, "This is lame." Nobody knew exactly which unfortunate circumstance she was referring to, but she was beginning to look like one of those sand kids we'd seen in the desert. I'm sure I was, too, had there been a mirror any-where that I could check. Luckily there wasn't. I couldn't recall the last time I'd seen myself in a mirror, and I was pretty sure I'd rather pass on that, anyway. We'd spent weeks and weeks living in baggy clothes with no make-up. I was even forced to wear my geeky glasses 'cause there was too much dust for my contact lenses. When I'd found out only two years earlier that I had to wear them, I was in complete dis-belief. I was the only person in my immediate family so afflicted. *A four-eyes. Me?! How did that happen?*

Cleaning facilities were generally non-existent in the countryside. Luckily, I had used the free laundry in our Beijing hotel before enter-ing Mongolia. Ammon was already happily into hand washing when we were in the city, but outside the capital, there wasn't a bucket or enough water to fill one to be found anywhere. After nearly a month out in the country, rolling around in dusty vehicles and practically sleeping with farm animals, I knew I, too, would have to hand wash my clothes. They stank. I stank. *Everything* stank.

There were never any showers at our rural accommodations, but on one rare occasion, we did find a very large metal pipe gushing with icy water from the earth. The six-inch-diameter hose located near a few gers and buildings in the open desert was used as the small community's water supply and wash site. Locals filled big plastic jugs and tin milk containers for cooking and drinking. These were then transported using a small wooden plank that was drawn by a rope and supported by two wheels on either side. When we arrived, a few teenage girls and children were doing laundry, and a very short but nonetheless well-toned man in tight underwear was taking a "shower." Freshly washed and still wet, he proceeded to clean his small motorcycle with a soapy rag. I could tell from the way the two girls were avidly watching him that he was the hot shot of the neighbourhood. I didn't think they were happy about our drawing his attention away from them, since they'd probably planned to do the laundry when they knew he would be there.

We all jumped at the opportunity to wash the twenty-eight layers of Mongolian grime off the limbs we could expose without stripping down. Then out came the shampoo; washing our hair never felt so glorious. Future ran around in his orange-and-grey-striped undies and white plastic sandals rinsing himself. Then he washed the van so it, too, could enjoy five minutes of cleanliness.

"Don't you love a country where you can run around in your underwear in the wild?!" Ammon said, smiling and accidentally catching Future's attention.

"Ammon! Help me, you must," Future laughed, waving his wet shirt around before stuffing it in Ammon's hand.

"You dirty guy!" he joked, as he scrubbed Future's back with the soapy shirt.

Though we were sopping wet when we jumped back in the van, we were completely dry only minutes later. Soon we were again sitting in puddles of sweat as we drove further into this strange country. There were still many herds of goats, sheep, horses, and even camels roaming free.

"Five sheep and ten horses to every person in the year 2000," Ammon reported, turning around in the passenger seat on the car's left-hand side.

"But I never owned a sheep!" Future said, perhaps surprised by Ammon's statement. We all laughed because we knew he'd never owned animals of any kind.

"Well Future, I guess your five went to those who have hundreds," Bree told him.

"Yah, I think so! They stole my sheep!" He pretended to be aggrieved.

"There are roughly three million people in Mongolia; forty-five percent of them live in the capital and thirty percent are nomadic. Most of the nomads sell raw wool to travelling traders or transport it to towns themselves," Ammon explained.

Future was among that forty-five percent. He relied on his intellect and personality to make a living; he was not meant for hands-on tasks like herding, mechanics, or other skills related to outback living. As I tried to understand how he fit into Mongolian culture, I figured that a big part of surviving has to do with your general outlook on life and not letting hard times get the better of you. With all the near catastrophes we'd encountered at every turn – running out of fuel, flat tires, broken parts, sand traps, and so on – it would have been futile for Future to react angrily. His positive persona and accepting attitude encouraged us to rely on him.

"This bumpy road is killing me. I'm going to have a broken back by the end of the trip!" Mom complained as we all climbed out of the van, still feeling a bit raw from the previous excursion. We were stopping at the desolate ruins of Ongiin Khiid, an old Buddhist monastery. It was constructed in the late eighteenth century to honour the Dalai Lama's first-ever visit to Mongolia. Once home to hundreds of monks, it was now the crumbling essence of what had once been a major spiritual spot.

We had only seen one or two cars the whole day, so we weren't surprised to have the place completely to ourselves. The few monks who came every morning had long since completed their rituals of worship. By the time we arrived, the blazing red sun was hovering low in the west.

"Here's an interesting fact. Mongolia has only a little under 2,000km (1,243mi) of paved road!" Ammon announced to our groaning, aching bodies.

"Meaning?" Bree prompted him for more.

"That is NOT a lot! To put it in context, Hong Kong – you re-member that place? You've been there---"

"Yah, I knooow!" Bree said sassily.

"Well, you never know. You did forget your tooth, eh?"

"HEY!" she barked, as she laughed and waved the retainer, to which her fake left eyetooth was attached, around on her tongue at him.

"Now you're being nasty!" Ammon protested.

I giggled, remembering how our waiter from a lunch break days before had run after us, frantically waving his hand over his head. He caught up to us, opened his hand, and said the equivalent of, "For you? For you?"

Bree had gasped and rushed over, swiping the object from his palm. "Oh my gosh, my retainer!! Thank you, thank you. I love you! I would have died without my tooth!" When she'd popped it into her mouth mid-sentence, the man first looked confused and then startled when he realized what he'd just been holding. Nonetheless, he seemed pleased to have made her smile. Literally!

"Put that thing away!" Ammon shuddered before continuing. "Hong Kong has more roads than all of Mongolia put together, and it's just a small island."

"That's not hard to believe! I don't even remember what paved feels like anymore. What does it even look like? Can somebody please describe it to me?" I went on, exaggerating slightly.

"And did you know Mongolia is the eighteenth largest country in the world? I could never understand why nobody ever mentions it when it's so big. And I'd seriously wonder, 'Is it real, or is it just there on the map?' Well, now I know," he smirked contentedly.

"You always loved maps. When you were just a little guy, you al-ways marvelled over them," Mom said, not for the first time.

"Eighteenth doesn't seem that big, though," I said.

"But do you know how many countries there are in the world?" Ammon asked, the answer ready on the tip of his tongue, as usual.

Bree, anxious to guess first, as usual, shouted out, "sixty-eight!"

"Ammon, I think I do not know! I did not know this. That it eighteenth biggest was," said Future, always ready to join the conversation.

"Ummm, I really don't know. Let's say, oh, I dunno. I probably only know, like, ten," I gave up quickly.

"Oh c'mon! You know more than that!" Mom said, a touch annoyed. "You know a lot more than that. You've *been* to five already. The U.S., Canada, Mexico, China, Mongolia. You know Russia, 'cause we're going there next, and Italy and France---"

"And Japan!" *Of course I know more!* "Venezuela, Brazil ..." I thought of every home stay student we had ever had, and before I knew it, I was over twenty-five countries. "Korea, twenty-five; Thailand, twenty-six; Singapore, twenty-seven---"

"And we're going to India and Nepal, which you should know. And here are two more that I'm sure you forgot: Kazakhstan and Kyrgyzstan. We're going there after Russia, so you better memorize those," Ammon said, as we explored the ruins further.

"Okay, so that's thirty-one. Oh, and the Netherlands, that's thirty-two."

"Okay, sixty-eight then!" Bree chose again, even more sure than before.

"No, you're way off. There are fifty-four countries in Africa alone!"

"What?!" We were both surprised.

"I'm guessing a hundred and two then!" I said.

"You guys are still way off. These are things you should know. There are one hundred and ninety-three countries in the world, give or take a few, depending on whose list you're going by."

"How many have you been to already?" Mom asked him.

"Mongolia is the thirty-third country I've been to," he reported proudly.

"Wow, Ammon!" Future gasped as he climbed back into the driver's seat.

"I can't even name that many!" I said. *He really does know everything off the top of his head!*

"Wow! I want to make it to a hundred," Bree said, announcing what was clearly a very recently set goal, given she'd guessed there were only sixty-eight countries just moments before.

"And you want to go to ALL of them?!" I asked Ammon.

"That's the dream," he smiled.

"You are a loooong way off, my friend" I chortled as I climbed back into the van. I was certain he would be dead and buried long before he got even half of them. I had only been to five so far, and it seemed an entire lifetime had passed.

"NOW I KNOW!!" Future announced, pointing his finger at Ammon and stopping him in his place just as he was about to climb in after Bree. The old ruins of the ancient monastery were beautifully lit behind him, golden in the fading sunlight. Ammon had grown an impressive beard rather than try to shave out here, and his hair was now long enough to curl around his shoulders. He was also tall, of course, and his bone structure was strong and prominent, like that of an ancient Roman.

"I know now who you look like, you. I see him before, this guy. This guy – JESUS!"

"I'm a believer!" Bree shouted out of nowhere.

"You reminded me all this time. Is Jesus. I have this man seen, Jesus, in picture. That is you!! I *knew* I see you before." He looked very pleased with himself, like he'd just figured out a riddle that had been puzzling him for a long time. And indeed, he had, if only to his own satisfaction. We all turned simultaneously to examine Ammon/Jesus anew.

Ammon stood perplexed for just a moment and then laughed uncontrollably. "Okay then. Now that my cover's blown, let's not talk about this here," Ammon joked, waving back at the once magnificent Buddhist monastery.

Trust from Dust
37

*A*side from the beetles leaving zipper-like tracks in the singing sands, Khongoriin Els dunes appeared to be completely untouched. Our footprints were gigantic next to the tiny threads the beetles left behind.

"They're so cute. I just love watching them!" Mom bent over to get a closer look at the shiny black bugs.

"They are incredible," I said, watching another one skitter along. Checking the bearing of the insect's path, I wondered where on earth it was headed, and from where it had come. There was absolutely nothing but the endless dunes in every direction. Getting anywhere significantly different from where it was would take much longer than his natural lifespan.

"These sand dunes stretch across 100km (62mi) and are up to 20km (12.4mi) wide. Some of them reach heights of 0.8km (.5mi)," Ammon told us before slipping his guide book back into his baggy, cut-off shorts.

A light breeze blew the golden crumbs uphill like ripples on water. Looking back, I could see that our footprints were already being washed away by the windswept dunes' ever-changing movements. From this distance, I could just barely make out the camouflaged figures of our camels where we'd left them below. The walk was too strenuous for them.

We climbed until we could climb no more, though Bree and Future somehow found the energy to chase each other playfully. *Some people never grow up!* He tried trapping her but she dodged him like a cat. In his attempts to jump and catch her, his hat flew off his head and rolled away, or perhaps she'd kicked it off his head while hand-springing out of his grasp. He dove down the mountain after it, somersaulting backwards and forwards and surely getting sand in each and every orifice imaginable in the process. Bree stood laughing triumphantly from the top while he and his hat tumbled downwards in a spray of sparkly brown sugar. Future's legs were swallowed up to his knees when he slid to a stop and waved his rescued hat above his head. I envied their ability to live in the moment like that. They never seemed to worry about dehydration, sun stroke, heat exhaustion, or the simple fact that there was only mutton fat to replace their spent energy. Not for the first time, though, I realized that he was on vacation, too, and having just as much fun as we were, if not more.

Crunching grainy bits between our teeth, we returned to the lower edges of the dunes where we'd left the camels and found a curious hole our two guides had dug. They explained they were letting the camels have a drink and showed us the little pool of mucky water sitting in the bottom.

"But how did they know where they would find water?!" Mom asked, amazed.

"Where ground is cold, this is how you finding. And green, life grows," Future proclaimed. Barefoot, I felt around and noticed that the ground was surprisingly cold, moist even. *Of course!* Suddenly, it made perfect sense and explained the small patches of green grass which unexpectedly sprouted up only steps away from the edge of the dunes. Getting down into the hole, Future dug deeper until a fair-sized puddle formed around his bare ankles.

"Hey, hey! You know what I was thinking?!" Bree started, "Here's another way movies can be educational! The cartoon *Dinosaurs* teaches kids how to dig for water. I remember that exact lesson about the cooler ground! Yah, I learned it from that show!!" she finished proudly. It never failed to amaze me how well her memory worked, if only when it came to movies.

"Good for you, dear," Ammon did an amazingly accurate imitation of how we'd so often heard our grandma encourage us.

The camels were lying on their bellies with all four knees buried in the sand. Though I'd not received instructions or read any handy camel-riding manuals, I managed to swing my leg up and over the blanket "saddle" that was fastened between the two humps and had stirrups fashioned from woven rope. My feet came within inches of the ground, unlike Ammon, who was still standing awkwardly on tiptoe with the camel between his legs.

With a blunt command and a smack on the bottom from the weather-worn owner, the camel abruptly straightened its rear legs and catapulted me forward. I clung to anything I could as it practically threw me over the first hump. While he stood there with his bum in the air, I was uncomfortably suspended for a very long few seconds before he leisurely manoeuvred his front legs out from beneath him and stood upright. When the front half rose, I was thrown backwards so rapidly that I again feared I would somersault backwards over the other hump. I barely managed to settle into my "seat" before I realized I was sitting at least six-and-a-half feet off the ground.

"Why are their humps so floppy?!" Bree asked as she rode up beside me. She lifted one in an attempt to make it stay upright, but it persistently fell to the side. "This is not how I imagined it would be!" She was almost devastated by the lifeless lump.

"Me neither. I thought it would be two full, rounded humps like in the cartoons, but these are so long and dangly," I agreed.

"Do you guys know why they have humps in the first place?" Ammon asked.

"Sure. 'Cause if they weren't there, we'd fall right off. They're built-in seatbelts," Bree joked. Ammon glared at her dismissively.

"Nooooo," he said, drawing the syllable out in hopes someone else might jump in to answer.

"They're basically just saggy boobs, aren't they? You told us this before," I recalled.

"They're used for fat storage. That's how they can last so long out in the desert."

"That makes sense to me," Mom chimed in. "The first place you lose weight is always in your boobs."

"Oh my gosh, Mom! Way too much information," Ammon recoiled.

"Well, it's true!" Mom supported her argument by indicating her own as an example, grossing Ammon out even more in the process. He shuddered deeply. I'm sure he was again questioning what he'd gotten himself into by agreeing to go on this trip with three females.

"I thought they stored water," Bree said.

"'They' meaning the seatbelts?" he teased. "No, the water thing is a common misconception. But it's more complicated than that. It has to do with the shape of their red blood cells," Ammon explained. "The way they're sagging like this tells us that they don't have much reserve left."

"Yah! Judging by their humps, it looks like they've been wandering the desert for years. No one has been taking care of them," Mom pointed out.

"Probably not that long ago, but they can go up to thirty days without a drop of water."

"What's the difference between a one-hump and a two-hump camel?" Mom asked.

"A one-hump camel can't last as long as a two-hump?" Bree guessed again.

"These are Bactrian camels from Asia. Asian camels are a lot rarer than the one-humpers that come from the Middle East," Ammon explained.

"Wow, really? I never realized that," I said.

"So, it's sorta like the African elephants having big ears and the Indian ones having smaller ears." Mom loves elephants.

"Why do the guides have to hold the reins? I wanna race!" Bree said loudly. The camels were led by ropes tied to wooden rings dangling from the hole that was pierced through the nose of every camel at a young age. "Why do you get to have the reigns, Future?"

"I is professional. I know camels!" he proclaimed proudly, grabbing my black flip-flop off my foot and using it to smack the camel's side to show it who was boss.

"I think it's because nobody ever comes out here to ride them, so they aren't that tame," Ammon began. "You see how many herds are just roaming around out here. They probably caught these guys last week---"

As if to prove Ammon's point, Future's camel had started to rebel and was twisting its neck around as it attempted to bite his foot. The camel emitted a cacophony of loud, high-pitched growling and snarling noises that echoed across the sand. Flailing his arms, Future pitifully tried to hide from its swinging head behind my small flip-flop, coming just short of losing both it and his fingers to the camel's teeth.

"Or maybe 'cause they just know we're stupid tourists and the closest hospital is a week away," Ammon added when Future's camel bolted off into the empty desert, the owner hollering after them both. This demonstrated just how undomesticated these camels were, but it also cast doubt on Future's claims to have expertise with them.

"I don't want to have this thing run away on me," I confessed, as I watched Future nearly fly off his ill-tempered beast as the owner continued pursuing them frantically on foot.

The sun was blazing and my face felt like a potato chip without the oil. Future had finally been rescued and was still laughing good-naturedly at himself. Though he and Bree seemed too cool to acknowledge the heat and Ammon was far too tough to allow that the sun could dampen his spirits, the scorching, forty-five-minute return trip was exhausting. To keep our sanity, we joined a mutual game of naming our favourite and most desired cravings.

"Strawberry milkshake with sprinkles," Bree started.

"Strawberry/raspberry Yogen Fruz," I jumped in right after.

"Dr. Pepper."

"Sushi," Bree continued.

"Mocha Frappuccino, with extra whipped cream!" I drooled.

"Cold water," Ammon's participation surprised us, even if his choice was a little lacking in imagination. He usually belittled our games.

"Yah!" we all jinxed.

"Yes, water cold. We get for you. They having," Future said, happy to be able to direct us to the first thing he recognized on our list. He leaned forward to talk to the local man, who now had his hand firmly fastened around Future's reigns. "Yes, yes. They get for us," he confirmed happily.

I was ecstatic over the prospect of drinking something as simple as water. *Cold* water! I envisioned pulling a bottle out from a refrigerator, so cold that beads of condensation rolled down its sides. *Maybe even slushy cold Sprite, like we had at the Tiger Leaping Gorge. That was heaven!*

Once the camels were tied up to a small wooden pole near the gers, the youngest of the family's three daughters volunteered to show us where the water could be found. She had braided pigtails and used little purple hairclips to try to control her wild hair. Chubby cheeks and big teeth made her nose seem tiny and rabbit-like, and her eyes virtually disappeared whenever Future made her laugh. Chucking the young girl in our van, we headed out, leaving the rest of her family to prepare dinner.

"Isn't it crazy that they just let us take her? I mean, really? They don't know us from a hill of beans. We could just as easily kidnap her!" Mom commented.

She told us she was ten years old, which started me wondering things like, *How do they celebrate birthdays? Would they actually know what the date was living out here, or only seasons and years? But then, how important could dates be in a place where there are no appointments or anything?*

The little girl's family had welcomed us to stay the night when we arrived unexpectedly on their doorstep that afternoon. People were always very helpful when we'd pull up unexpectedly, hoping to get pointed in the right direction or have a warm place to stay and get a nibble of anything they had to spare. We initially tried to reimburse the gracious occupants in these situations, but soon learned that doing so was not their custom; in fact, offering payment usually caused them to take offense. Their custom seemed to be based on a general belief that if everyone helps when they can, everyone will always have what they need, so it was much better to humbly accept their warm hospitality and friendship.

Another vital custom to understand was the need to shout out "nokhoi khor! nokhoi khor!" when approaching any ger. I didn't understand the importance of the phrase, which translates roughly to "hold the dogs," until we drove up to a ger that had been left temporarily vacant by local nomads who'd gone off to tend their flocks. Future had called out "Nokhoi khor! Nokhoi khor! Nokhoi khor!" but no one was home to keep the canine guard in check. As we drew nearer, the most vicious-looking, shaggy dog I've ever seen exploded from the shade of the ger. We turned and fled the moment the beast charged towards our van, its brutish teeth bared. He'd pursued us as diligently as a lion running down a gemsbok as we'd quickly scrambled behind the van's doors. If Future hadn't quickly rolled up the window, he'd have had one seriously badass dog sitting in his lap, making for some interesting company. If you were to learn only one word or phrase in Mongolia, this traditional greeting would be it – Nokhoi khor!!

The girl squatted in the front passenger seat and pointed left and right for about half-an-hour before she abruptly signalled that we should stop. It looked no different from anywhere else we'd seen, but she jumped out of the van and waved at us to follow her on foot. Having spent so long in the desert, I ached for the feeling of ice water washing down my throat; I'd have gone to the ends of the earth for it.

It was easy to see why we'd left the car behind. It became far too sandy and bushy to drive on, even if we'd had four-wheel drive. As the girl led us down an invisible path identified only by simple bumps in the terrain, it started to sink in that we were not getting any closer to a fridge. My unrealistic expectation of reaching a small town that had cold water died. *Where was I expecting to find electricity out here anyway?* I questioned myself. *Obviously, the sun is getting to me.*

"If you guys weren't here, I wouldn't go anywhere with her! I don't trust this tiny girl to get us there, let alone back!" I worried, glancing behind at our unmarked path.

"Yah. Especially now that our guard's down and we're miles away from the van, even if we knew where it was! I'm sure it's a plot," Ammon agreed just to scare us.

"But Ammon! You are *Jesus,*" Future began, always putting the same emphasis on his second name. "You can find your way." Amused, he tromped behind the girl as if in a parade.

"You know there's no sense in worrying about stuff like that, Savannah. People should just trust because otherwise, you could go crazy with suspicion. What happens, happens," Mom said.

Although I was beginning to get nervous, my curiosity was increasing. *How on earth is this supposed to lead to water?* The land became even more sandy and lumpy, and now there were lots more bushes that made it almost impossible to navigate. It had been a while since we'd left the van. Who knew how far we were from the ger? But with the sun sinking along with my heart, we kept on.

"What time must it be getting to be?" I asked.

"About ten if the sun is starting to set." Ammon didn't even have to glance at the watch clipped to his belt.

It crossed my mind that when I was her age, this would've been bedtime, *but I suppose with no school to get up for* ... The young girl was twisting and turning, ducking and weaving through the desert bushes, appearing and disappearing just often enough that we could follow her.

"Where on earth is she taking us?" Mom voiced, sounding more fascinated than worried.

"Are you sure she understood what we asked for?" I whispered, not wanting Future to overhear. "She's probably getting us lost in these bogs, like Gollum did to the hobbits, and then the next thing you know--- Hey, where is she?!"

"Oh, stop it!" Mom snapped.

"No, really. Where did she go?" I asked, looking side to side.

"Over here, you guys. Stop slacking," Ammon called from our left. "You see how authentic this is? This is awesome!"

"What do you mean?" Bree asked.

"You can't tell? This isn't a tourist set up, this is a real family. This is their life, and this is how they live it. Remember the ice canyon yesterday at Yolin Am? How the camels were all decorated with bells and ribbons? Yah right! They can't afford that kind of stuff, and even the few who can would only bring it out for special occasions. That whole show was for us. They know tourists go there to see the ice canyon so they can charge five thousand togrog for it. That's why it was kind of expensive."

"You call five dollars to ride a camel expensive? Gosh, it costs more than that just to go look at one in the zoo!" I retaliated.

"It's all relative," he insisted.

Our chatting didn't seem to make the time pass any faster. It still seemed like forever before the grassy mounds of earth opened up into a small oasis built around a natural spring. Fields of green grass framed by an elegant sand dune presented an ideal setting for cows, horses, and a few camels. The whole scene was washed in perfect lighting from the setting sun. The silent girl led us around the marshy edges on a crudely made boardwalk to where the water spewed up from the ground. Covering it was a small metal cage of sorts to prevent roaming livestock from contaminating it, though it hadn't kept the frogs and small, grey, fresh-water shrimp out.

"We didn't bring any purifying tablets," Mom pointed out.

"Well, we've survived up until now. Let Bree try it first, just to be sure."

"Ammon! That's not very nice! But we are taking it directly from the source. If it's coming straight from the earth, it should be okay."

"Good, 'cause I'm not waiting until we get back," I said.

"Here, then," he handed the dusty bottle to me. "You try it first."

Getting down on my knees next to Bree, I rinsed the bottle out first. Feeling the tepid water on my hands was wonderful, though it wasn't the kind of cold I'd been dreaming of. I was so happy to see fresh water and lots of it that I ignored the smell of sulphur and other such minerals. I didn't even bother trying to strain out any tiny shrimp that I might have caught; I simply held the bottle up in a salute in the dim lighting and glugged it back, focussing only on the wet sensation.

Prehistoric
38

*B*y the fourth day of our journey, the van was looking a lot worse for wear. A few times a day, Future had to ask Ammon to get out and reconnect the battery wires that constantly came loose in the engine. So far, the van had made Future proud and always worked again after a bit of fiddling. Despite the constant threat of breaking down, we felt we had no choice but to go on with our trip, having come this far.

Because the scenery didn't change too much here in the south, I often found myself with my nose between the pages of *Gone with the Wind*. I literally couldn't put the book down and regularly gasped and commented aloud as I read. I got so involved in the story that I sometimes forgot anyone was listening or that I was in Mongolia at all.

"What you really should be doing is looking at the scenery," Ammon suggested. I think he was just tired of hearing my comments: "Oh, my sweet Rhett," "Oh, my heart," "Oh, Rhett!"

"Oh. Counting dead horses, you mean? Gotta love doing that," I replied, barely looking up from the sand-covered pages.

"I've already counted thirteen today!" Mom sounded oddly cheerful given the morbid subject matter.

"Good for you." I much preferred to concentrate on the lively mares pulling carriages loaded with beautifully dressed women in my novel.

"Oh! Fourteen," Mom shouted, and sure enough, there was yet another dried up skeleton. Half buried, its backbone was displayed prominently enough to play it like a xylophone. Its deep, dark eye sockets were surrounded by bits of brown hide, and tufts of hair still clung to its white skull.

In the northwest parts of the country where it was greener, we'd seen flocks of huge vultures feasting. We watched once as dozens of them bashed heads as they fought for their share of a young goat's flesh, its newly dead face mangled and already chewed to bits. The vultures were like no other bird I'd ever seen in the wild, given the sheer size of them and their very pronounced slouch. Though it was a bit bizarre, we were fascinated by the way they pecked at the goat to get a good meal. One eyeball was missing and the other was dangling from a smaller vulture's beak before he threw his neck back and gobbled it down. When we got too close to the gory scene, they either hopped away with their heads sweeping down below their shoulders or took off, spreading their wings so wide they cast shadows over us.

Given the country's harsh, unsheltered winters and blazing summers, I guessed that animals would drop like flies and feed them well. I wondered why we hadn't seen any vultures here. Had they already picked all those horses clean? Or did they not usually travel this far south?

"Yesterday I stopped counting at forty." Bree's comment reminded me of the dog-counting game Bree and I had played, somewhat addictively for a period, when we were kids. We literally could not see a dog without counting it, but before I knew it, dog counting was only a memory. I couldn't remember when or how it was that we'd quit playing that game and marvelled at how we came to be counting dead horses in the desert instead. I felt better about the substitution when I realized that this, too, would be just a memory one day.

"Wait! What was that sound?" Mom shouted over all the other noises, bringing me back to the present. "Future! Future! Turn down the music." He was singing away and we had to wave at him frantically to adjust the volume. "Something is dragging!"

Ammon checked it out while we waited and an apparently disinterested Future continued to hum along to the muted tune. "So.

Did anyone notice that the whole bottom of the car is falling off?" Ammon asked casually when he popped back up from his quick inspection.

"What do you mean, the whole bottom of the car?!" Mom insisted.

"The bottom of the car is dragging on the ground."

"It doesn't look too bad," Mom decided after she'd checked it out, too. "That's just the protective shield. It could be worse."

"It could be worse? This is only the beginning of it being worse!" Ammon warned. "We better just be extra careful not to go over anything crazy and scratch the real important stuff all to crap, 'cause now everything is exposed."

"We are already *on* careful mode. We can't even go a couple of hours without stopping for something. This car is doomed!" I felt like it was my job to convince them of it, especially Future, who only ever "tck tcked" with his tongue and shrugged. He didn't even flinch at the huge metal slab that we pulled loose from underneath. He just threw it in the back and went on driving.

"Well, no sense in worrying about it now. Let's just see how far we get," Mom said.

"Before we get stuck again?" Bree asked.

"Yes," Mom answered frankly.

"Yah, I knew it. It only took two hours," Bree bragged, looking up from her watch. It was dryer and hotter and deader here than anywhere else, if that was possible. We were in the heart of the flaming cliffs of Bayanzag, and it looked as if we really had entered the burning pits of Hell. The land was completely desolate, and the brilliant reds and oranges of the magnificent cliffs only seemed to increase the heat.

"Oh geez, seriously? Again!?" I cried in response to Future's, "Oh no. Oh, no good. Tck, tck, tck."

"Yep. We're stuck," Ammon confirmed.

Only an hour earlier, we'd been standing at the top of a ridge looking out as Ammon told us the incredible history of the land we stood on.

"That used to be lush vegetation out there," Mom said as she surveyed the huge red valley.

"Yup! And seaside property, too, complete with dinosaurs," Ammon added. "This was the first place they ever discovered fossilized dinosaur eggs. Can you imagine what that would be like!? Now they've found, I think, fifteen different types of dinosaurs here." It was crazy to imagine that if we went back in time only a few hundred million years, I would be standing in the presence of dinosaurs! I was awe-struck by the very idea of it.

"You were always crazy about dinosaurs as a kid. You used to know the proper, scientific name of every single kind. Did you ever think you'd come here, Ammon?"

"Who knows? Why not? Life is full of mysteries and surprises. I'd believe I'd come here before I'd believe I'd be travelling around the world with you bunch."

"That's true enough," I agreed.

Now we were stuck right in the heart of that sea/desert, surrounded by the burning cliffs. We all crawled out of the minivan and took our usual places. Mom jumped into the driver's seat and moved the seat forward so she could reach the pedals, while the rest of us positioned ourselves at the rear of the van with our hands flat on the burning hot, hatchback trunk. With all hands pressed hard against the car, we shouted, "Ready? Three, two, one – HEAVE!" The tires spun rapidly and spit hot sand up in our faces until the van suddenly went sliding over to the side.

"What the heck, Mom?!" Ammon snapped as he walked around the front, eying the mess she'd made.

"What? What did I do?" she exclaimed, leaning out the open window to look.

"You just made it worse! You were supposed to turn the wheel the *other* way!"

"Sorry, it's confusing 'cause the steering wheel is on the wrong side," she protested helplessly.

"But now we're really screwed!" Ammon barked, throwing up his hands.

"No, we're not. It's okay, I'll fix it. It'll be fine," she said, anxious to relieve everyone's frustration. Ammon clenched his teeth and growled deeply, but quietly. Clearly, he was just as sick of the sand and the heat and the frequent problems as I was.

"Don't act so stupid!" Bree remained completely unfazed by his temper. His displays of anger always made me timid as a mouse, but she was never frightened. In situations where I felt I needed to tiptoe carefully and wouldn't dare start fussing, she tromped right in like a bull in a china shop.

"Is okay, Mama," Future said, possibly feeling guilty himself.

"What do we do now?" Bree asked Mom.

"We need to ground the wheels so they have something to grip. It would be good if we had some trees or rocks or wood or anything to---"

"But we don't," Ammon said accusingly. "Unless you wanna go dig up some dinosaur bones and use them. That's about all you'll find out here."

What if we can't get out? There's nothing and no one to help us. Nobody will even know we've gone missing. I was uncomfortably aware of the heat and the fiery red earth that had swallowed up the dinosaurs millions of years ago. At a blazing 45°C (113°F), even the wind hurt. *A car and a few humans is nothing but a teensy snack for this land.* I pictured our bones in the sand, just like those of the horses – unnoticed and left to rot. Even worse thoughts occurred to me then. *We wouldn't even rot! We'd just shrivel up like mummies and our intestines would spill out and shrink up like baked worms. But there aren't even any worms out here to eat us. Not even those ugly vultures would find us.*

"We'll just have to dig a little to at least free the wheels," Mom suggested.

"Okay, then. I'm pumped; let's just do it!" Bree got down on her knees and started digging with her hands. "Ooh! Ow! Ow, ow, ow!! Dang! That's bloody hot," she yelped as she shook them out after each scoop.

"Here, dork. Use something else. Try a flip-flop," Ammon chucked one at her from the van. Future got right in there with Bree, and soon they were using flip-flops for shovels and digging like dogs with their butts in the air, shooting sand out between their legs.

"Okay, that should do it. Let's try again," Ammon advised after ten minutes of serious digging. It took a few rounds of pushing and digging and pushing and digging before the car finally came loose and jolted forward. Everyone stopped pushing abruptly, everyone but me, that is. I fell forward and crashed onto my bare knees as the black smoke from the muffler spewed exhaust in my face. When I hit the ground full force like that, my almost healed scabs were scraped off, and coarse sand filled the wet, open sores. I'd hurt my knees exactly the same way just a couple of days before, but at least we were safely out of another sand trap. I knew it wouldn't be the last. I was sure glad to be putting some distance between me and those flaming hills. I was hopeful, too, that eventually, I'd learn to time my pushing better and avoid any further injuries.

We were truly living moment to moment every day, never knowing where we would eat or find fuel. Accommodation was always a surprise, too. We didn't know where we'd be sleeping until we got there, wherever "there" was. More often than not, it was in a ger with a local family, usually on the floor or on a tiny cot with wool blankets. We once stumbled upon a campsite filled with small gers, and we rented a room in a small town that had cement block buildings another time.

This night we rolled in late to a town close to Bayanzag. We searched for accommodations, but many of the places were booked or cost at least thirty dollars each. Poor Future was running in and out and driving all around to find availability for a price we could afford. As a last resort, he drove us back to the town where we'd visited a little dinosaur museum earlier in the day. They offered to let us sleep on the floor in the back room. *Bingo!* We spent a few bucks and saved a lot more, so it benefited everyone. Future and a couple of guys from the museum dragged in some rugs and laid them out to cover the hardwood floor. It was intriguing to know that I was sleeping amongst long-lost dinosaur eggs and wild, fossilized beasts.

Dinner by candlelight on the floor with a roof over our heads was exactly the comfort we needed after a long, stressful day. Future joined us as we all ate straight from the pot. With a final goodnight, he opened the door and headed for the van where he usually slept. An unexpected gust of wind whipped the door out of his hand and slammed it shut. The draft killed the light from our small, flickering candle.

"I guess that's our cue," I heard Ammon say from somewhere to my left.

"But I still need to brush my teeth," I said, a yawn catching me off guard in mid-sentence.

The scent of candle smoke tickled my nose and I seemed to float away with it. Sitting there in the pitch dark, exhaustion suddenly caught up with me. I considered searching for a match, finding the candlestick, fumbling through my daypack to find my toothbrush, and taking a water bottle outside where the cool air was already beginning to settle in for the night, but it all just seemed like way too much work. Instead, I groped around to find my irregularly shaped daypack/pillow and laid my head down.

Tow Truck
39

*T*he sun felt hot and somehow soothing on my bare knees as they hung from the van's open sliding door. They were just starting to heal. Slowly stepping out, I lifted my elbow to test the wind. *I really hate this place,* I thought as I squinted desperately at the emptiness around me. Scanning the baked, bare earth, I felt as minuscule as an ant reaching towards the sky to shout at nonexistent birds above. *Nobody would hear our desperate cries.* I heard Future's soft "tck, tck, tck," and I knew it wasn't good. It never was.

His legs protruded from beneath the car, where he was scuffling about in the dirt. I crouched down beside our broken vehicle, which had been falling apart piece by piece over the course of our jaunt. We could've found our way back just by following the trail of parts and leaks we'd left in our wake, but this time was worse; the van had completely given out.

After everything the past week had thrown at us, I didn't dare ask, "What now?" It appeared we would be given no more chances. When he noticed my shadow and sandaled feet, he raised himself onto his bent elbow to deliver the verdict – "No. No oil. Is leak everywhere."

After a freakish seven days together, I had a much clearer understanding of this man stretched beneath the van. You couldn't say he'd been thoroughly vetted before we'd leapt into his car and allowed him to "guide" us around parts of his country that he knew barely any better than we did, but in uncontrollable situations, every attribute of a person's character is inevitably revealed, whether they like it or not, and relationships tend to develop more quickly and deeply. To be fair, our group's occasionally quixotic behaviour and general lack of preparation probably contributed to many of the incidents we had dealt with along the way, yet I didn't regret any of it, even now, when things looked so bad for us. Judging from what I had seen of his character, tested on almost every level by now, I knew Future was sincere. Despite his many faults, I loved his positive attitude and energy.

Recent circumstances had generated another life lesson, and he'd played an important part in that process. As we took each step towards a new destination, we were forced to live nowhere but in the present and with the people who surrounded us. We weren't playing by any set of rules or competing to impress peers; we'd had to just get on with life. I never once felt judged for my wild hair, dirty clothes, or the mere fact that I had no makeup on and looked my worst (or my most natural, depending on your perspective). I felt loved and accepted by Future, no matter what.

"I don't suppose there is any spare oil in the back, eh?" I was grasping at straws now. He shook his hand from underneath to signal no, as I suspected, but I couldn't let it go. "Nothing? No small containers? Like, for emergencies?" I emphasized, reminding him that most people stash some somewhere.

"No, did not bring," Future confessed, apparently not having put any prior thought into his namesake in this instance. Considering he had never previously dealt with foreigners, it's quite possible that his interactions with us offered the first opportunity to actually *use* the English version of his name. We had asked him the first night we met where the name Future had come from.

"That is me," he answered, obviously not understanding the question.

"Yah, but what is your real name? In Mongolian," Bree asked.

"Ireedui Pureve."

"So, it's nearly as unpronounceable as the rest of your language," I laughed, but I now understood why he preferred to go by the name Future.

He threw his head back and laughed, "Oh, Little Savannah!" He smiled at me gently for a moment before adding, "Ireedui is future. Means future. That is me. I have good future."

As the wind loosened my tangled, two-day-old braid and blew it in my face, I remembered that conversation and hoped he was right about that. My skin felt as tired and dry as the land around me, but I couldn't be bothered by that now. Future's bodiless, lower limbs were twisting and shuffling so his rear-end could clear the van. Sand streaked his naturally black hair, which was now plastered to his head from the sweat of his exertions and from lying in the gravel. His round face was smudged with grease, and his mocha-coloured skin revealed what a week's exposure to the sun could do, but that might have been just the thick layer of dirt that had built up. I wiped the dirty strands of hair from my eyes and climbed back in to seek whatever shade our vehicle afforded and to tell the others his news.

"The oil is leaking, and he doesn't have any more," I told them. What I didn't have to say was that we would not be going anywhere tonight.

"What? Like none?" Bree asked incredulously.

"None," I assured her.

"Like, nix?" she pressed on.

"Zip. Zilch. Nada." I said to remove any hope that an easy fix was available to us.

"Oh, dear. Well that's not good," Mom said simply, now that we were all on the same page.

"So what does that mean?" Bree asked.

"You can't drive without toasting the car completely!" Ammon said matter-of-factly. *Oh, geez! Now what!?* "Don't tell me you're surprised!" Ammon said sarcastically, acting even a little more superior, if that was possible, before he jumped outside.

"Jesus!!" Future shouted out, surprised by the suddenness of his arrival, "Look what you are did. Why?! Why you do this to me?"

"Because you have enraged me," Ammon joked back.

"Oh no! I know, it was wrong. I am sorry for joke about you. It is because I make joke that van broke!" I heard Future making light of the situation, but now that the van was toast, he and Ammon decided their first move was to scout the area for any sign of civilization and help.

As much as I hated the sand constantly trying to swallow our car, I didn't like sitting around thinking about our current situation any better. The desert had hardened and turned into a barren wasteland, broken only by some gravelly patches and scraggly patches of grey-green. The van was our only source of shade.

About 200m (656ft) away, a dozen or so camels roamed freely. Wild herds were a common sight, but these were the only living creatures we'd seen all day. These camels all sported the typical forked, wooden nose pegs commonly used in Mongolia, a sure sign they belonged to someone, but there was no way to know when the owners might return. We weren't nurturing any false hopes at this stage; getting us out of this mess was completely up to us!

"Savannah, what are you doing?" Mom asked as I stepped out of the van and started walking towards them.

"I'm going to go catch a camel. What does it look like?"

"You'll never be able to," she replied.

"I can at least try!"

"REALLY?! Okay. This'll be awesome!" In a flash, Bree was at my side.

"Go that way, and I'll come in from the other side," Bree commanded. We ran at them with outstretched arms to make ourselves appear bigger and more intimidating. She approached them from one direction as I came at them from the other in an effort to trap them into nonexistent corners, but they didn't seem to be falling for it. Mom's curiosity got the better of her, and she came out to assess our chances. She wasn't long in delivering her verdict, putting her hands on her hips as she turned and left with an emphatic, "Oh, yah. Right! There's no way, but good luck, anyway."

The camels' hides were splotchy: thick and fluffy in parts, bare and bristly in others. Their legs looked like those you see on some dinosaurs, and their feet had only two toes protruding from big, squishy pads. They seemed to be unwilling to expend any more energy than necessary so didn't flee outright, but they did maintain just enough distance to avoid us. It was as if they were teasing us, and somehow knew we would never be able to outrun or outsmart them. Their big feet seemed awkward beneath lanky bodies, yet they moved surprisingly swiftly across the hot ground. As they circled around us, their heads bouncing loosely on their narrow shoulders, they appeared to be laughing at us. *They are deliberately humiliating us. Mom was right. We'll never catch one.*

We eventually had to give up, with the herd still mocking us only metres away. Future had returned from his scouting expedition and was walking towards us when we headed back to the car, a long towing strap bundled under his arm, "What are you doing? Coming to join us?" we joked.

"Yah. I catch camel."

"No way!"

"I is professional. I know it camels!" I couldn't help but roll my eyes at that. I'd heard it before. I had difficulty envisioning how his attempts could be any different than ours, but he proceeded to hurl the strap at the closest unsuspecting camel with everything he had. Time after time, it either didn't reach the intended target or merely bounced off harmlessly.

Future was about to give up when one ran right past him and his strong Mongolian spirit took over. He instinctively chucked the strap as he held tightly to the other end.

"Now rope should falling down, tangle in the legs," Future explained as the strap landed perfectly between the humps and then swung around and fell into place. We held our breath, smiling broadly as the rope got tangled up in its hind legs, leaving the camel no choice but to stop. Future hastily bent over to untie his shoelaces and knot them together. Easing in beside the camel, he patted its side. He moved closer and soothingly whispered, "Sook, sook, sook." The camel's cheeks were puffed out and it foamed at the mouth excessively, like a kid who'd used half a tube of toothpaste while brushing. Confidently reaching for the nose peg, Future fastened his shoelace to the forked stick.

He calmed the beast for a few more moments with gentle pats and whispers before leaving me to hold the laces while he untangled the tow rope from the camel's back legs, wound it carefully around his arm, and then slung it jauntily over his shoulder. Together, we led the extremely unhappy camel back to the van, feeling quite pleased with ourselves.

Bree and I marvelled over what the simplest things could be used for in the middle of the desert. "This kind of thing only happens in movies," Bree was saying, "like the one where---" The next thing I heard was a loud OOMPH as she flew off her feet. The camel's leg swung out to the side and roundhouse kicked her right in the stomach, sending her soaring through the air. It happened amazingly quickly and quietly; one second she was there, the next, she was doubled over on her bum in the sand.

She sprang back to her feet, somehow unharmed, and laughed, "I just got SMOKED by a camel in Mongolia. That's awesome!" Luckily, the wide, round surface of the camel's padded foot dispersed the intensity of the impact, and she was not so much hurt as she was surprised by the kick.

The others' voices carried on the light wind as we drew nearer to the van. "Let's look on the bright side. It's a lot cooler today than it has been." Mom looked up from her daypack where her thermometer hung on a carabineer clip. "How lucky is that?"

Ammon reflexively picked his up and said, "Yah, it's only 35°C (95°F) today." Given that the temperature had been ranging from 40–50°C (104–122°F), this was a distinct improvement. Remembering Future's reaction when we'd first read those extreme temperatures made me giggle even now, during this time of uncertainty.

"What?! No! Let me see. How hot?? Fifty! I cannot believe. This my first time ever so hot! Oh my, I cannot believe. Jesus! How can you do this?" Future was always jokingly blaming our misfortunes on Ammon/Jesus.

Reflecting, I regretfully came to terms with what Future's reaction said about him. He was a brilliant man with a calm, cool, and collected approach to life, but he was a city boy. His skill as a doctor couldn't prevent death if there wasn't food to eat; his knowledge of languages couldn't rescue us from a wreck when there was no one to communicate with; nor could his beautiful, operatic voice sooth our nerves under such extreme circumstances. *Then again, he did catch us this camel!* I thought, smiling over at him leading the foaming camel by his shoelaces.

Mom and Ammon were still discussing the weather, there being little else to talk about at this point. "The cooler temperature will at least buy us some--- Wait! WHAT is *that?!*" Ammon shouted. I loved seeing the effect our entrance had on him.

"A camel," I answered casually as we strutted proudly into their midst.

"Yah, I can *see* that! But what the heck are you going to do with it? EAT it?!"

"No! Of course not!" I was caught off guard for a second by the thought of killing this animal that promised to save our sorry butts.

"Pull. Pull," Future started to explain.

"It's going to pull us to safety," I said, clarifying what Future was trying to tell Ammon.

Ammon laughed so hard he almost fell over. "And how is this fat thing gonna do that? I mean, geez, did you *have* to catch the one pregnant camel in the bunch??"

"HE'S not pregnant!" I declared about the admittedly rather large-bellied creature.

"Well, he sure isn't happy at any rate! It looks like he swallowed a can of shaving cream, he's foaming so much!" Mom commented.

But this fuming camel was about to become our personal tow truck! Once the tow strap was wrapped around the camel's two humps in a figure eight, we tied the other end to the front bumper. Ammon and Bree manned the rear bumper; Mom was again in the driver's seat, this time with very clear directions; and Future and I tended to the camel. We desperately tried to motivate our "engine" by smacking him on the bum with a flip-flop and dragging him forward. Despite his many squeals and groans, he grudgingly and tortuously pulled the van. I was grateful that he was at least polite enough not to spit on us. I'd heard that camels were prone to some nasty spitting behaviour, but if a camel doesn't resort to spitting under these circumstances, when would be a justified time? One more long-held belief bit the dust that day.

We made it all of 30m (98ft) over the next twenty minutes, when Future stated the obvious. "Enough. Is too heavy! Is better I go. I ride camel, bring help." He shouted "Down! Down!" as he tugged on the shoelace in his first effort to mount the beast. The camel's head bobbed up and down like a slinky toy as he pulled, and he wasn't one bit closer to getting him to lie down.

He tried soothing him first, clucking "Sook, sook, sook, sook" as he patted him and tugged gently. He tried sudden outbursts of "SOOK SOOK SOOK!!" Running around to the creature's side, he pushed his back end down, but the camel only reached around to bite him. It was man against beast, and man was losing. Future leapt here and there, pushing and pulling and tugging like a Nintendo character to absolutely no avail. When he tried to climb onto the camel from the roof of the van, we knew it was game over.

"Is impossible," he said as he led the camel over to secure it to a tiny shrub, but no one heard him because, by this time, the rest of us had migrated back to the van to come up with a plan B.

Stranded
40

"*I* must walk. Little Savannah, you have paper and pen?" Future smiled at me as he asked, as if I really was his baby sister. I pulled my daypack from beneath the seat and reached in for the two things that I always kept immediately accessible.

He took his time crafting a beautifully written Cyrillic "help/rescue" note for anyone who might come by. Despite the fact that none of us could read his note, we derived a lot of comfort from it somehow. He handed the paper to Ammon as the leader. Trusting that he'd done all he could for us, Future took his leave, saying, "Give to anyone who come. I am come back with help."

"WAIT!" Mom stopped him when she noticed his empty hands. Searching around a bit first, she held the last of our water out to him. "Here, take it."

"No, no. There is only that. I am okay. You keep," he insisted.

Her motherly instincts compelled her to try again, "Future, we'll be fine. What about you? You need water if you're without shade and using energy, especially in that wind."

He simply shook his head, "No, Mama. You can no doubt me, I am okay. You take for family."

"Are you sure you'll be alright?" Mom asked one last time. This time he didn't respond; he simply smiled like he always did and leaned over me in the van to flick the headphones glued to Bree's ears. He smiled and waved his fingers inches from her face to say goodbye.

"Bye Future! Good luck," she said, and he turned to go on his way. I heard the sound of his crunching footsteps on the desert fading, and held my breath to listen for as long as possible.

"So. What's the verdict, then?" I asked, turning to Ammon.

"Yah. What did you two find out when you went scouting earlier?" Mom asked.

"Let's just say that, if you look out as far as you can see in any direction," he stopped, mulling over his next words, "you don't see much of anything."

"Meaning?" Bree dared him to continue.

"Meaning that, this could potentially be very ..." he paused, resting his foot on the door ledge to move in closer to make his announcement. Then he delayed a while longer, resting his elbow on his thigh and chin on his fist. After wiggling his bristly jaw side to side waiting for the right moment and rehearsing exactly how best to tell us what we needed to know, he asked, "Okay, fine. Do you want the good, the bad, or the not-so-good news first?"

"Just tell us the good news," mom said, always preferring to see the positive side of any situation.

"Well---" he began.

"WAIT! The bad news. Definitely the bad news first," I interrupted, not wanting to wait another second to find out if we were as doomed as I suspected we were.

"If you just shut your mouth, you'll find out sooner," Ammon snapped, then continued, "Okay. Well then, the not-so-good news is this." He decided to start in the middle, something he'd always thought to be a sound strategy when dealing with women. He scanned the van's interior and reached under the bench when he'd spotted the tip of a blue lid. "We only have this much water," he said as he presented the half-empty, litre bottle of water. There was no point in trying to pretend; the fact of the matter was, it *was* half empty, and we really could have used the other half.

"What's the good news, then?" I asked, deciding that the bad news didn't make me feel any better.

"The good news is that there are some gers out there."

"Well okay, then," I stifled a sigh of relief.

"The bad news is," he carried on, careful not to miss a beat, as if there was any chance we might lose interest in what he had to tell us, "they're pretty far away and there's no guarantee someone is there. Even if there is, well, we're kind of stuck in a low spot here." Future had promised, when he volunteered to be our search and rescue hero, "I find you again. I can this place remember. You do not worried." Now Ammon, the seasoned traveller and still our fearless leader, seemed to think that might not be possible. Our morale, which was none too high to begin with, slipped even more. "As soon as you clear that little hill, we're completely out of sight. Who's to say if it's even possible to find the car again out here? So. There you have it." He looked around soberly, as if waiting for hands to be raised in the classroom.

"So where are the gers?" Mom asked, trying to calculate our odds.

"And how many are there?" Bree put in.

"Let's just say, one ger is off in the distance that way," he said, leaning slightly out the door to point us in the right direction, "and there are two gers that are further away out in that direction," turning the other way completely. Our view was blocked by rugged hills anyway, so we were left to imagine just what "further away" meant.

"And he went off in the closer direction?" Mom half-asked, half-stated.

"Yah," he agreed.

"How far was the closest one, would you say?" I asked.

"Well, if you stand at the top of that hill, it looks to be about this far," he said, holding his thumb and forefinger a fraction of an inch apart. This was an effective way to convey distance out here. "And the two out there must be about," he began opening and closing his fingers, prolonging it to consider his newest information.

"Oh, c'mon Ammon. You're killing us," I protested.

"Hey, you asked," he retaliated, showing he was in control if we wanted answers.

"Okay, so how big then?" I gave in, playing his game.

"About this big." With that he abruptly pinched his fingers together.

"So, it's basically nonexistent?" I collapsed.

"Yup," he agreed

"Why do you toy with us like that?" I demanded.

"What? I wasn't!" he laughed, knowing he was.

"Yes, you were!"

"It's no wonder Future went that way, then, if the choice comes down to one ger that's relatively close by or two practically non-existent ones," Bree said.

As Future wandered off into the desert horizon, I wondered if we'd ever be rescued. Before long, he would drop down behind the hill and out of our sight. *How will he ever find us again? All that empty land, and we're stuck here beside one tiny car in all this vastness.*

"Do you want to hear the rest of the bad news?" Ammon said aloud, still gazing after Future's elongated shadow.

"No, not really!" Mom said.

"Oh yes, please! I'd love to," I said sarcastically.

"Let's just hear it then," Bree said, wanting to stop the fussing.

"Okay. I'm really hoping he'll be able to make it both ways without any water. There had better be someone home." We all looked worriedly at one another. Future's incredibly elongated shadow seemed to be one of the few anchors left in the desert.

"Do you think Future will come back?" I whispered to the solitary camel standing beside the van. My words expressed doubt, if only for a moment, wondering if our Mongolian guide had just abandoned us. But no. He was also our friend, and I knew we were all in this together.

"He'll come back." I guess Mom had been listening, and she affirmed my gut instinct about Future. "If he can, he will."

"If he can," I echoed with a profound sense of foreboding.

Her words reminded me of the seriousness of our situation. This wasn't just a game. It was real life, and I was all too aware of the perils we faced. Reaching toward the camel, I placed my open palm against the dusty window. Gazing into eyes that resembled golden flakes of sand framed with lavish dark lashes, a strange connection sparked between us. Maybe I was looking for reassurance of some kind or to somehow humbly share his intimate knowledge of the desert. My attention was diverted to my hand at that point and I thought it should have been sweaty or at least a bit moist against the glass, but I was already severely dehydrated. Every nail bed and wrinkle was caked with dirt. *What happened to you, Savannah?* I wondered, crinkling my forehead. This was not the "me" I remembered. *Where on earth did you go?* I asked myself.

I pressed my forehead against the window and heard nothing but silence. I began hopelessly hitting my head against the glass. With the exception of the irregular drafts of wind through the open sliding door, the planet seemed frozen in time, and I felt completely isolated.

"Hrmph," I grunted as I continued to reflect on this different world I found myself in. *Is this the kind of isolation people were talking about when they'd refer to Timbuktu, wherever that is? I knew I was going travelling, but nobody ever mentioned anything like this!* I'd officially shaken hands with "the middle of nowhere" and I wouldn't call it an amiable meeting. Perhaps off-roading in a housewifely minivan should've been seriously reconsidered.

It seemed ironic and somewhat cruel that this should happen to us on our last day in the Gobi Desert. Dirty, tired, and hungry, we were all in need of a power wash and a hearty, Las Vegas-style buffet. My craving for spaghetti cramped my bowels, and I was afflicted by an overwhelming desire to watch *The Simpsons* again. The very idea of a shower brought tears to my eyes. I debated whether I'd be more grateful for the layers of dust washing off or for the cold water I'd be drinking straight out of the tap. My mouth hung slightly open as I subconsciously drooled in anticipation. The water I had in mind was just a little trickle coming from a rusty pipe poking out of a stone wall but as the hallucination deepened, so did the water gushing out. Soon the trickle turned into an explosion cascading all over me, and I could feel my mouth grow wider and wider so as not to allow a single drop to escape.

When I wasn't daydreaming to pass the time, I was actually very frightened, but I didn't know who to look to. There was no sense in asking Mom questions. She had no way of knowing how long it might take, or whether anyone would come in time. *Surely, someone would come, right?* The problem was that, even on a busy day when we drove anywhere near a village, we *might* see six cars all day, sunrise to sunset, and that would be considered heavy traffic. Three scattered gers was a far cry from a village. *Most likely, no one will come.* I could deduce that much. Maybe after a few days, we would have a chance, but given how limited our supplies were, it wasn't looking good. Amongst the four of us, we had only 500 millilitres of water and a Cadbury bar which was only a mug away from being hot chocolate.

I stretched my legs lengthwise on the bench and clouds of dust spewed up from the woven fabric. I was keeping watch for Future – or anyone else, for that matter – to show up, but time was dragging. Noticing how quiet I was, Mom tried to allay the worry that was etched on my face, despite my efforts to hide it.

"Future is a native, Savannah. He'll know what to do," Mom said, trying to sound confident.

"Yah, a native *city* boy! How is that going to help us way out here in the boonies?"

"Well, his whole camel idea kinda got shot to hell." Ammon's reminder prompted me to glare over at the fat quadruped still foaming and still tied to the pathetic little bush. One good, strong tug would free him, but he just kept circling the shrub aimlessly, nibbling at it once in a while.

"Really, how was that whole camel thing supposed to work anyway? What were we thinking?!" I suddenly found myself laughing, despite our circumstances.

"I think Future was just doing it to humour us," Ammon laughed. "Really, were we all just gonna jump in once it started rolling and then whip him from the window and roll to safety? As if!"

"Stupid idea." Bree nodded in agreement.

"If it hadn't been so sandy, then maybe it might've worked?" Mom suggested.

"No, Mom. Don't even go there," Ammon interrupted. "Like I said, it was an incredibly retarded idea, but it was fun to try anyway."

"Well, now that we apparently have a camel friend, what should we call him?" Mom asked.

"Chewy!" I suggested.

"Like Chewbacca from *Star Wars*. Good name!" Bree added. "He sounds just like him."

"Man, you guys pissed him off royally!" Ammon marvelled, not for the first time.

"And you should have seen him drop-kick Bree! It was hilari---" I was halted mid-sentence by Bree's glare, and backtracked as quickly as I could. "It was totally not cool and mean. Bad, Chewy, bad! And because all he does is chew and chew. Do you see how he swallows and then brings it up again and chews some more," I added.

"Disgusting!" Mom said.

"You can even see it going down, like a tennis ball ...." A long discussion that began with regurgitation eventually led to the evolution of dolphins from dogs, which led to the random hypothesis that your forearm is the same length as your foot, which led to more of the same inane kinds of things we often got into. Meanwhile, Bree left for a brief visit with nature. When she hadn't returned fifteen minutes later, I got to thinking about the little bit of toilet paper she had taken, and debated whether she truly had to go, or if she was perhaps simply avoiding Ammon's spiel again. It turned out that neither was the case.

"Look what I caught!" she announced excitedly when she finally came back, holding out her hands to show us. The lizard's head was slightly oversized for his skinny body. It was the same shape as a bearded dragon, but much smaller and had no spikes. Its colouring was striped with green and blue meshing into brownish grey scales. It reminded me of the mating pair of gorgeous geckos I'd given away before this trip. They'd had soft marshmallow-like bellies and enormous round eyes that looked like green marbles with silver threads sinking into another universe.

"How on *earth* did you catch that?" I asked baffled.

"You savage!" Ammon congratulated her. "You were meant to live in the wild!"

"Oh good, that'll be perfect for dinner," Mom said. "Go catch some more." She handed one of our empty water bottles to me and instructed me to go with her.

"Geez! Just what I always wanted, lizard soup," I smiled.

"Hah! You wish. Not unless you're planning to use camel blood as stock."

"That's sick, Ammon," Mom protested.

"And that's coming from someone who wants to eat lizard sandwiches," he retorted.

"C'mon Norman," I said, quickly naming the lizard, "let's go find your friends." I'd thought there was nothing out there in the desert, but there was actually a lot more life in the harsh terrain than you might expect. The skinny, palm-length lizards darted around our bare feet in the relative coolness of late afternoon. As we leapt around chasing after them, they dashed quickly from tuft to tuft of grass on their hind legs, holding their tails erect in the air. They were astonishingly easy to catch, providing you were willing to dive onto your belly in the fine gravel with your arms outstretched, and we were. We developed an effective lizard-hunting method, going from bush to bush to chase them out into the open where we could pounce on them.

"Okay, okay, I got him. Quick! Bring the bottle!" Bree would shout at me. I'd come over holding the bottle carefully to keep them from being squished, jumping and tiptoeing between low shrubs and then skidding in on my knees beside where she huddled on all fours, her hands cupped securely on the ground.

"Okay, careful now. Careful! Okay, and whoop!" she'd say, dropping another one in to land on the pile of brothers and sisters.

When we returned with a prize-winning collection of beautiful lizards, Ammon was busy writing in his journal. Mom had already finished one of her typical, two-sentence-long journal entries: "We are sitting here stuck. Refer to Savannah or Ammon's journals for more details." She was now busy sewing flag patches to the rain jacket of her backpack. Praising our success in providing for the family, she grabbed the bottle to examine the fourteen Normans.

"Aaww, Normy, you're so cute. You want to meet our other pet, Chewy? Say hi to Chewy!" she said, holding the bottle of lizards up so they could see him amiably chewing and regurgitating the shrub he was tied to. Passing the bottle back, she went on with her project.

"Mom, you're nuts," Ammon said.

"Well, sewing on the Mongolian flag patch may be the last thing I ever do in this life," she joked, as she repetitively pushed and pulled the needle to finish the task at hand.

Awaiting our Future
41

*W*e had yet to see a soul eight painful hours later. Even Chewy's friends had not come back for him. Stranded and lost out in the desert, we were completely vulnerable. My stomach started to growl, despite my efforts to maintain control. *You're not hungry. You're not hungry.* I had gone longer than this without food before, but with worry about our situation nagging at me, I started imagining camel steaks. I knew we could survive at least a couple of days on Chewy's meat, but hoped it wouldn't come to that. For one thing, we would eat the lizards raw first. I wondered how long it would be before we'd have to do that. It seemed a bit of a waste to eat such beautiful lizards. We tried to play cards, but my mind wasn't in it, and I lost a few rounds in a row. Mom appeared unbothered, Bree was happy to be winning at my expense, and Ammon was in control as always. I was amazed that they could wait so calmly.

The sound of crunching caught my attention first, and I caught sight of a small horse with an oversized rider heading towards us. My heart leapt as I smacked Mom, who was dealing the next hand onto the bench and my knees.

Typically, though, my initial reaction to the approaching rider – *Thank the Lord, we're saved!* – quickly became – *Yikes! What if it's the camel's owner? We have Future's note, but it probably doesn't say anything about Chewy. How will we ever explain to him that we weren't trying to steal it?! Geez, this must look so bad. We just wanted to eat him if we got really hungry. Oh man, he's going to kill us!* I almost expected the rider to have the kind of shiny spurs at his ankles and a gun strapped into a leather holster that you'd see in an old western.

As the stranger rode up I was just beginning to make out the faint outline of his face when Bree shouted, "FUTURE!!" Imaginary background music played as he rode in triumphantly on his newly acquired horse. I could've kissed him! I'd never been so happy to see anyone in my life.

Stepping from the van, Ammon greeted him casually with a smile, "Good to see you, Future, but if you brought us a horse to help Chewy pull the van, I don't think this one will work." Future's steed was no bigger than a donkey and even skinnier than others we'd seen.

"Where on earth did you get a horse?!" Mom then voiced the next obvious question. "And where'd the kid with the bike come from?!" In our excitement, we hadn't noticed the little boy trailing behind Future on a blue bicycle.

"And how did you get turned around like that?!" Ammon asked, wondering how he'd managed to come in from the opposite direction he'd left from. Future swung his leg over the horse and practically walked off it before he began a very animated re-enactment of his adventure.

"See black mountains? I walk to there! But no one home, so I climbing in roof and taking a rice for you. In my hat, I taking it. From there, I see another ger, so I keep walking. So, so tired. Then, then, when closer, I see smoke in chimney so I running. When I hearing dog, I am crying, I am so happy! I was knowing there was somebody home." When he arrived, tired and thirsty, they welcomed him, just as we'd been welcomed at so many gers we'd stopped at along the way. Once he was revived, they provided him with the horse and the boy to start a search and rescue party. He'd given his hat full of stolen rice to the family living there. "Then I come. I coming for you!" A delighted smile was stamped on his face. He almost forgot to give us the jug of water he'd brought back; we quickly guzzled it down.

I was amazed that he had found his way back after hours of wandering the desert. I tried to imagine how in this world he managed to walk as far as the first ger where no one was home, and then walk to the ger he saw from there to circle around and come up behind us. Since the sun was rapidly setting, we had to focus on packing up and getting back to the young boy's ger. We left the van there in the desert after loading our gear onto the backs of Chewy and the horse.

"Oh, wait. There's one more thing." I let all the Normans go as the spare tire was being fastened onto the horse's wooden saddle. *As if someone's going to steal our spare tire out here!*

Future and Ammon took the lead with the camel that carried four backpacks tied together and slung between its humps. The boy pushed his bike and kept up with us effortlessly. Bree and I walked side-by-side pulling the horse, and Mom made sure the spare tire didn't fall off the saddle. I turned back every so often to watch the van get smaller and smaller. The ger was forty-five minutes away, "in that direction," but we hardly noticed the walk at all. We'd been saved.

A second, "supposed-to-be-white" horse was tied to the fence of a poopy, goatless goat pen next to the two gers. The family consisted of grandparents and their two grandchildren: the boy with the bike and a younger sister. The children's parents worked in Ulaanbaatar to provide for their family and came home only occasionally to visit and bring supplies. The grandparents were both worn and small, their skin leathery and darkened over the years by the sun.

The smaller of the two gers was used for storage, and we found the grandpa busy cleaning it out for our use as we arrived. When Future told us that, my heart swelled in response to them and their unreserved hospitality.

We released Chewy once we'd stored our backpacks in the storage ger, but he didn't seem to understand that we were freeing him when he was untied.

"Shoo, shoo. Go! Be free!" we shouted at him, but it had no effect. Seemingly indifferent to states of freedom or captivity, he hung around for quite some time before finally wandering off. I did feel a little sad at the time and hoped he would be able to find his friends again.

The rice provided by Future and the unsuspecting, absent neighbours was already cooking, and we were ushered into the family's ger for salty, milky tea. As desperate as I was for water, I drank the hot, salty liquid and tried not to wince too obviously. *At least we're safe, but now what? How long are we going to be stuck here?* I thought, staring down into my cup, knowing I would have to finish every last drop before I could have some dinner because the family rarely had this many guests at once and owned only a few dishes.

The sustenance from the black pot was warm, well intended, and very much appreciated, so I choked it down. I didn't ask for seconds and decided to eat the hard, if slightly more palatable, flour biscuits instead.

After dinner, Future told us his plan. "Ammon, you come. Neighbour has car, we go to him." Future, Ammon, the boy and his dog left. Absent our trusty leader and translator, I once again felt stranded, this time with elderly folk who looked like they might fall over dead at any given moment.

Ammon and Mom had both warned us not to count on getting back to the capital tomorrow. We gave up waiting for him to return around midnight, and Mom told us, "Well, I guess he'll be back later. Let's just leave the candle burning so he can see when he comes in."

When I woke the next morning, Ammon was sleeping next to me. His dark brown mop shooting out from the tangled, green sleeping bag reminded me of a hairy caterpillar.

"What time did you get in last night? And tell us what happened," I said, as I unravelled my feet from a wool blanket.

"Starting from what point?" he asked, crawling out of his cocoon.

"The beginning." I slithered over to the bowl on the floor and reached for one of the hard biscuits. "From the time you left." The usual thick, sheep hairs weren't hard to find, but the biscuits were so stale and dense that the hairs broke off inside and were impossible to avoid.

"Well, we went off trying to find the neighbour up and over some hills in that direction," he started, waving his hand to show us, "looking for the ger which we eventually spotted in the distance. When we got close to it, the guy's five dogs came charging out at us, barking like crazy. Future actually swung the kid around to protect him, kind of thing!"

"He used the kid as a shield?!" Bree interrupted.

"No, silly! Behind his back! So the kid wouldn't get mauled by the dogs. Then some dude came out of the ger and yelled at the dogs. They stopped *right* in front of us, just before we were attacked and made into minced meat. It was kind of scary, actually. They were big dogs!"

"Yah, I know. I've seen 'em. Those dogs are insane!" Mom agreed.

"So then he invited us inside." The household consisted of the man, his wife, and one daughter. Ammon told us the man appeared to be a miserable drunk, but Future informed him of our problem over tea. The ferocious looking dogs were still glaring in at them from the doorway only a few feet away. The man didn't have a car, but he did have a couple of simple, basic tools. Eventually they agreed on a course of action and headed out to take a look at our vehicle.

"So off we marched, up and over the hills and up and over more hills, and we somehow ended up exactly where the van was. I don't know *how* that happened! I was totally lost. It all looks the same out there to me!" He was still struggling to comprehend the Mongolians' amazing navigational skills.

Once back at the van, the men gathered around to inspect the damage before crawling under to see what they could do. Because the protective shield was inconveniently sitting in the trunk, the oil pan had been bashed almost beyond recognition. They started trying to fix it using Future's cell phone as a light, but decided against it given its limited battery life. Future then promptly sent the boy to collect shrubs and twigs so they could light a little fire next to the neighbour, who was on his back hammering away. At this point in Ammon's story, I was shaking my head and thinking, *Is it totally crazy that they apparently had a small fire under the car, or is it just me?*

Whatever the case, it must have worked, but it was fully dark by the time Future told Ammon, "Okay this is take a while. It not be quick fix. Go back to ger and sleep." When Ammon asked him how the hell he was supposed to find his way back, he replied, in typical Future fashion, "Yes, following kid. You go. Sleeping."

"So then the kid, the dog and I walked back in the dark. I had no clue who knew the way, the dog or the kid, but I just picked a star on the horizon and followed it, and after over a half-an-hour I was, like, 'Okay, are we lost? What the hell?' but I couldn't talk to the kid anyway, so I thought, 'They seem confident enough, so I'll just go along.' A bit after that I saw a tiny light in the ger and made it back to you guys." He ended his tale with a nod and a big bite of his biscuit.

"Wow, you *did* have an adventure." Mom said.

"It was kind of scary," he admitted.

"I would've died!" I said, but I was amazed by the kind of trust these people shared.

"So what's the verdict for today, then?" Bree asked.

"Well, last I saw, they were under the van banging away. I really doubt they'll get it fixed. So the next option is waiting to get a ride. There will be transport at some point. Didn't Future say the kids' parents come with supplies? It could be days, weeks, months – who knows?" Ammon waved her concern off and looked like he was prepared to become the little nomadic family's adopted son.

"But can't they get word out? They must be in some kind of contact," Mom said, taking her turn at a hairy biscuit.

"Nope. They just have to wait. I don't think they have postal service, and what use would a cell phone be way out here without any reception?" he asked. "Future couldn't use his, except as a flashlight. Nobody has transport, and that scrawny horse isn't going to get very far. The neighbour didn't have a car, only some tools. We're not getting out of here tonight, let's just say that. Or were you guys thinking of maybe tying all the goats to the front like reindeer and flying to U.B.?" he added when he noticed our dirty, disappointed faces.

"I'll just die if I have to eat another bowl of that disgusting, nasty---"

"Don't even go there, Savannah," Ammon warned without looking at me.

"Horrendous," I continued in the background, "fat-tailed, lard-butt---"

"Stop it!!" Ammon growled, this time training his cold, blue eyes on me. "We get it, alright?!" I pinched my lips together until he turned away again.

Watching cautiously, as if for a swinging backhand, I finished my sentence quietly with, "dead sheep," and immediately felt a bit better.

"Well, how long do you think it'll take?" Mom asked. I couldn't believe how desperately I wanted to be back in the hostel that had initially made me cringe. *I'm so stupid not to appreciate the luxury of food, a bed, and a shower. Gosh, it seemed so safe there, with people and vehicles and communication and everything.* Every day, I realized more just how much I'd taken these simple things for granted back home, and even back in *Ulaanbaatar.* My grateful thoughts were interrupted, though, because just then, the little wooden door to our ger swung open and Bree shouted, "FUTURE!"

"Oh, ho, ho. Good morning!" he chuckled as he burst into the room. "We go! We are go!"

"What do you mean? You found a car?"

"No, my car. Is good! Is fix," he announced as he stepped aside to let us see it there outside the door. Our eyes adjusted to the sunlight as gradually as our minds adjusted to the miracle of the resurrected car.

"We are go!"

Last Lap Before a New Start
42

"**D**o you want to hear joking?" Future asked, possibly for the hundredth time. "I making funny jokes."

"Oh no, not again!" we laughed, amazed that he was not yet bored with his homemade jokes.

"Ammon and some friends swimming in the beautiful lake. Suddenly some girls crying from beach, 'Look, look. Is that crocodile?'" Future squirmed, howling again at his favourite part. "'Hurry up guys, they have dangerous crocodile. Let's come out water.' Every guys quickly come out from water, but Ammon not. Only crocodile slowly swimming and coming near the beach and stands up, and asking, 'what's happened?' in human language. But everybody knowing the crocodile was not real crocodile – was Ammon!" Future banged his head against the headrest in a fit of laughter. "Oh Ammon, so funny!"

As his laughter began to slowly die off, the car began complaining far louder than the usual clunking and banging noises it had a habit of making. The shock absorber had come off, and our ride was even bumpier and slower from then on, something I could hardly believe was possible.

"Jesus, I sorry! I think Jesus not like that I joking. Forget last night's joke. Just forget," he begged. *But how could we forget that one?* He'd told it at least half a dozen times. Despite the newest dilemma, I smiled as I remembered it. "'*What is that big white thing in the sky,*' *they asking*

Ammon. He saying, 'I don't know, I not from here.' But everybody knowing it is the moon."

On our way to the capital, we needed diesel urgently and finally drove past a very small town. Our relief turned into consternation when we found that the whole town was deserted, including the gas station where we'd hoped to fuel up.

"I'm so hungry! Are we ever going to stop for food?" I asked as we approached.

"Not if you want to make it to Ulaanbaatar tonight. It's still 360km (224mi) away! That's pushing it as it is. Here's another biscuit. Eat that," Ammon replied as he threw one back at me. Bree and I instinctively parted like the Red Sea to dodge the edible bullet. As a final farewell, the granny where we'd stayed while the car was being fixed had given us a woollen bag full of flour biscuits for our journey. We were extremely moved by her generous offer, a feeling we'd experienced often over the past few weeks, but despite our gratitude, they were still the same hard, tasteless biscuits that Bree and I, in particular, had a hard time choking down.

"We've been chewing on those all day," she muttered.

"But after a while you kind of get used to them. They're just like water. They don't taste like anything. You just eat them because you know you need to," Mom said.

"You should be happy you're not eating mutton," Ammon reminded us.

"I am glad, but either way, I'm still eating wool," I complained as I pulled another long, dark hair from the cracks.

Under protest, we both managed to choke down a biscuit before we finally found a rare passer-by who we could stop to ask where everybody was. Apparently, the entire population had gathered on the outskirts of town for their own local Nadaam Festival celebrations. He waved for us to follow him; he was headed to the same place.

"Crap! Now we really won't have time to stop and eat if we've got to go find this guy." My complaint was completely ignored in light of our obviously more pressing need for fuel, but I didn't push it. I was learning, even if I couldn't always keep quiet about it.

It took a while to find the owner. We received various answers when we asked the spectators in the crowd if they knew who and where he was.

"Yah, my neighbour has a car. He will know!" one had told Future, sounding proud of his neighbour's success and pointing across the large sea of heads. "He's over there." We chased down a number of such vague leads but eventually, by following a series of pointing hands and pushing through the throng of onlookers, we "found Waldo" and took him back with us to get refuelled. Unfortunately, we also noticed that the new patch job had been leaking oil. Judging by the visible puddle forming underneath the van, it had been dripping for quite a while. After purchasing what we hoped would be enough oil and diesel to make it back to Ulaanbaatar, Future leapt back into the driver's seat and exclaimed, "Okay, we are go!"

As if we didn't have enough problems, Future then slowly turned around holding only half a key. He looked surprised, but not the least bit angry.

"Where is the other half?" I asked carefully.

"Is broking in ignition." He'd bent it the night before locking the trunk, and now it had broken right off. "But is okay, I have spare," he quickly continued.

"Oh good! Phew! Where?"

"At home." When I laughed at what I thought must be another funny joke, Future did too, but then when I asked where the spare key *really* was, he began describing the drawer where he kept it in his house. I couldn't believe my ears! *After all the car problems we dealt with, this is what is going to bring us down?* As luck would have it, though, there was still a piece of the key sticking out of the ignition. Future's calm demeanour and naturally positive attitude kicked in again, and he somehow used the hole in the upper half of the broken key like a wrench to turn the part that was still sticking out of the ignition, and it worked. The engine actually turned over!

It was a good thing Future was able to rig up that key contraption, given all the repairs we were forced to make thereafter. We stopped to jiggle the battery back into place, refill the oil, and investigate weird noises coming from the tire. We even had to rip out the shredded engine-fan-housing that was blocking airflow and causing the engine to overheat. We were determined not to allow these minor issues to keep us from reaching our target, but it was hard. We waited on pins and needles to see what the next disaster might be.

Future kept the mood so light that it was hard to remain negative, though. At one point, he laughingly proclaimed, "I retire from tour guide AND mechanic." We were amazed that, as the owner of a van now literally falling apart in more ways than we could count, Future was still, by far, the most happy-go-lucky member of the group.

It was completely dark when we finally reached the tarmac road on the outskirts of Ulaanbaatar, only to have the van break down one last time. *Yes, yes, yes – NOOO! And we were so close!* The brakes had seized, but Future refused to give up. He stepped on the gas hard and the poor car struggled to move a few feet until the brake pads started burning and smoking. After a few more tries, the discs were worn down to metal on metal and were glowing red hot.

"Umm, he's about to blow up the whole car if he keeps doing that!" Ammon's voice reflected a sense of urgency. I didn't need to lean out the window to see the glow from the brakes on the dark landscape.

Future finally admitted defeat. We pulled over to the side of the road and perched desperately around his cell phone, watching the weak reception signal fade as he made an SOS call to Baagii. It was past midnight by the time Baagii came to the rescue with a vehicle and food – real food. Having not eaten anything but the infamous biscuits, we were starved. I shovelled scoop after scoop of the tasty and, most importantly, non-mutton-based meal into me and revelled in the last lingering remnants of its warmth.

While the men transferred the backpacks from Future's vehicle to Baagii's, it was somehow decided that Future would stay behind with his van and we would go on to the hostel without him. Even though I felt a mixture of guilt and relief at hearing about this arrangement, I dozed off a bit as I experienced the deep and calming satisfaction of a full belly. *Everyone in this kind of culture has to rely on one another. In such harsh conditions and scenarios, it is likely that their experiences and lifestyle make them all the more appreciative of their fellow man.* I'd seen how quickly people who value family and help strangers became friends in this culture. I thought of the grandparents who had nothing but shared their biscuits with us anyway, all the families who welcomed us into their homes, Khongorzul helping at the border, and the many others who'd helped along the way, none of them expecting anything in return. I couldn't forget their bountiful generosity despite their limited means. These were the most hospitable strangers I'd ever met. In all fairness I don't think there is a word for 'stranger' in Mongolia. The closest translation would probably be, "friends that haven't met." *After all, isn't that what a stranger should be?* I was beginning to wish I, too, lived in a culture where that's what being a stranger meant. I looked out the rear window as we departed and saw Future standing in his headlights waving. He was truly a selfless warrior.

We were completely fried by the time we arrived at the hostel, but it sure felt good to be in a familiar place. Bree and I were forced to share a bed because only three were available in the twenty-bed dorm. I was so tired that all I needed was to be laid out horizontally somewhere – anywhere – to sleep peacefully. It was hard to locate an empty bed without turning the lights on, and I had no desire to feel my way into an occupied one. Once again, though, Bree saved the day.

"Over here!" she whisper-shouted to me. She'd found a free bunk. We could sleep in the top bed, and there was one for Mom below. Ammon was fending for himself in the darkness.

For a couple of minutes, I could hear Mom shuffling about below. I could feel Bree's rhythmic heartbeat and knew from her deep, even breathing that she was already in dreamland. I was not far behind. My heavy eyes closed and I was gone before my head even hit the pillow.

Three days later, Future and Baagii arrived for the final time to drive us to the train station. To our amazement, this time they pulled up outside the hostel in the van we thought we'd murdered in the desert.

"Future, you did it again! I don't know how you pulled it off!" Ammon inspected the refurbished van to see if it really was the same vehicle we had driven through the desert.

Tickets in hand and bags fully packed and ready, we stood on the platform saying our final goodbyes. Bree and Baagii were off to the side undergoing an emotional, somewhat painful, parting.

Future stood before Ammon and said, "I want you have," as he twisted his silver, horse-head ring off his middle finger and placed it in his palm.

"Oh wow, that's beautiful Future, but I don't know if I---"

"No, you take. Is for you, my Ammon. You know, you really looking like Jesus. Please take care of girls." Turning to Mom he said, "Good Mama. You good," and gave her a hug. Finally it was my turn, "Little Savannah, when you are grow up, you getting pretty girl, 'cause I naming you Pretty Savannah."

"Thank you, Future." I gave him a big hug, too. "You are a good guide, but an even better friend."

"Bree, you nice girl. Funny girl," and he stole her from Baagii for a hug.

"C'mon Bree. It's time," Mom reminded her gently. Bree was barely able to hold back her tears and needed a few more moments.

"Good luck on your trip! And have fun in Russia," Baagii called as he waved. "Come back to Mongolia any time. We'll be here."

As I was climbing onto the train after Ammon, Future called out my name. I reached back to him and he took my hand and squeezed it tightly in a final farewell. I didn't need to open my hand to know what was there. I could never mistake the shape and feel of those hard, round biscuits. I grinned as Bree and I lingered a few moments longer at the door. We were sad to be leaving, but the whistle blew and we had to find our seats. I staggered as the wheels started to turn and the train jerked slightly, but Bree was there to steady me, as always. I used this excuse to wrap my arm around her, hoping to comfort her at least a bit.

From the window, I saw Future give Baagii a soothing pat on the back as they turned to leave. *Sook, sook, sook,* I thought with a smile. The platform slipped away and I wondered if I would ever see either of them again. We'd made some good friends, and the time for the painful inevitability of farewells had already come and gone, but I knew there would be plenty more hellos ready to welcome us wherever we went.

Ammon and Mom were already settled into the four-seat cubicle which would be home for the next thirty-six hours. I found I didn't mind too much. It was a perfect chance to get reacquainted with my dear, sweet Rhett, but then Ammon pulled the deck of cards from his daypack and began shuffling, his new ring reflecting the sunlight.

With an exaggerated shiver, he plainly stated, "Given what happened the last time I was there, I am NOT looking forward to going back to Russia."

Secretly, I was!

To Be Continued…

Acknowledgements

I originally had no clue how to write a book, but am so grateful that I was given this opportunity. I want to thank not only the three family members who accompanied me on this life-altering trip, but the members of my extended family, as well. You always encouraged my various endeavors and have been listening to my nonstop motor mouth from the moment I was born.

Mom: You kept things together while I sat for months at the computer. Although I was rather horrified at the time, I am so glad you typed out all of my journals for safekeeping. And thank you for all the hard work you put into creating the website. "I like it – A LOT!"

Dad: "I'll bring the coffee." Thank you for all the long days of reading, rereading, and rereading again. I couldn't have done it without you.

Bree: Who would I laugh with if you weren't around? Though we've had our moments, as all sisters do, you are a great big sister and always there to protect me. I owe you a life – or three.

Ammon: Thanks for teaching me so much and being my substitute father through this exciting, formative period of my life. I truly value your advice and help.

Sky: I couldn't live without your gentle heart.

My siblings are the best gifts I've ever been given. Thank you for them, too, Mom and Dad.

Terri: One day you will understand and come back to me.

Sandra Fok: You've been there since the beginning, and the trip was worthwhile if only to meet you. "I bring Sushi and Pizza." And don't forget the Starbucks and treats for early morning math sessions. Damn you, Strawberry – You are a life saver!

Mary Anne McCall: I am so proud to have you for a grandmother. Your intelligence never fails to impress me. Even separated by oceans, you were one of my biggest supporters.

Shean Stacey: You were always our family's number one fan. If it weren't for you and your big bear hugs, we never would have come so far.

Rhiis Lopez/Ana Kefr: I love all of our Sodomatroglofantasmodyte memories in you-know-where (I don't even want to record the ugly word in my book). Thank you for the write-up!

John Volken: I love how, from the time I was ten years old, you introduced me to friends as a future author. You believed in my writing before anyone else, even me.

JoAnn Cleaver: Your guidance and polishing touches on my manuscript were much appreciated.

Heather UpChurch: You were so patient and helpful through the process of designing my cover. You put in more time and effort than I ever would have expected. I am extremely grateful to have found <http://www.expertsubjects.com>.

Rae McWhirter: I only met you recently, but it feels like forever. You've helped me so much. I'm so glad you fell into my life.

Greg Wallis: We all admired your random appearances and your incredibly upbeat enthusiasm. You always gave me a boost when I needed it.

Brandon Baumgardner, Adriana Watkins, Aileen Tien, Hein Lok and **Tish Stacey**: Thanks for all your help, encouragement and amazing support during the writing process.

Kees Kleef: You are one of a kind, and I am incredibly lucky to have you, particularly when I couldn't stop talking and "giving you blisters in your ears" way past lights out – even when you had to get up early to work to support me and my writing. I can't thank you enough for everything you have done for me. O.W.Y.

A special thank you to all the nameless folk I met along the way who supported both my travels and my attempts to write about them. I cannot tell you how grateful I am to all of you.

Finally, to all the characters referred to by name in the book, thank you for being a part of my journey.

6942072R00219

Made in the USA
San Bernardino, CA
18 December 2013